German Jackboots
on
Kentucky Bluegrass:

Housing German Prisoners of War in Kentucky, 1942-1946

German Jackboots on Kentucky Bluegrass:

Housing German Prisoners of War in Kentucky, 1942-1946

By

Antonio S. Thompson, Ph.D.

Diversion Press

Thompson, Antonio, 1975-
German Jackboots on Kentucky Bluegrass: Housing
German Prisoners of War in Kentucky, 1942-1946 /
Antonio Thompson
p. cm.
Includes bibliographical references and index.
ISBN 978-1-935290-00-1 (alk. paper)
I. Title
Library of Congress Control Number: 2008907251

Published by Diversion Press, Inc.
P.O. Box 30277
Clarksville, Tennessee
www.diversionpress.com

Acknowledgements

I owe a debt of gratitude to all those who helped and supported me throughout this project. I begin by acknowledging the staff at numerous archives, libraries, and museums who provided information and enabled me to conduct research for this book. The list includes the National Archives II at College Park, Maryland and The Military History Institute at Carlisle Barracks, Pennsylvania. Numerous libraries within Kentucky deserve thanks including those at Danville and Shelbyville. The interlibrary loan office at the University of Kentucky proved instrumental in the research process. The Kentucky Historical Society and *The Register* have been a tremendous support network for this work and other projects including my recently published article in *The Register of the Kentucky Historical Society* and my dissertation and forthcoming book of the same title "Men in German Uniform." The Kentucky Historical Society awarded me a graduate student fellowship in 2005 that allowed me to continue my POW studies. I offer thanks to John O'Brien at the Don F. Pratt Museum at Fort Campbell, the James D. Veatch Breckinridge Museum and Arts Center, and the Patton Museum at Fort Knox. Matthew Rector at the Historical Preservation Office at Fort Knox provided a great deal of support. I also graciously acknowledge my professors at Western Kentucky University, where I finished my Master's thesis and first started work on German POWs, and at the University of Kentucky, where I completed my dissertation on German POWs in the U.S.

A special thanks goes to those who provided interviews, photographs, and other related items and information including Monroe McGhee, Patricia Ellis, Junior Mathis, Paul Gardner, Bill Columbia, Myron Pool, Edgar Radford, Barbara James, Mary Ellen Lilly, E.T. "Hammer" Smith, Thomas Harper, Shea Godwin-Harper, Tony DeName, Margaret Rudd, and the Broadbent family. I am sorry to say that for some of these individuals, the thanks are posthumous.

I also owe a debt of gratitude to Walter Mathis, who not only provided an interview, but became one of this project's biggest supporters. Without his help I would not have located several of the individuals that I interviewed. Furthermore, I thank the former POWs who gave freely of their time, Paul Mengelberg, who patiently listened to my questions, and Heino Erichsen, who actually called me first. I am thankful to Horst Blumenberg who not only invited me into his home, but shared much of his memories and life with me. As most of Horst's experience was in Texas and Louisiana, more details of his life will appear in a forthcoming work. A special thanks to Howard Tromp, who invited me to spend time with him on several occasions and to his family who graciously hosted me for a week. Howard's interviews and material are so in-depth that most of them will also appear in a forthcoming work. I also thank the family of Egon Hessenthaler, who allowed me to use Egon's memoir.

I would also like to thank those who have taken time to read the drafts of this work and encouraged me throughout the process including Dr. Richard Gildrie, Dr. Tom Dixon, Joseph Bailey, and Shannon Gurwitch. Additional, thanks to Natalie Dovanne for her help and support.

I am always grateful to my wife, Dr. Amy Thompson. She painstakingly read each draft, commented on it, and discussed it with me at length. If this work meets with any success, it is largely due to her efforts. In closing, I thank my children, who provide a constant source of inspiration, and God, who has graciously provided me with joyful companions, endurance to weather adversity, and bounties immeasurable. If I have left someone out, I apologize as it was not done maliciously.

To my loving wife Amy

To my beautiful children Madeline, Julian, and Sophia

I hope I can give you the joy you have given me.

Table of Contents

There have been many rumors about the P.W.'s in this country. Rumors can be harmful in the operation of our P.W. camps, and every citizen can help the War Department by squelching rumors. No one is attempting to hold back information on prisoners, except in those rare cases where immediate disclosure might hamper security. I believe when more people learn the rules of the Geneva Convention and its background and become familiar with the policies of the War Department, they will realize that the handling of prisoners of war is probably one of the most misunderstood rather that the 'most outstandingly mismanaged part of this war.'

-Major Hugh M. Patton, Public Relations Officer at Camp Breckinridge*

Preface

German Jackboots first trod upon Kentucky Bluegrass in 1943 when several hundred prisoners of war entered captivity at Camps Campbell and Breckinridge. Over the next three years more than 9,000 German POWs, out of nearly 371,000 housed in the U.S., lived in, worked in, played in, and escaped from Kentucky's POW camps. Kentucky's experience housing these men and their impact on the Bluegrass State remains largely untold, although three broad national overviews exist. Judith Gansberg published *Stalag: U.S.A.: The Remarkable Story of German POWs in America* in 1977. Arnold Krammer followed with *Nazi Prisoners of War in America* in 1979, and republished it in 1991 and 1996. Lewis H. Carlson followed in 1997 with his book, *We Were Each Other's Prisoners: An Oral History of World War II American and German Prisoners of War*, which covered the American experience in German camps as well as German POWs, held in the U.S. These authors benefited from living sources and made good use of interview material.

My work owes a debt of gratitude to these authors who paved the way in the research of German POWs in the U.S. and opened the historical inquiry for those who followed. I utilized these works and many others in my own national study dissertation, "Men in German Uniform: German Prisoners of War Held in the United States during The Second World War." Among other points, I argued that the U.S. maintained a history of generally good treatment of its prisoners following policies that dictated fairness and humanity. I demonstrated that good treatment of captured enemy personnel peaked during World War II with the implementation of the 1929 Geneva Convention.

While conducting my dissertation research I discovered numerous state monographs. While each has its own merits a few remain notable for their academic treatment of the topic including Allen V. Koop's *Stark Decency: German Prisoners of War in a New England Village* (1988) and Allen Kent Powell's *Splinters of a Nation: German Prisoners of War in Utah* (1989). Two other works followed this successful pattern, Robert D. Billinger Jr.'s *Hitler's Soldiers in the Sunshine State: German POWs in Florida* (2000) and David Fiedler's *The Enemy Among Us: POWs in Missouri During World War II* (2003). Billinger recently published another state study *Nazi POWs in the Tar Heel State* (2008).

In May 2001 I completed my Masters Thesis at Western Kentucky University titled "World War II German Prisoners of War held in Kentucky and Tennessee." My thesis provided the first study of German POWs in Kentucky and Tennessee. The only other academic treatment published on Kentucky held German POWs was an article by Richard E. Holl "Swastikas in the Bluegrass State: Axis Prisoners of War in Kentucky, 1942-46," which appeared in *The Register of The Kentucky Historical Society* in 2002. After finishing my dissertation, I returned to thinking about the experience of my home state, Kentucky, and the German prisoners of war held there.

I decided to pursue an academic monograph and in preparation of this work I used various materials

2

from the archives at Fort Campbell, Fort Knox, the Camp Breckinridge Museum, the Kentucky Historical Society, and other local Kentucky and Tennessee archives, libraries, and newspapers. I spent untold hours poring over newspapers on microfilm at the University of Kentucky, Northern Kentucky University, and Eastern Kentucky University libraries. I also researched at the Military History Institute at Carlisle, Pennsylvania, and at the National Archives II in College Park, Maryland. Additionally, the Interlibrary Loan service at the University of Kentucky became an indispensable source for material. One of the highlights of this research was the correspondence and interviews with former POWs, their employers, U.S. servicemen, and others who interacted with the Germans.

Kentucky's German POW housing experience is as rich and varied as any other state and provides both a view of the American home front and U.S. foreign policy. The POWs resided at three large permanent camps, Camp Campbell, Camp Breckinridge, and Fort Knox as well as over a dozen branch camps, including those at Shelbyville, Frankfort, Owensboro, Eminence, Maysville, Lexington and Danville.

The German prisoners of war impacted Kentucky in numerous ways. They demonstrated the strength of youth and willingness to do hard work that the state desperately needed to overcome the labor shortages facing Kentucky's tobacco and corn farmers. They came with their military arrogance, often displayed as a strong sense of defiance, with which they caused problems including escapes, violence within the camps, and refusal to work. Prisoners of war in Kentucky brought the war to the Bluegrass State.

Kentuckians saw the enemy up close and personal, took stock of what a German was and was not, and formed their own theories about Nazis and "Teutonic Supermen". Kentucky gained economically and culturally from the Axis men and in many ways the POWs benefited from their experience as much as the state gained from having them. Through interaction with local civilians, friendships formed with farmers and guards, an education program, and numerous perks, all obvious signs of good treatment, the POWs learned firsthand about American democracy, and what being a Kentuckian meant.

Chapter 1
Axis Prisoners in the U.S.

When the Second World War began in Europe in 1939, U.S. neutrality seemed a natural extension of its post-World War I isolationist policies. Americans still groaned under the yoke of the Great Depression, but by the end of 1941 the nation found itself thrust into the war with the bombing of Pearl Harbor. As the country turned the gears of war, military preparations took precedence over the planning for, handling, and housing hundreds of thousands of enemy prisoners. Few could have fathomed that during the course of this war nearly half of a million enemy prisoners would be housed in over 500 camps in the country ranging from California to Maine and from Florida to Minnesota. Initially the government relied only on the outdated experience gained from handling prisoners in previous conflicts, using the incomplete and already outdated plans created between the wars to augment new emergency planning. By the time the smoke cleared after the Pearl Harbor attack no facilities existed in the U.S. for the housing of POWs, despite the fact that the first prisoner of war, Kazuo Sakamaki, a Japanese mini-submarine pilot involved in the Pearl Harbor invasion, had just entered into captivity.

The War Department tasked its subordinate agencies, the "newly" created Army Service Forces (ASF) and the recently reactivated Provost Marshal General's Office (PMGO), with the lion's share of the

5

responsibility for planning POW operations. The ASF closely resembled its World War I counterpart the Service of Supplies and held responsibility for much of the military organization, including logistics and supply, within the continental United States. The capable Brigadier General Brehon B. Somervell led the ASF assisted by the Service Commanders of each of the nine recently created Service Commands. The responsibility of PMGO, which arguably had a greater role in the actual "on the ground" POW duties, included the Aliens Division, which monitored enemy civilians, and the Prisoner of War Division. General Allen Gullion, a University of Kentucky graduate, had previously headed the Aliens Division and received a promotion to Provost Marshal General. General Blackshear M. Bryan aided Gullion as the newly promoted Assistant Provost Marshal General. Nearly all POW program policies came from the War Department and its subordinate agencies, the ASF and PGMO, and various civilian agencies, such as the Department of State and the War Manpower Commission (WMC).

Because of the size of the task ahead of them and the number of civilian and military agencies involved, lines of responsibility often remained blurred and frequently overlapped. The War Department underwent a major reorganization in 1942, but even this overhaul failed to completely solve the dilemma of what agencies would oversee the various aspects of the prisoner program. The growing influx of POWs throughout the war forced an expansion of department responsibilities resulting in frequent changes to these agencies. Eventually, however, the U.S. successfully housed nearly 425,000 Axis POWs in what became the largest and most humane POW program in this nation's history. Since past experience had been seriously outdated and also circumstantial, the U.S. relied heavily upon the 1929 Geneva Convention which provided a rough blueprint of international law on the treatment of prisoners of war.

Forty seven nations met at Geneva, Switzerland in 1929 to produce both the Prisoner of War Convention and the Red Cross Convention jointly referred to as the Geneva Convention of 1929.[1] The quest to eliminate the suffering and poor treatment of combatants in enemy custody began on August 22, 1864 with the first Geneva Convention negotiated by sixteen nations.[2] This multilateral treaty signed in a time of peace concerned the humane treatment of prisoners, wounded, and protected personnel and differed from most treaties that were bilateral and negotiated by the belligerents to govern the current conflict.[3] This first Geneva Convention paved the way for future treaties and as legal scholar Jean Pictet stated "for the first time, war had yielded to law."[4] Other international treaties followed, the most notable being the 1906 revision of the Geneva Convention, which had twenty-six member nations, and the Hague Conventions of 1899 and 1907.[5]

The Geneva Convention of 1929 revised a major flaw in the Hague Convention which prevented its widespread use during the First World War. Under the terms of Article II, if all belligerents were not signatories then the treaty "shall cease to be binding from the time when, in a war between Contracting Powers, a non-Contracting Power joins one of the belligerents."[6] The 1929 Convention clearly stated that the signing nations were bound by its terms regardless of whether other co-belligerents had signed. It also provided for greater benefits for those captured. It detailed neutral rights and protected personnel (medics and chaplains) and provided general terms for humane treatment. Neutral nations served as protecting powers, and enforced these terms by inspecting prisoner of war camps and reporting their findings to the holding nation and the nation of the prisoners' origin.

The Convention monitored treatment in other ways. The men within the camps elected spokesmen who could request a meeting with a neutral representative. The prisoners were to be permitted to write to their families to inform them of their status and the holding nation submitted the names of housed prisoners. These methods served to keep the signatory nation straightforward in its prisoner relations, if not for the sake of honest dealings, then for fear of international censure and retaliatory treatment against its own nationals in enemy hands. The U.S. ratified this new treaty in 1932 and during the Second World War the U.S. honored the Geneva Convention despite treatment inflicted upon U.S. servicemen at the hands of their enemies and the discovery of atrocities such as the death camps in Europe. The German government signed the Geneva Convention and attempted to adhere to its tenets. International law and government policy, however, do not always reflect the behavior of men in the field. Numerous instances exist of mistreatment, massacres, and atrocities of captured or surrendering men by all belligerents in all conflicts, regardless of official policies. Governments know that this happens;

otherwise international law like the Geneva Convention would serve no purpose.[7]

The Geneva Convention required holding nations to provide the captive enemy with food, clothing, and shelter equivalent to that given to its own personnel. These nations also had to ensure the safety of prisoners by removing them from the combat zone immediately upon capture and housing them away from any potential counteroffensives or bombing. While these stipulations had obvious merit, implementing them proved expensive, time consuming and impossible in the theater of operations. Bringing these prisoners to the U.S. presented a relatively simple solution.

Troops and supply ships going overseas were filled to capacity with men and material directly related to the war effort. Once empty, these ships returned to America. The U.S. loaded these returning ships with captured enemy personnel. Using this method, the transfer of POWs to the U.S. proceeded swiftly, smoothly and quite inexpensively. At the time the biggest fear of German prisoners and American personnel was being sunk by a German submarine. However, no U.S. ships transporting soldiers or prisoners were lost.

Housing the men in converted barracks or other space already existing on military facilities provided cost effective housing. Usually a section of a military base could be cordoned off with fencing and barbed wire and further secured by guard towers. Unoccupied barracks typically had the requisite electricity, water, and sewage. Even with new construction the military cut expenses by using prisoner labor. The cost of shipping food, clothing, and other materials to U.S.

camps was cheaper than sending them overseas. When the decision was made to bring these men to the North American continent the Allies lacked a foothold in Europe or North Africa to safely house these men, but once in the U.S. the safety of the POWs would be assured. The Luftwaffe did not raid the U.S., and no Japanese planes bombed Californian cities. Little chance existed for the men to escape to rejoin their lines and U.S. officials assumed that this would significantly reduce escape attempts. While in the country the prisoners would be put to work to help alleviate the labor shortage caused by the war. On paper it seemed like a wonderful idea.

Housing was at a premium since The War Department stipulated that sites for camps had to be located away from areas sensitive to the security of the U.S., ensure the safety of the local population, and provide maximum economic feasibility. In Kentucky the War Department agencies converted space on the existing military bases of Camp Campbell, Camp Breckinridge, and Fort Knox into base camps, or semi-permanent facilities, each equipped to hold 3,000 prisoners. The military used branch camps, which housed between 250 and 1,000 men, as temporary overflow and to locate prisoner labor to needed areas. The construction of these camps often reflected their temporary nature and the "cost-effective" maxim of the War Department. The branch camp at Eminence was built on an old fairground and the one at Maysville on a park. A Lexington camp used an old school building, while one of the branches at Danville was nothing more than a tent city. These camps typically lasted only long enough to meet the area's labor needs, sometimes as short as several weeks, and few operated more than one season.

While U.S. officials worked on preparing camps for the arrival of POWs, Allied forces in North Africa began capturing enemy soldiers by the thousands. These captured Axis men were first disarmed and searched and once the officers and enlisted men were placed in separate groups they were moved to the temporary holding camps in Oran, Algeria; or Casablanca, Morocco. Depending on the time and place of capture, the trip across the desert could take days and included long marches with intervals of truck rides with American or British guards, or train-rides under guard by Free French or French colonial troops. Once at the camps the POWs were again searched and processed. The holding camps offered few amenities. Food, water, and shelter could be scarce and the overcrowded conditions were sometimes made worse by the heat, blowing sand, infestations, and infrequent washing. The prisoners in these holding camps remained for weeks, sometimes months, awaiting transport to Glasgow, Scotland; Halifax, Nova Scotia; Norfolk, Virginia; or New York, and permanent captivity for the duration of the war. Once they disembarked and received transfer to their new holding nation they were again screened, searched, and segregated. The pilfering of souvenirs from Axis personnel, in the form of medals, knives, wallets, jewelry, and insignia became a common side effect of all the transfers. Many men arrived at their permanent camps with only the clothes that they wore in the desert.[8]

The prisoners entered their new base camps in the U.S. amid the bustling activity already taking place near the train stations where they disembarked and on the military bases around them. The guards divided the prisoners into the 1,000 man compounds and then further sub-divided them into companies of 250 men. They had to abide by U.S. policies and they remained under the same discipline as if they were still on active duty. In juxtaposition to life in the Third Reich, these Axis men enjoyed a great deal of freedom behind barbed wire while learning American democracy and the U.S. style of captivity. They received new clothes, generous food provisions, food cooked to their preference, and canteen coupons to buy items from a prisoner operated store. They also wrote letters home and strolled around the camp at leisure. The size of the POW camps grew during the war. The camp usually included three large barracks, a mess hall, and eventually a library and a chapel. Each camp also established indoor and outdoor recreational space stocked with equipment and the POWs organized sports teams that battled for camp championships in soccer. Others held boxing exhibitions or table tennis tournaments. With the full support of the American government, these men eventually put on plays, conducted musicals, had orchestras and libraries, and even published their own newspapers. Interested prisoners took classes to earn their high school diploma or college degree through numerous correspondence programs or through the use of qualified prisoner instructors.

These benefits did not come free of charge. The Geneva Convention allowed prisoners to work and the

U.S. enforced prisoner labor. The cost of the housing program drained the already strained American economy while the home front suffered from a lack of manpower. Employing the POWs solved both of these problems. Although the Geneva Convention permitted the holding nation to require enlisted men to work, it provided little direction. It stipulated that POWs would be paid the same as men of equivalent rank of the holding power and that they could not be employed on "unhealthful or dangerous" tasks or work directly related to the war effort, such as working on tanks or in munitions plants. The Convention also required the captor nation to treat its prisoner labor humanely and equal to that of its own soldiers. Using these basic provisions the U.S. created its own labor program. The U.S. had previously employed German POWs during the American Revolution and on a small scale in World War I, but neither experience could prepare the nation for the logistical considerations of the World War II labor program. Like every other administrative effort during the Second World War, several agencies cooperated in designing this program. Numerous new policies and interpretations of old ones became laborious in themselves.

A multitude of problems surrounded the housing of POWs and all of these national problems had counterparts in Kentucky's camps. Many prisoners maintained a general defiance; others escaped, went on strike, or fought with and murdered each other. Yet, they worked and formed friendships too. They benefited the labor starved economy of the state. They maintained contacts with former employers long after the war. They learned American democracy and

Kentucky hospitality. After the war ended, many of these men returned several times to visit former camp sites and look up old friends. Often these reunions preceded a permanent transition to becoming a U.S. citizen. Finally, the story of Kentucky's housing program and German prisoners of war can be told.

Chapter 2
The Day the Earth Stood Still: Bringing German POWs into the Bluegrass State

On a hot July day in 1943, an Army truck carrying reporters whirled past the gates at Camp Breckinridge, Kentucky. The men on board included some of the first civilians in the United States to see German Prisoners of War. After the truck entered the newly constructed POW enclosure through the double-barbed wire fence, the officer, riding shotgun, spoke over the humming of the engine as they approached the men with PW stenciled uniforms, "Here's the first of them . . . Don't stop." [1] The passengers, as if on a bizarre safari, watched the bronzed and youthful men from North Africa at work. Many of the Germans took the time to return the silent, questioning glances. The reaction left a lasting impression on the reporters and likely on the prisoners. Tarleton Collier, a reporter for the Louisville *Courier-Journal*, recalled the encounter in his aptly titled article "Mute Germans Give Prison Camp Air of Unreality."[2]

Kentuckians across the state expressed apathy, bewilderment, empathy, and morbid fascination, often alternating the feelings, as the captive enemy poured into Camp Breckinridge and Camp Campbell beginning in 1943, and Fort Knox in 1944.[3] Seemingly without warning, thousands of Axis prisoners began to take up residence in the state's military bases and the shattered tranquility of the Bluegrass State appeared irreparable. Despite the media blackout concerning prisoner of war transport and treatment, and the regulations forbidding interviews or pictures with these men, few Kentuckians remained ignorant of their presence for long, thanks to ample radio and newspaper coverage. Placing prisoners in the community through the contract labor program allowed farmers and other civilians to become as accustomed to the presence of the captive enemy as they dared. The ensuing escape of dozens of Germans from Kentucky's camps and the manhunts that followed helped acquaint the rest of the state's residents with their newest neighbors. Civilians who yearned for information about the war prisoners greeted their arrival with worried concern and often nagging questions. How were they being treated? Where were they being held at on the military base? Where would branch camps be located? How secure were these places? And why during a period of heightened national insecurity and rationing were these men from North Africa and Europe transferred all the way to Kentucky?

Although the POWs began arriving in Kentucky in 1943, the first Axis men to enter U.S. captivity came in 1942 after being transferred from British custody. The British suffered under the strain of several years of war and lived with the reality of Luftwaffe bombing and losing supply ships to U-boat depravations. Housing and feeding their Axis POWs became a heavy burden and guaranteeing their safety and preventing escape became increasingly difficult. A transfer agreement with Great Britain enabled the U.S. to assume these responsibilities. Thousands more Axis prisoners captured during the North African and European campaigns entered the U.S. in the coming years.

Temporary holding camps, slightly removed from the battlefront, prepared the POWs for transfer to England, Scotland, Canada, or the United States. German and Italian prisoners often waited months to leave the sun-exposed, dirty, and hastily constructed camps at Oran, Algeria, and Casablanca, Morocco, and finally board empty Liberty Ships making the return voyage after dropping off men and supplies at the front. Those intended for the U.S. arrived days or weeks later after a harrowing Atlantic crossing where both Allied and Axis eyes searched the waves for prowling U-boats. Being sunk by their own U-boats would be an ironic fate for the German prisoners. Despite many sleepless nights through the countless voyages, none of the ships transporting prisoners were sunk.

Arriving in the U.S. the ships unloaded their captive cargo at either Camp Shanks, New York or at Norfolk, Virginia, where a more detailed screening and registration process supplemented the rudimentary one received upon prisoner capture. By the time the prisoners embarked upon the trains that crisscrossed the nation bringing them to permanent compounds, most of this motley crew had been picked clean of weapons, watches, medals, and anything else souvenir worthy.[4]

With few exceptions the period of captivity provided the Axis men their first glimpse of the U.S. They found the country in stark contrast to the Nazi propaganda fed to them by the Third Reich. As the trains clicked off the miles, prisoners commented about the size of the U.S., the level of prosperity, the vastness of the rural areas, and the sprawling cities that never knew a war-induced blackout. Europeans knew well that bombers used city night lights to guide them to their target and because of that passing lit up U.S. cities at night must have been a rare treat. As hours turned into days, many of the men commented that Germany woefully underestimated the size and power of the U.S. German press reported that the Luftwaffe bombed U.S. cities and some of the POWs found it amazing to see that the skyscrapers and large cities had not been reduced to rubble. A few men argued that the U.S. must build quicker than the Luftwaffe could tear down, but the savvier among them quietly realized that this too had been a lie. Former POW Heino Erichsen commented that "each night, replete with a good meal, I would stay awake as long as possible to peer through the dark [as the] lights of towns, cities, and farmhouses flashed by."[5]

Railroad lines delivered Kentucky its first prisoners in 1943 to Breckinridge and Campbell. The men in German uniform who entered U.S. POW compounds included a conglomeration of volunteers, draftees, criminals, hardened veterans and new recruits; Nazis and anti-Nazis; and from all over Europe and Asia. Fritz Nessler, a former German paratrooper captured near Mateur, North Africa, recalled his initiation at Camp Campbell, "August 1, 1943! There was a big thundershower over Fort Campbell. I remember this day like yesterday."[6] Nessler arrived soon after the POW camp at Camp Campbell opened. At that time only two compounds had been constructed and the camp housed slightly over a hundred men.

Finding adequate space became one of the first and most pressing requirements of the POW program. The Geneva Convention required that prisoners be accommodated the same as American soldiers. This included providing them with running water, laundry and bathing facilities, electricity, and barracks housing among other things. If existing facilities lacked these requirements, the War Department located alternate housing or acquired land to build new facilities. The U.S. Departments of War and State also stipulated other requirements, most of which aimed at safety, escape prevention, and economic feasibility. The subordinate departments of the War Department, the Army Service Forces (ASF) and the Provost Marshal Generals Office (PMGO), scrambled for solutions. During the transition, fairgrounds, former Civilian Conservation Corps camps, and similar locales provided temporary facilities while POW labor created more suitable housing. When the POWs did without, as was the case when they had to sleep in tents while completing construction, then so too did their American guards. From 1942 to 1945, across the U.S., the Army converted unused sites, built new camps, and utilized additional space on existing military installations to house the 371,000 Germans, 51,000 Italian, and 5,500 Japanese war prisoners.[7]

The POWs in Kentucky entered existing military bases, expanded to become their semi-permanent residence for the duration of the war. By the end of 1942 the government approved less than a dozen sites to house POWs in the U.S. Camps Breckinridge and Campbell in Kentucky and Camp Atterbury, Indiana, were earmarked to hold prisoners as early as

September 1942. At this early date these were the only camps in the Fifth Service Command, which was the branch of the ASF tasked with regional control over Kentucky, Indiana, and Ohio. Many of the Italians and later German war prisoners housed at Camp Atterbury shuffled back and forth from Fort Knox during the later part of the POW program.[8]

As preparation of the Kentucky camps began, the War Department announced the commanders of the POW installations. Lieutenant Colonel Einar W. Chester, of the Infantry commanded at Breckinridge, and Lieutenant Colonel Frank A. Hunter of the Infantry Reserve commanded at Campbell.[9] When POWs stayed at existing military bases, as at all three Kentucky base camps, the POW camp commander controlled POW activities and answered to the Fifth Service Command, but remained subordinate to the post commander in all other matters.[10]

Designs for both Campbell and Breckinridge allowed for 3,000 prisoners to be sufficiently guarded and housed within the established guidelines. Camp Campbell differed from many of the other POW camps in the nation in that their barracks, DD, XO, and VW, were not adjoining and were located in separate parts of the U.S. military installation. The barracks and other facilities at Breckinridge and Knox, as well as most other camps, were separated by barbed wire, but otherwise connected.

Construction changes, modifications, and additions continued from the planning stages in 1942 through the late stages of the program in 1944 and 1945. Some of these changes created unforeseen problems which led to conflicts amongst military personnel. Late design changes at Breckinridge reduced the size of the recreation space available to POWs. The camp commander felt that the slight hill between the recreation field and the fence created a blind spot between the two proposed sentry towers. He requested that a third tower be built between the two perimeter towers to cover that area and prevent POWs from slipping through the wire and into the nearby woods.[11] Major S.T.B. Johnson of the Corps of Engineers received the request and forwarded it, along with his opinion that the third tower would serve no useful purpose, to Fifth Service Command Headquarters in Ohio. They examined the blueprint and felt that the two towers provided adequate coverage and declined the third tower, perhaps to the joy of all future POW escape plotters.[12]

Arrangements for Breckinridge changed again in October 1942, when planners discovered that the military police escort company barracks (MPEC), located there to provide security, housed 510 men exceeding its 450 person capacity. New designs accommodated the full MPEC and included an officer's mess and a guard tower near the front entrance. The officers at Breckinridge agreed that these last two additions needed to accompany the request for the enlarged MPEC barracks. In order to ensure the implementation of these new plans they contacted the Chief of the Aliens Division, and later Assistant Provost Marshal General, Blackshear M. Bryan for his approval.[13]

Despite the added step, heated debates erupted between officers at Breckinridge and the Corps of Engineers who argued that these additions "were not included in the typical plan for internment camp construction at posts."[14] Captain Smith, representing both Camps Breckinridge and Campbell, insisted to Lieutenant Colonel Marsdon of the Corps of Engineers, that Bryan agreed with the proposal. Since Smith had no documentation of the agreement Marsdon personally checked with Bryan. Marsdon then informed Smith, who had again been trumped, that these buildings "had been authorized 'when [and if they would be] considered necessary'." Official records indicated only that Smith "expressed dissatisfaction with this arrangement," although his unofficial response could be guessed.[15]

General Bryan noted their next conversation, only fifteen minutes later, this time discussing the construction of guard towers at Camp Campbell. Campbell operated completely as three distinct compounds, each equipped to house 1,000 men and each with a central guard tower of 20' x 40'.[16] Last minute changes threatened the speed at which Campbell would become operational. When Marsden authorized additional guard towers on December 1, 1942, it conflicted with those indicated on a previously revised blueprint. Colonel E.G. West, tasked with interpreting these changes at the site, had to clarify if Marsden wanted each compound to have five or seven guard towers. West received a reply on December 17, over two weeks after Marsden's first directive, obviously delaying the project. Campbell's XO and DD compounds would each have seven total guard towers, while the VW compound would only have four in addition to the existing one.[17]

Military officials and citizens alike waited out the waning days of 1942, unsure of when the "Nazis" would actually arrive, or what exactly to expect when they did. Camp construction and other preparations in Kentucky became a situation of hurry up and wait as the days of anticipation turned into weeks, and then months. As Kentuckians waited out 1942 and through 1943, thousands of Axis men fell into U.S. hands and began transferring to prisoner camps statewide. German POWs entering the U.S. fell into one of four broad stages. The first was an agreed upon exchange from the British in 1942. While sources vary on the actual number of men transferred, at least 50,000 men to as many as 175,000 came to the U.S.[18] The U.S. also housed as many as ten thousand other Axis POWs consisting mostly of naval personnel captured prior to major U.S. offensive operations. The second stage began with the Allied invasion of North Africa in November of 1942 where defeated soldiers serving under General Erwin Rommel, the elite Afrika Korps, became captives. The subsequent invasions of Sicily and southern Italy were considered part of this stage. These veterans of North Africa were among the first POWs transferred to Kentucky. The D-Day invasion of France, beginning June 6, 1944, marked the third broad stage. The final stage included the men captured in late 1944 and 1945, part of a last transfer to the U.S. as Allied forces conquered Germany.

For Kentuckians, the waiting finally ended in June 1943 as Breckinridge joined ten other U.S. locations in housing the newly arrived 36,688 POWs.[19] The number of war captives being transferred to the U.S. nearly doubled by July, reaching 65,058. The military announced that most of the 267,000 captured in North Africa would also be sent to the U.S.

With preparations for the first of three POW compounds at Camp Campbell complete by December of 1942, residents of Christian County, Kentucky; and Montgomery County, Tennessee waited nervously for the prisoners to arrive.[20] Colonel Marsden commented that the officers at Campbell were "most anxious to acquire one thousand prisoners of war in order that they could be utilized on post."[21] One form of anxiety subsided and another began as the first 500 German POWs entered into confinement at Campbell on July 24, 1943. Although it seemed barely enough time to forget the dust of North Africa, the Germans had been permanently transported far from the battle fronts. While the enlisted POWs gauged their new surroundings, their officers promptly inspected the men, and as if in an attempt to ward off notions of defeatism among Hitler's elite, reported them to be of high morale and "in fine physical condition to a man."[22] Kentuckians learned, as did the rest of the nation, that the Germans may have been defeated on the battlefield, but their spirit was not broken.

U.S. personnel, civilians, and reporters visiting the camps agreed with the assessment provided by the German officers at Camp Campbell. The men were in good shape and, with little preparation on the part of the prisoners; they could immediately begin the labor part of the housing program. After watching the young POWs at Breckinridge one reporter stated that "if it weren't for the bright yellow 'PW' stamped on their trousers you'd swear the captives were just a group of American boys thrown face to face with the discipline and G.I. living of Army life."[23] Some did not like the comparisons of the "Aryans" with "blue-blooded" Americans. Others found the situation unsettling. After visiting POWs at Breckinridge one reporter uneasily commented about being among "the mute, tanned, stocky young men whose steady gaze enfolds you as you pass."[24]

The POW compounds created the only bilingual spaces in Kentucky as signs in both German and English designated buildings and other locations within the compound. Civilian observers noted that the POWs operated their camp with "typical" German efficiency. However, all POW camps in the U.S. operated under guidelines established by the Geneva Convention and the U.S. government. A typical compound housed 3,000 men, divided into barracks of 1,000 men and then further subdivided into companies of 250 men. Barbed-wire enclosures separated each barrack from the one adjacent to it. Watch towers and armed guards warily eyed the men as they traveled throughout the camp conducting their daily activities. POWs trekked to the canteen to purchase needed items such as soap or toothpaste or luxury items like magazines, or paint and canvas for artwork. Prisoners also had access to an outdoor recreation area and a day-room within the compound's double barbed-wire fences. American officials and guards, always mindful of the potential threat that the POWs presented, operated under a "buddy" system within the compound. The Compound Commander entered the camp with an escort of the Assistant Compound Commander, while the tower sentries maintained visual contact with at least one of these men. Security measures dictated that when any inspection of the camp was made by a third party, such as a representative of the International Red Cross (IRC), the Swiss Legation, the State Department, or other War Department personnel, the Compound Commander accompany them, once again with the Assistant Compound Commander in tow.[25] Although American officers kept a watchful eye on the POWs and ultimately represented the highest direct authority over them, their daily governance fell back to German officers and Non-Commissioned Officers. The POWs knew that they still held membership in the Wehrmacht and their officers maintained at least a semblance of military decorum and discipline.[26]

Each compound also elected a spokesman from among their number. This man had access to the POW camp commander and any visiting government or international agency or representative and could also contact the Swiss Legation with complaints. His job consisted of relaying orders, communication, and compliance, and provided him, and the German officers through him, with important access to channel grievances back to Germany if necessary. When representatives of the IRC visited, for instance, he met with them privately and relayed POW dissatisfaction back to the Third Reich. His opinion therefore could have consequences for American POWs held by Germany. One of the most noted situations of this nature involved the British and their shackling of German POWs being transported. Using restraints of this nature violated the Geneva Convention and the German government threatened reciprocal action against all British men in their custody.[27]

The spokesman obviously had a powerful and desirable position. The highest ranking POW officer was typically offered the role of spokesman, but many passed it up in favor of allowing the enlisted men to elect a representative. After the prisoners elected their spokesman, the American POW Camp Commander approved the candidate and reserved the right to remove him if he abused his position. In some cases, such as large compounds or where the barracks remained completely separate, as was the case at Camp Campbell, each compound had a spokesman. The highest ranking officer of the POW camp, with few exceptions, became the commanding officer over the German POWs as well. By the time POWs swept up after D-Day arrived in Kentucky's camps, the hierarchy within the compounds had already been clearly delineated. The camp spokesman, commanders, and "leading" men from North Africa filled these posts nearly a year before the liberation of France and generally did not allow their newly arrived comrades access to these positions.[28] Regardless of their arrival date, officers received privileges that included having quarters separate from enlisted men, use of orderlies, and a pay rate equivalent to that received by American officers. German officers did not have to work, but if they volunteered they filled only supervisory roles. For these men, life behind the wire in the U.S. offered a fairly privileged and relatively free existence.

The efficient organization of the POW camps required constant communication between U.S. officials and German prisoners. Supporting free elections of spokesmen and giving the POWs opportunities to channel complaints and voluntarily organize some of their own activities demonstrated a preliminary lesson in American democracy. Robb Inez, writing for the *Courier Journal*, remarked that "it is a cosmic joke on these sons of totalitarianism that each company compound and the stockade itself has been organized along democratic lines. At the request of the American authorities, each company has formed an association and elected its own spokesman."[29] He continued that "this basic lesson in democratic government has delighted the prisoners."[30] Lieutenant Colonel Einar W. Chester, commanding officer of the Breckinridge POW camp agreed, "It's a lesson in democracy, sure enough . . . The prisoners are certainly in favor of it too."[31] The POWs, however, could not organize in any manner not approved by the Camp Commander. Their newfound freedom prohibited them from singing when on work details outside of the camp, at least officially, and forced them to get permission to sing within the compound. Other prohibitions included not being allowed to display the Swastika or any other Nazi related paraphernalia. Officers and soldiers could still wear medals and rank bearing insignia, but many of these items had already been lost or pilfered.[32] All this aside, however, there did seem to be a degree of democratic absorption and appreciation that took place over the course of the POW program. Much of this stemmed from the treatment and privileges given by the U.S. above and beyond the basic requirements set forth by the Geneva Convention.

All POWs received new sets of clothing after they entered the camps. These articles, which the Army kept track of and prescribed to the finest detail, represented the only changes of clothes that many of these men had for months. Their new uniforms differed from their military uniforms in that they were dyed dark blue and they all had large PW stenciled on each outer item. POWs could not obtain any additional clothes, but they could exchange worn out or damaged clothes.[33] Officers, however, could purchase additional uniforms or alter PW ones "to be distinguished from those of enlisted prisoners."[34] Even toiletry and cooking items were parceled out to the exact dollar and did not exceed Army regulations in price to the military or quantity to the prisoner. The "bean counters" at the Quartermasters Department doled out items like soap, towels, toothbrushes, combs, and shoe laces, but limited these things to a maximum of one dollar per month per prisoner. The POWs met any supplemental needs by using their pay allowance at the canteen. The number of kitchen utensils and cooking pans received by the POWs also had a predetermined allotment, including one meat cleaver for every seventy-five men, one salt shaker for every ten men, one frying pan for seventy-five men, and of course one cake pan for every six men.[35]

      Basic rules for the men included adhering to the military courtesy expected of U.S. enlisted personnel. Prisoners stood at attention during the playing of the National Anthem, and also during To the Colors, Escort of the Colors, or Retreat. They saluted U.S. officers, just as they did their own Wehrmacht officers, and practiced any other decorum carried out in the U.S. that differed from that in Germany. POWs followed the same military discipline within the camp as they did on active duty. This included respect and care for their uniform, belongings, and surroundings. Inspections arose suddenly by either U.S. or German officers and failure to maintain their barracks, belongings, or clothing resulted in reprimands. U.S. officials inflicted more severe punishments for serious infractions. Prisoners attempting to escape or refusing to work, for instance, lost privileges, suffered confinement, and ate a diet restricted to bread and water.[36]

The operations and handling of POWs changed continually during the program including new rules and interpretations that only slightly impacted the day to day running of the camps. As the war progressed, the Allied forces captured hundreds of thousands of men and nearly 371,000 Germans eventually entered the U.S. as captives. Once in the U.S., the POWs, with some exceptions of escaping and prisoner on prisoner violence, remained a relatively benign lot. The War Department and the media made the POWs seem more threatening than they actually were. American perceptions, however, improved from capture to repatriation. Actual military gains coupled with perceived future success in ending the war helped create this cognitive shift in the minds of Americans concerning their captive residents. Once U.S. forces landed in France, Americans read the reports of victories and of the thousands of POWs taken into captivity and created their own gauge of success and a timetable for victory. Kentuckians also read of "Nazi Prisoners Scooped Up By Hundreds" and followed these stories with news that 300,382 POWs were held in the U.S. as of October 5, 1944. Even in June 1945, months after the war in Europe ended, over 300,000 Germans remained behind American barbed wire. Kentuckians knew that there were over two-million

Axis POWs being held in Europe, thanks to the flow of news through newspapers, periodicals, radio broadcasts, and government press releases.[37]

Other stories belied the ease of the fighting and the willingness of the Germans to surrender. One article from the Clarksville *Leaf-Chronicle* described how a group of 31 Military Police Officers from the 26th Infantry Division made two trips to the Mediterranean in 1943 to escort POWs back. For these boys, the second trip proved a "wonderful adventure" where they couldn't name one city as their "favorite." They did make "friends with most of the local population" and commented that "the girls were friendly" and that the "magnificent white sand beach at Mondello made great swimming."[38] Another article in *The Cadiz Record* explained how the Army allowed the German soldiers a "trial surrender." They paraphrased the message as "try it out for three days. If you don't enjoy being a prisoner with us, you can return to your units."[39] The paper claimed that eight men took the Army up on the offer and four only stayed for three days then left long enough to bring back fifty more men.[40] There are many reasons why it seemed counterintuitive for the "Nazis" to not come pouring into the camps. Surely, at least from post-D-Day on, they received post-cards and letters from their comrades, brothers, sons, and cousins, in U.S. prison camps describing their proper and often exceptional treatment. Nazi and non-Nazi alike received the same benefits of U.S. "hospitality" which often set the maximum Geneva standards as the minimum standards in U.S. operated camps. Even the wounded received the best care, as General H.C. Pillsbury stated "there is no place in an Army hospital for sentiment . . . when a soldier is sent to an Army hospital for the removal of some slivers of shrapnel the method of his treatment is not decided upon by the question of whether the shrapnel was American or German made. He simply is a man who needs attention and he gets it."[41]

The message became too clear to some, such as the German Army's 82nd Corps, which surrendered in its entirety to the 101st Division on May 8, 1945. These men brought with them all the belongings they could pack in their cars and trucks, including cigarettes, beer, and wine. One Nazi officer reportedly dropped a Swastika flag from his luggage. A GI spotted it and helped himself to the souvenir. The German stated "You Americans . . . After the war you'll need a ship apiece to take the souvenirs home." To which the GI replied, "Well, we've got the ships for it."[42] The Union County *Advocate* even provided a typical American, if not typical Kentuckian, explanation for why so many Germans surrendered after the D-Day landings. They claimed that the "enemy likes our brand." According to American Private First Class Wilbur Worden "the first thing he [the German prisoner] does is try to bum you out of a cigarette [sic]."[43] The *Advocate* found other opportunities to provide amusing stories and lighten the mood about the POWs being in the community. The paper's editor ran an article titled "What's In a Name?" which told of two guards, one named Seymour Pow and the other Herbert Camp, the names of these men at Breckinridge combined created "POW camp".[44]

Whether these reports and dozens of others like them were sensational or accurate, the important thing was that the U.S. upheld the Geneva Convention, a fact that the combatants and civilians of the Third Reich understood. Many of the men fighting on the Eastern Front faced a harsh captivity in the Soviet Union or risked being killed out of hand by their Russian captors. The Russians refused to sign the Geneva Convention, a decision made obvious by their actions toward German captives in their custody. Wehrmacht forces realized their fate if captured by the Soviets and eventually entire units hastened to retreat from the East to surrender to the Americans and British. Some of these captives made up the contingent of POWs at Fort Knox.

Knox began holding Italian prisoners in February 1944 and the Germans replaced them later that year.[45] Half of the Germans housed at Knox were captured after D-Day, while the other half had been captured in North Africa. Soon after the arrival of the Germans, reporters visited the compound at Fort Knox. Louisville *Courier Journal* reporter, Poucher Coleman, described them: "some of them are blond, with chilly blue eyes; others are dark, with eyes like dull black agates. What they're thinking about is anybody's guess."[46] This description certainly did not mesh with the earlier reports from the Union County *Advocate*, and probably did little to ease the fears and stress of Kentuckians living near the camp. He continued "as a rule they're a healthy looking, well-disciplined lot, not inclined to be ingratiatingly friendly or openly hostile. They don't seem to be particularly unhappy, and yet they're not apathetic. Rather, they seem detached, to possess stereotyped personalities molded by Nazi discipline."[47] It must be noted again after such a generalized statement that the U.S. allowed reporters to only observe and not interview POWs and they could only take pictures if the POW and camp authorities both consented.

Newspaper writers like F.G. Alletson Cook admonished readers of the *New York Times* that "Nazi Prisoners Are Nazis Still." Having been to the White Sulfur Springs camp in West Virginia, he reported that many of the men clung to their faith in Nazism. One German, perhaps in a mockery of American democracy, placed a sign reading "Give me Liberty or give me Death." Cook reported that the men in general are unmoved by pictures of German cities that had been bombed, claiming them to be "fakes."[48] An American officer that Cook interviewed called the Germans "well trained, excellently disciplined automatons. As individuals they don't exist; as a team, magnificent."[49] Such narrow-minded interpretations might hold true for some Nazi elements among the prisoners, but lumping all the POWs into such groups was at the root of future problems encountered within the camps nationwide.

On the other hand, authors like Tracy Strong reminded readers of the *Christian Century* that "there is still such a thing as international law, and that in an important area of international relations it is still being observed."[50] Strong's statements represented one of the few instances where the *Christian Century* and the U.S. government saw things eye to eye on the issues of prisoner of war handling. James H. Powers, writing for the *The Atlantic Monthly*, urged that the prisoners of war should be studied and the results from these observations pooled. The best way to handle the German POWs, he believed, could only be determined after a critical analysis of all the data thus collected.[51] Anita De Mars, in an editorial to the *New York Times,* suggested that the well-fed POWs be put through "a systematic bleeding . . . once a month" to supply blood for U.S. soldiers.[52] She wrote this article in response to learning that German forces murdered 150 surrendering U.S. soldiers. Another woman quickly retorted to this editorial that she was repulsed by the suggestion, stating that "we women will hurry to the nearest station to donate all the blood that is needed. Good pure blood, full of the clean corpuscles of love, charity and kindness, but never must we permit our menfolk to be injected with the fiendish and ruthless blood of the enemy. Spare them the humiliation."[53] Kentuckians and other Americans disagreed on how to view the prisoners. Some accepted the Army logic, that these men would be here for the duration, presented no clear danger, and provided needed labor to area farms. Others felt that housing enemy prisoners in their own "backyards" should not be taken so lightly. Officials often cited that the good treatment of German POWs ensured that American captives received similar treatment. Many Kentuckians put aside feelings of uneasiness and made the most of the situation. The press often reported on the high spirits and good physical conditioning of these war prisoners. Many Americans agreed that something more needed to be done to protect civilians and curb "Nazi" mischief. Some of the ideas held merit, while others less so. Kentuckians, in the middle of the confusion and often rash interpretations, formulated their own opinions on how to handle these men. Emotions over the war obviously intensified reactions to the treatment and handling of Axis men in American hands.

The War Department understood the difficulties and passion that the presence of the captive enemy raised. Arguments about care and treatment hardened with a mixture of practicality and emotion, but the final say came from the U.S. military, not from communities or individuals. A Camp Campbell press release reminded concerned citizens that the handling of prisoners of war "is a grave, often grim, business, as all issues of war must be" but the final estimation needs to be one "shorn of galloping prejudice, proving that common sense and humanity are finally the successful methods for solving a problem that might easily become hysterical in war and foolhardy in the peace that follows."[54] This basic policy echoed the War Department's stance and defined how Kentucky's three base camps and numerous branch camps operated between 1943 and 1946. The program in the Bluegrass State uniquely provided a mixture of military discipline, recreational diversions, and character building hard-work, to impart upon the POWs a respect for American democracy and for the Kentucky way of life. Kentuckians also had an answer for the lingering question "how to occupy these men"; they worked Kentucky farms by the thousands over the next three years.

Americans of the World War II generation, or the "greatest generation" according to Tom Brokaw, a praise not undeservedly given, lived through the Stock Market Crash, the Great Depression, and the attack on Pearl Harbor. The Second World War created an outlet for some of the emotions and rage built up over the course of these events and created a solution that helped to end the Depression. Although entire towns turned out to watch Axis POWs load trains or march, and others worried about the security measures at the camp, the concerns over the POWs paled in comparison to concerns over the war effort and even the industrial output and economic stability of the home front. On the other hand, the POWs presented a measure of the success of the U.S. war machine. This tangible result could be measured, since more enemy prisoners generally equates to military success, and could be interpreted as a sign of impending victory. The Axis POWs also presented a tool to ensure that the American boys captured by the Germans and Italians remained relatively safe. Maybe the "earth stood still" for some Americans, but those who thought the POWs would enter into camps under heavy guard where they would not be seen or heard from again until the war ended would soon be proven wrong.

Chapter 3
Working for the Enemy?
German POW Labor in
Kentucky

They aren't supermen—they're just healthy misguided boys
-Reporter Hugh Morris after meeting POWs at Breckinridge[1]

On a fall day in September 1944 a school bus pulled into the little town of Trenton, Kentucky. The bus brought Kentucky's newest farm hands, German POWs, to Christian County farmers. Watching the bus enter town was one of the highlights of Edgar Radford's memories. His family employed POWs in their tobacco crop earlier that season and the Germans returned to work the corn crop. For Radford and others in Trenton this had become a familiar sight. Like many other Kentuckians he was skeptical of the men at first, but after working with the prisoners he realized that he "liked the idea of being around them a little bit."[2] Walter Mathis, another Christian County youth, vividly remembered the POWs working on his father's farm. "I can still recall and see them bringing wheat to the wheat thrasher, bringing hay to the hay bailer. I can still see them loading tobacco on to the wagon and taking it to the barn."[3] Walter and his older brother,

Junior, a teenager, felt that having the POWs around not only helped their father and other farmers, but according to the men, provided both with an exciting memory. Walter wondered about security and at first thought that there were too few guards for the prisoners. Soon he realized that the POWs had no malicious intentions. He remembered talking about the matter with his siblings, none of whom admitted or expressed "any fear at all of German prisoners."[4]

Other Kentuckians, however, like Patricia Ellis, found the situation less appealing. Her family employed German POWs on their Fayette County farm and she "was very afraid of them." She recalled people talking about fighting against the German and Japanese soldiers and to her "it seemed like it was bringing the war into your own backyard." Watching the "truck with cattle racks full of these men and a guard with a gun, maybe two guards with guns" approaching her house proved unsettling for an already leery Ellis. She admitted that "we were not ready for German prisoners to come up to the house."[5]

Like it or not, between 1943 and 1946 thousands of German prisoners from thirteen Kentucky camps worked in agriculture and industry across the state. Getting these men from the camps to the farms proved no easy task. Local farmers wanted to hire the Germans, but bureaucracy, government regulations, and lack of adequate housing, hindered the speed at which they became available for work. These delays seemed understandable in light of the confusion and difficultly farmers and U.S. officials experienced in implementing what became the largest prisoner of war labor program in U.S. history.

While the attention of Americans had been distracted by the events taking place overseas, the War Department and its subordinate agencies, the Army Service Forces (ASF), and the Provost Marshal General's Office (PMGO), tried to use the mandated media blackout to discreetly transport and house approximately ten thousand war prisoners in Kentucky camps. An operation of this size, however, could not be accomplished without the public taking notice. Before the war ended Kentuckians had a good understanding of the POW program and its impact on the state. The labor vacuum on the home front reached epidemic proportions. As working men rushed off to war or served in arms factories, the nation relied on women, secondary school aged children, and imported foreign labor to staff agriculture, pulp-wood production, and other essential industries. A correlation existed, however, between the equipment and supplies used in the war effort and the growing demand for production at home. The POWs, young, healthy, and otherwise a drain on the nation's resources, presented a ready source of manpower. The military debated their potential use in the American economy long before they housed them, but questioned their reliability and usefulness. How safe would the American public be once the compound gates opened and Germans mingled with Kentucky farmers and civilians and had increased opportunities to commit sabotage or escape? These concerns loomed large and as Americans contemplated them, the POWs filled the camps.

Most German veterans entering into camps Breckinridge and Campbell in 1943 served with the vaunted *Afrika Korps* under Field Marshal Erwin

Rommel. These elite young men possessed the élan, youth, and bronzed bodies gained from service in North Africa, and many undeservedly earned the dubious honor of being labeled hardcore Nazis. Regardless of classifications, Army officials wanted these men to work, and, thanks to having seen hard service in the military, they had already been acclimated to manual labor. While waiting on the War Department agencies, the War Manpower Commission (WMC), and state and local labor agencies to iron out a contract labor program for civilians to utilize, the POWs carried out work on military bases. These jobs included anything that related to their own upkeep and the maintenance of their living areas and camp. Army regulations created a classification system that categorized the types of labor performed and which categories received pay. Most of the work done by the POWs on Army bases or around their camps fell into two of the three newly created categories, Class I and Class III. If the work was classified as routine tasks related to housing and maintenance, it went unpaid. The military required POWs to clean and beautify the barracks and compounds and carry out minor repairs. Both German and American officers inspected their facilities and demanded of the prisoners the same level of promptness, cleanliness, and attention to detail, as was required of active duty soldiers.

Officials at Breckinridge invited reporters from the Louisville *Courier-Journal* to tour the POW camp during the summer of 1943. Although not allowed to photograph the prisoners without their consent or interview them at all, reporters observed them at work. Reporter Hugh Morris noted that "the compounds themselves are kept immaculate by the men themselves, who obviously take pride in the appearance of their new home."[6] Colonel Einar W. Chester, the commanding officer of the POW camp at Breckinridge happily told the visiting reporters that "you can eat off the floor of any German barracks or mess hall."[7] Another reporter concurred with Chester and added that "the precision of the camp itself and the barracks on this hot June day [June 20, 1943] was mathematical."[8]

The POWs also tasked themselves with planting gardens. The fact that this type of beautification project went unpaid did not faze the POWs who saw this labor of love as a reward itself. Using money earned in canteen coupons the POWs purchased plants and seeds. Sometimes the guards made these purchases for the prisoners or simply donated the seedlings. The POWs also transplanted shrubbery from land that they cleared on other parts of the base. Some of the gardens had been adorned with small picket fences, one with miniature windmills, and all had been heavily planted with clovers, irises, and gladiolas.[9]

The war prisoners took their flower gardens seriously. Experienced and caring hands supervised by a former landscape gardener, turned prisoner, tended the gardens. Newspaper reports covered this aspect of the camp as one of the most prominent and important parts of POW life. One reporter remarked that "you are struck . . . by the infinite amount of labor which the young Germans apply to the grounds of the camp. Not a structure but is encircled by garden plots of geometrical design, some tasteful, some grotesque, and adornments flourish everywhere."[10] Another noted that "within a few weeks the compounds are going to bloom like Grand Central Palace."[11] Yet, even the casual Kentucky observer noticed a flaw in many of the garden plots that apparently some non-native Kentuckians would miss; some of the POWs planted ragweed. Captain H.S. Rice, the internment officer, exclaimed to the reporters that the POWs would "be sorry" when they discovered their folly.[12] The flower gardens not only occupied the POWs, but gave them a sense of empowerment, a source of pride, and a feel of home. The POWs even offered to volunteer their time in constructing similar gardens around the officer's buildings and some Americans, impressed by the work already done, took them up on the offer.[13]

The POWs transferred their flower gardening skills to a large scale vegetable garden, full of cabbage, squash, eggplant, and tomatoes, among other things that augmented the POW diet. [14] The project started respectably "small" in 1943 with only 35 acres. This provided free food to supplement the meals of both the Germans and Americans at the camp. The sale of the surplus brought the camp a profit of $9,000. In 1944, the POWs planted 240 acres of crops, with approximately 80 acres tended primarily by the POWs, while military and civilians on post tended the other plots around Breckinridge.[15] This vegetable garden, not only provided the POW camp with food, it earned $11,000 from the surplus raised in 1944. The venture proved profitable enough that by 1945 the Breckinridge prisoners had 180 acres of their own garden under cultivation.[16] No records indicate what area farmers thought about this competition coming from the forced labor of war prisoners. Likely the demand exceeded the supply so much that the Breckinridge experiment did not make much difference in the overall scheme of things. Most Kentucky farmers had bigger concerns with finding help for their tobacco and corn cash crops.

Early into the labor program the military created a screening process to determine what skills the POWs brought with them from civilian and military service. This classification system allowed U.S. officials to more efficiently group these men for future tasks. POWs with special skills, such as clerical abilities worked as aides and clerks, those with language skill as translators, and those with medical skills staffed POW infirmaries. Soon, the larger pool of unskilled POWs began contract work on the bases, including clearing land, constructing buildings, and paving roads. Unlike other labor connected solely with POW upkeep and maintenance, POWs utilized in this manner, labeled as Class II labor, received 80 cents per day instead of the basic 10 cents for non-working POWs. With the military effectively organizing the prisoners and finding tasks to employ most of them regularly, the days of lounging around the camp and volunteering for work ended. The Army invoked the mandatory labor clause of the Geneva Convention and thereafter sought ways to fully employ all POWs. The contract labor program on the military bases set the precedent that the POWs, for the most part, were reliable workers who could be depended upon if employed on civilian contract jobs. With regulations for off-base employment nearing completion the final cog in the labor program had seemingly been removed.[17]

This early contract labor for the military operated so well that other branches of the military and other bases that did not yet have access to POWs wanted to contract them. Soon POWs transported from one base or branch camp to other military installations to perform large-scale tasks like building or road construction. Fort Knox officials were so pleased with the performance of the Italian POWs working on base in 1944 that when the Germans replaced them later that year they originally planned to use them only on base and not hire them out to farmers.[18] Central Kentucky's agricultural needs spoiled this plan, however, and following the completion of camp construction Knox prisoners joined their counterparts from Breckinridge and Campbell in tobacco and corn fields across the Bluegrass State.[19]

The civilian contract labor program in Kentucky began in the late summer of 1943. Although at this early date only several hundred POWs occupied the two functional camps in the state, farmers in the nearby communities eagerly employed them as soon as contracts became available. Even though POWs worked on military bases, the process of generating public contracts created new difficulties for government officials. The ASF, PMGO, and WMC, and the War Food Administration, cooperated in preparing the labor regulations. These agencies also balanced union concerns, the needs of civilian laborers and employers, and the hiring out of hundreds of POWs daily, all while still processing thousands of new prisoners arriving from Europe. As preparations and debates continued, U.S. officials dealt with the fact that the POWs were prisoners who, like it or not, were being forced to work. This brought the additional concerns of reliability, prisoner escapes, and public safety. All of these issues had to be accounted for before the prisoners could be sent into Kentucky's rural farm communities.

The program for allowing prisoners to work in the civilian sector reached its final stages of readiness once U.S. officials established policy, which included allowed tasks, required pay, and military guard allotments to accompany work details. The POW camp commander then notified the public of the availability of these men, often through announcements in local papers and meetings with the Farm Bureaus. At first the employer and POW camp commander negotiated the contracts. The commanders needed to know how many days the farmer wanted the men and how he intended to use them. If these things seemed suitable then the commander ensured that the farmer knew the regulations concerning time to pick them up, drop them off, how the men could be utilized, and POW rights. The contract then went to Major General Fred C. Wallace, Commanding General of the Fifth Service Command, and the local branch of the WMC for final approval.

The labor regulations underwent constant revision, often benefiting the employer. The process of procuring a contract, for instance, became decentralized. New contracts emphasized a closer relationship between the employer, local Farm Bureau, and POW camp liaison. Farmers visited the local camp for a contract, which now could be approved by the camp commander, sometimes the same day. Lieutenant Colonel Carl B. Byrd, Commanding Officer of the 1539 Service Unit at Camp Campbell, sent a press release to the *Kentucky New Era*, the newspaper for Christian County, and the Clarksville *Leaf-Chronicle*, the paper for Montgomery County, Tennessee, on July 30, 1943. It announced the availability of 500 German POW laborers currently housed at Campbell for contracted farm work.[20] Byrd informed farmers that these men could not be employed more than 25 miles from the camp and that they could only work in agriculture.[21] W.D. Talbert, Christian County Farm Bureau Agent, further explained that farmers wishing to contract these men had to pay Camp Campbell $2.50 per man, per day, and had to pick the men up at 7 a.m., bring them back by 5 p.m., and provide their own transportation. The military provided one guard for every ten men and lunches.

Byrd, anticipating the speed at which contracts would start coming into his office, warned farmers to start the process early. He suspected that some employers desired to hire these men well in advance to guarantee that they had them when needed during the season. He warned that some farmers might wait on preparing contracts for several weeks thinking he did not immediately need the men only to find out that all of the POWs had been contracted months in advance. Before the decentralization of the contracts Byrd stated that he expected delays in processing the contracts due to the number of channels they had to go through, including being sent to the Fifth Service Command Headquarters in Columbus, Ohio.[22]

Even at this early stage, before any problems surfaced, some local farmers seemed skeptical about hiring prisoner labor. By August 16th, 1943, nine Christian County farmers, already entered into contracts and waited for their final approval.[23] By the 19th of August the first fifty POWs, allotted out in groups of ten as stipulated by War Department regulations, began working on five different area farms. Kentuckians must have been amazed, or at least amused, at watching these Germans, clad in their blue uniforms stenciled in bright PW letters, working in tobacco fields for the first time. Surely the POWs found the situation odd and perplexing, since just months earlier they had been fighting in North Africa and now they worked for the enemy. The heat of a Kentucky summer with bent back and tobacco rows blocking the wind did not present a new challenge to these men with desert warfare experience. Cutting and spiking tobacco proved more of a problem. After some on the job explanation the POWs followed the farmer's example. Despite the likelihood that these newcomers to a tobacco field suffered several spiked fingers and hands, their first experience on Kentucky's farms passed without incident.[24]

Meanwhile, a couple of hours northeast of Camp Campbell, the POWs at Camp Breckinridge also started their first days with the contract labor program. The men at Camp Breckinridge performed the same jobs, namely in tobacco and corn, with many of the same problems. Camp Breckinridge also farmed out some of its POWs to work in Indiana canning factories. John Edwin McClure remembered the confusion that he and other Daviess County farmers faced in navigating the contract process for hiring POWs. McClure recalled that the farmers heard of the available labor at Breckinridge from a variety of sources, including the newspaper, but they did not know how to actually hire them. The solution seemed simple, go to Breckinridge and find out. So, McClure and several others loaded up and drove over to the camp. He recollected that they "went down there and drove right up to the camp, beyond the barbed wire" and directly to the commander's office. McClure knocked and the Colonel who answered was "raising all kinds of hell" about their being on the base. The Colonel chastised them 'don't you know this is a prisoner of war camp'." McClure stated that he straightened out the man by stating "we are not wearing uniforms and you can't argue with me like that." Then he explained that they "came down here to see about the possibility of getting some of these fellas to do work," which seemed to put the Colonel at ease. He then replied "well, why didn't you say so, come on in." At which point the Daviess County reconnaissance mission proved successful and they returned with the necessary contracts.[25]

After the labor program operated for several weeks, Kentucky officials again simplified the contract process by reducing the daily cost from $2.50 to $2.00 per day. Almost as an added bonus, the military offered transportation for a minimal charge. The Christian County Farm Bureau became a strong advocate for county farmers by negotiating with Camp Campbell officials to allow farmers to contract labor directly from the Farm Bureau rather than going through officials at the base. Lieutenant Colonel Byrd also cleared up some of the farmers' confusion by clarifying that the POWs could be used in corn, sweet potatoes, and hay, in addition to tobacco.[26]

Byrd proved to be a tireless spokesperson for contracting POWs. He maintained contact with the Farm Bureau, newspapers, farmers, and community organizations, constantly advocating the work ethic and cost-effectiveness of the German workers, and addressing questions and concerns. He met with the Kiwanis Club in October and praised the labor program. He explained that "two German prisoners of war accomplish about the same amount of work in one day that three ordinary day-laborers produce" and that "in the past month 5,000 man days had been put in by the prisoners on more than 100 farms." [27] During the presentation the discussion moved away from POW labor and into POW treatment. Byrd carefully outlined to the community group that the POWs "are treated according to certain mutually agreed upon standards, and the compact is a reciprocal one whereby our prisoners are given like treatment."[28]

The next month he spoke at the Christian County Farm Bureau luncheon, where he again cited the advantages of using POW labor and the necessity of the Geneva Convention. [29] This time, however, he showered most of the praise on the Farm Bureau itself for cutting through the red tape and simplifying the contract process which, in part, led to 6,300 man days of labor by November 1943. While speaking in Hopkinsville he noted that Christian County farmers entered into 95 percent of the available contracts, the remaining five percent were held by Trigg, Todd, and Montgomery County employers.[30] At the same time, however, Byrd expressed concern that farmers had been treating POWs too well. Byrd stated that the gifts of extra food doled out by the farmers, such as the "fried chicken, ice cream, or cigarettes" and that doing favors such as mailing letters for the prisoners, had to stop. He added that the farmer must not enter into conversations with the POWs beyond giving instructions. The guards needed to perform their duties, facilitating communication between farmers and prisoners *and* preventing fraternization. He warned that "if the guards permit" these activities to take place between the POWs and the farmers then "they are breaking military regulations and would face punishment."[31]

Byrd's interaction with the nearby communities proved unique among POW camp commanders and important in the relationship between the military and the civilian population. By demonstrating the usefulness of the Germans, their general reliability, absence of malicious intent, and the need for adherence to the Geneva Convention, he also put the community at ease and avoided much of the insecurity and anger that accompanied the arrival and employment of POWs in other parts of the U.S.

The harvest season of 1943 drew to a close along with Kentucky's first experiment with employing German POWs. The experience of the Bluegrass State that year was mirrored across the U.S. as 45,500 POWs worked on farms, industry, and other non-war related tasks in 27 other states.[32] The new year brought many changes to Kentucky's POW camps. As thousands of new prisoners arrived from overseas, new rules regulating POW employment were handed down from Washington. Over the next two years new branch camps dotted the state and areas like Danville, Shelbyville, Eminence, Louisville, Maysville, Lexington, and Frankfort, began housing some of the thousands of additional prisoners that flooded Kentucky's farms. Kentucky's POW labor experiment finally reached beyond a handful of rural counties to nearly two dozen in Kentucky, Tennessee, and Indiana.

Camp Campbell announced on July 12, 1944 that POW labor would again be available for contract for the harvest season. The Christian County Farm Bureau cited only positive benefits from farmers who employed the men in 1943. The Bureau negotiated with the WMC and the Extension Service at the University of Kentucky to provide a long-term contract between the Christian County farmers and Camp Campbell for 1944. This new contract allowed Christian County access to 15,280 man days of POW labor from mid-July to October 11 to cover the peak tobacco and corn harvests for that year. With the exception of some minor changes passed down from Washington, the contracts were identical to those of the previous year. Trigg and Todd County farmers negotiated similar long-term contracts for Campbell's POWs.[33] As in 1943, Byrd warned farmers that they needed to fill out the contracts promptly before the opportunity passed. The demand for prisoner labor from Campbell became so great that many farmers who waited too long could not get access to them. Byrd also addressed a growing problem, that of farmers signing the contract but not fulfilling it. He passed a new rule cautioning employers that if they agreed to hire the war prisoners, but did not fulfill the contract they could be liable for the cost of the days of labor lost and would not be able to utilize POW workers in the future.[34] G.G. Wadlington, Farm Labor Assistant at the Christian County Farm Bureau, reminded his constituents that "officers at the prisoner-of-war camp are doing everything possible to supply the prisoners so every farmer using them should cooperate to get the maximum benefit of such labor."[35]

As early as April 1944 John A. Sugg, Emergency Labor Assistant, and R.H. Ford County Agent for Union County informed area farmers that Breckinridge POWs would again be available for summer and fall employment. As the WMC limited the number of prisoners allocated to seasonal labor based on expected regional need, Breckinridge officials urged farmers to consider their labor needs and obtain contracts no later than two weeks in advance. Otherwise, the WMC might determine that the POWs at Breckinridge could be put to better use on different tasks unrelated to local agriculture or even transfer them to a branch camp or another base camp temporarily to fill that area's labor needs. Breckinridge officials clearly understood this "use them or lose them" logic and hoped to impart it upon all contractors who used POW labor.

While local farmers prepared a preliminary list of manpower needs, the county agents tried unsuccessfully to obtain the men for more hours each day. Many felt that the existing rule that only allowed the men to be away from camp between 7 a.m. to 5 p.m. seemed insufficient. They cited that civilian labor worked later during the longer Kentucky summer days. They also griped about the time lost in transporting these men to and from work sites which could be as far as 25 miles away from the camp. Regulations concerning the total amount of time worked each day came from the ASF and PMGO, authorities above the camp. POW labor, unlike civilian labor had to be back in order to observe the meal time, curfew, and lights out.[36] The process of preparing contracts began again in October as Union County issued another notification to area farmers, this time urging the need for immediate contracts for corn shucking.[37]

When the Germans arrived at Fort Knox in 1944, officials at that base immediately put them to work in different areas within the camp. Heino Erichsen was among the first 500 German POWs to arrive at Knox and like the rest of the prisoners housed there initially only worked on the base. He fondly remembered his time in the post laundry, the first time he worked side by side with American civilians, "they exchanged first names with me right away." This stood out to him because he was a prisoner of war and it was in stark contrast how things were in Germany. He recalled that "even with Germans of the same social class, it could take months or years to get on a first-name basis."[38] He eventually transferred from the laundry to the officers' mess in August 1944. "I was given a job in an excellent, practically four-star kitchen. This was the kitchen of the headquarters unit, which had a professional German restaurant chef and professional German pastry chef." He enjoyed this job much better than the previous one, recalling that "I hadn't seen meals like these in years. I translated for the mess sergeant, plus washed dishes and peeled potatoes." He added that "since I dined like an officer, I was as satisfied with my job as I could be under the circumstances."[39]

Kentuckians were initially hesitant to have masses of prisoners working throughout their communities. Yet, by the middle of 1944, none of the POWs, even those who had escaped, had committed any wanton acts of destruction. Therefore, by September 1944, agricultural and state and local government officials began exploring the possibility of employing the POWs on a wide-scale across Kentucky's farms. Fort Knox began hiring out its Germans for the first time during the fall 1944 harvest season. At a September 15 meeting in Lexington, Lawrence Bradford, State Farm Labor Supervisor announced that the Fifth Service Command was prepared to release as many as 1,500 POWs to Central Kentucky's farms as long as suitable housing could be found. The labor shortage in Fayette County had been so acute that Mayor R. Mack Oldham of Lexington and Mayor George Doyle of Paris asked businesses to release men from work to help with the harvest and in other counties schools closed to allow the boys to help.[40] When the meeting adjourned the representatives agreed to try to find suitable housing primarily near Lexington, Shelbyville, and Maysville. They presented the results of their findings at a second meeting the following night.[41]

Despite the fact that 650 POWs had already been allotted to area farmers, with the exception of using the fairgrounds at Eminence, little other housing could be found. Central Kentucky farmers worried about losing their access to these vitally needed workers[42] Bradford argued that housing for 1,000 to 1,500 POWs at one location could not be found and that several camps housing about 250 men were needed. Time was of the essence for Central Kentucky farmers, as they needed these men "within the next ten days to save the burley crop" worth "nearly $125,000,000" in 1943.[43]

Preparations at the Eminence Fairgrounds progressed swiftly and within the week that site had been inspected and approved by the military to house 250 POWs. By mid-September prisoners worked on Henry, Shelby, Oldham, Trimble, Spencer, and Carroll County farms.[44] The Henry County Farm Bureau and Extension Service, in cooperation with the WMC, brought the prisoners to the Fairgrounds branch camp from Fort Knox and allowed interested farmers to inspect the prisoners and their work potential, and to learn how best to utilize the men. Despite this, some farmers who could use the men did not sign contracts, expressing a "general uneasiness" about the matter.[45] On September 20, the first day the POWs were released for local contracts, eight Henry County farmers employed the men. The process of filling the contracts had been simplified by the experience garnered by Kentucky officials the previous year and through additional changes made at the national, state, and local level. Farmers appreciated the opportunity to hire labor at a reasonable rate of 40 cents an hour, or about $3.20 per day, as opposed to some local civilians requesting exorbitant amounts as high as $7.50 per day. The Army provided guards and lunches for the men. Restrictions required farmers to pick up their allotment of men, whereas some other camps, like Campbell, provided transportation for a fee. By allotting the prisoners out in groups of ten, few problems existed for labor starved farmers. Officials at the Eminence branch camp implemented a lesson learned from Campbell concerning deadbeat contractors and required payment in full once the contracts received approval.[46]

The editor of the *Henry County Local* rose early on Wednesday morning, September 22, to observe and report on the procedures on the first day that farmers picked up POWs at Eminence. Camp and local labor officials met the farmers as they arrived outside of the compound gate and explained the process of how to utilize these men. The wording of one of the orders to the farmers stood out to the editor, "they are not to be given anything other than something which can be consumed [strictly lunch], such as cigarettes, tobacco, candy, and the like."[47] This order meant that farmers could give the soldiers lunch, but that was it. Officials at Eminence relied on the experience gained the previous year at Breckinridge and Campbell and wanted to nip favoritism in the bud before it became a real problem. The entire process, from the official meeting with the farmers to loading over twenty trucks that carried the entire contingent of 250 POWs and 25 guards had been completed by 8:30 a.m. The editor found the prisoners' enthusiasm on the first day of work surprising, noting that they all "sing, laugh and joke."[48] He further commented that they all seemed "orderly and neat . . . physically fit" although generally short, remarking that only about half of the men were as tall as 5'11".[49] As October 1944 drew to a close so too did the 105 contracts signed for POW labor from Henry County. The termination of the harvest season also marked the end of the camp's usefulness and by the end of the month all the Germans had been returned to Knox and the fairgrounds returned to its pre-war functions. Area farmers expressed gratitude for the opportunity to get their crops in and POW labor saved a crop estimated in value of $3,090,000.[50]

As soon as other sites had been approved, additional branch camps appeared in central Kentucky for the 1944 harvest. The housing of 560 men at the Fayette Militia Armory on the Old Frankfort Pike made this one of the largest branch camps in the state. By September 23 farmers in over ten counties began hiring Lexington's allotment of prisoners.[51] Army regulations dictated that area employers pay POWs the prevailing wage rate of civilian labor. This measure, designed to protect civilian labor and appease labor unions, appeared in the earliest drafts of the POW labor program. This law created an interesting situation, however, as farmers from Franklin, Fayette, Jessamine, Bourbon, Scott, and Woodford counties hiring prisoner labor had to pay the government 45 cents an hour whereas farmers hiring labor from other branch camps, or even from other counties hiring from the Lexington camp only had to pay 40 cents an hour. Regardless of the prevailing wage, which differed all across the nation, the POWs only collected 80 cents per day and the surplus went to the Department of the Treasury.[52]

Many central Kentucky employers commented that the POWs were slow, but willing workers. Most agreed with the evaluation of S. Headley Shouse, a Fayette County employer, that "you couldn't expect these prisoners to go down the rows suckering tobacco like veteran farmhands, but they are doing alright so far."[53] Robert L. James, also of Fayette County, thought speed and production would increase once they figured "out what suckering tobacco is all about."[54] The farmers found the prisoners in high spirits since they often joked with each other and sang in unison while working. Shouse echoed the opinion of many employers when he stated that the prisoners were "certainly willing to listen to instructions and then go and do the best they can."[55] The patience of the farmers is made more remarkable when realizing that because of the crisis in central Kentucky, regulations stipulated that each farmer could only employ prisoners for two consecutive days. As all 560 men had been contracted, allowing an extended contract for some farmers would deny others the labor that they desperately needed.[56]

By the close of 1944 thousands more POWs worked in Kentucky crops as compared to 1943. Labor demands still loomed and the War Department continually urged full employment of POWs. The War Department pressured the ASF and PMGO to ensure that all prisoners worked and these concerns then trickled through to the Service Commands and individual camp commanders. Robert C. Goodwin, the Regional Director of the WMC for the states of Ohio, Michigan, and Kentucky, urged officials to "study possibilities of making fuller use of war prisoners."[57] In September 1944, all three states employed only 5,000 men combined, while thousands of others remained unemployed.[58] Camp commanders argued that they had filled all the contracts. They wanted to work the POWs too, but could not force civilians to hire them, and establishing branch camps in areas that would use the available labor took time. Most commanders desired that the POWs in their charge be employed for other, more pragmatic reasons; it kept them out of trouble.

As early as the spring of 1944 industries in Indiana, located in the Fifth Service Command, and

Illinois, located in the Sixth Service Command, realized that emergency government methods in place would not solve the dire labor crisis in food processing and looked towards the POW program for help. The WMC inquired if POWs could be utilized in this industry and Ralph Strong, WMC representative for Region V, added that the situation was dire enough that, even if all POWs available within the Fifth Service Command had been switched over, more manpower would be needed. [59] The War Department responded that they preferred farm labor over food processing. While POWs could not handle the food being canned, for fear of sabotage or poison, they could load boxes, trucks, apply labels, and do most of the manual labor."[60]

Kentuckians realized that Indiana sorely needed their help and quickly came to their aid. Officials at Breckinridge established a branch camp at Austin, Indiana, where the Moran Packing Company signed contracts for the POWs. A second branch camp established at Elwood, Indiana, allowed the Everitt Packing Company to employ POWs in the tomato canning industry. The POWs worked alongside active duty members of the U.S. military, who volunteered or had been assigned up to a two month period to aid these industries. After the peak canning season ended, the servicemen returned to duty and the POWs replaced them entirely in the factories. The need to keep the POWs away from the canned food required some delay in releasing the military men until enough civilians could be found to fill those positions. The POWs marched and sang while labeling cans, packing cases, and loading railroad cars leading their Indiana employers "[to] call [the] German prisoners 'mighty good' cannery workers."[61]

As 1945 rolled around it ushered in new changes for the POW program. Most POWs entering Kentucky camps in 1945 came from the battles in France and Italy. These newer men came from battle hardened units, although the Germans experienced a manpower strain to keep these divisions up to strength. The result was an increasingly large number of men being green recruits, while others seemed too young or old to serve in combat, and some were not Germans at all, but conscripts from around Europe. Yet, this influx of manpower available for labor made 1945 the peak year for POW labor usage, as the U.S. reached the maximum capacity of Axis men within its borders of approximately 371,000. Kentucky camps swelled to well over 9,000 prisoners during the early fall of 1945 and Kentucky farmers worked them from over thirteen different camps throughout western, central, and northern Kentucky.

In January 1945, Kentucky POWs returned to Indiana industry, this time helping construct an addition to the Indiana Ordinance Plant in Charlestown. Colonel Gilbert Wilkes, U.S. district engineer for Louisville, planned for as many as 500 POWs to build and man the site once suitable housing could be found, but stated that the POWs could not be involved in the manufacturing of weapons or explosives. [62] By the time the war in Europe ended, so too did the restrictions against employing Germans in military factories. They soon replaced many of the factory workers, often military men needed elsewhere, with a labor pool that swelled to 1,000 German POWs. The employment of the prisoners in these South Indiana factories met with opposition from both the American Federation of Labor and the Congress of Industrial Organizations. The Unions argued that the Germans took away jobs from civilians and this argument marked only one of the many disagreements between the War Department and various U.S. labor unions. The Unions finally conceded, however, after the WMC and War Production Board informed them that even with the prisoners and civilian workers available these factories remained woefully understaffed.[63]

Jeffersonville Quartermaster Depot served as one of the new locations to house POWs in 1945. Located across the river from Louisville in nearby Indiana, it began receiving POWs from Fort Knox. In addition to local farming, these men also loaded and unloaded trucks, made saddles, and constructed buildings. Like other Kentucky operated camps, the military occasionally invited reporters on a guided tour to snap photographs of POWs who gave their consent. Richard Renneisen, of the Louisville *Courier-Journal*, toured the camp in February 1945 and provided the first press coverage of the installation. His article, despite the limitations imposed by the War Department which forbade interviews with POWs or publishing POW names, painted a pretty clear American view of the prisoners. He found them to be very young, and felt that due their age they were probably heavily indoctrinated by the Nazis. He quickly added that "if these boys believe they are members of a master race, this reporter would say right off the cuff that somebody did a whale of a selling job on them." [64] With one exception, a young man he described as having a boxer's physique, he thought that most of them looked like Civilian Conservation Corps boys of the previous decade or like the young men being employed so readily by needy businesses locally. Watching a labor detail in the camp he concluded that "nobody in the prisoners' uniforms I saw looked hang-dog or surly or eager to goldbrick on the job, and some of them were doing outdoor construction work that required physical exertion and stamping around in cold, muddy ground on a frosty morning. They were well equipped with big overshoes, however, and gave no evidence that they didn't believe themselves pretty well off."[65]

Poucher Coleman, also from the *Courier-Journal*, visited Jeffersonville in April. He agreed with Renneisen about the prisoners age, but not appearance, "some of them seem too young to be top-notch combat soldiers; a few seem too old; but in general they are husky, barrel-chested, very tough-looking young men." Coleman added that "I have seen very few prisoners at Fort Knox, Campbell, or Jeffersonville who wouldn't be tough in combat."[66] Coleman concluded that the POWs seem "happier in Jeffersonville than they ever have been in Nazi Germany."[67]

April 1945 found Lieutenant Colonel Carl B. Byrd again speaking at the Christian County Farm Bureau. He pointed out that POW labor in 1944 amounted to 36,000 man hours and hoped that the POWs would be put to similar good use in the coming season. He desired to end the lingering problem of fraternization between farmers and POWs. He lamented that, despite many warnings, farmers still provided extra food and sweets as incentives and stated that a continuation of these activities was simply unacceptable.[68]

As the 1945 season began Farm Bureau officials announced that as of June the WMC and War Department approved of only 860 POWs for the entire state. Camp Campbell provided 320 of that number for use in Christian, Trigg, Todd, and Logan counties, as well as Montgomery County, Tennessee. One hundred and twenty of these men had already been contracted to work on twelve farms by June 8, 1945. The small number of men available in what farmers felt should be the peak year of employment troubled many Kentucky employers. Farmers increasingly relied on POWs and expected larger numbers to become available. Since the war ended in May and with the small number of prisoners approved for farm work, many Kentuckians wondered if the Army planned to start sending these men back to Europe. Kentucky Senator, Alben W. Barkely, addressed these concerns. His correspondence with the War and State Departments revealed that no immediate plans existed to cancel contracts and that employers could use these men unhindered through November. This news relieved Kentucky farmers who knew that they could get in their 1945 harvest before the POWs returned to Europe.[69]

The relatively small number of POWs being released for farm work, however, bothered Kentuckians who began contacting local and state officials requesting more men. These concerns moved up to the regional headquarters of the WMC for Region V and to officials of the Fifth Service Command who agreed to release a total of 3,100 POWs for work in Kentucky. The men thus released had initially been assigned to other various duties, including base labor, military contract work, industrial work, or as potential labor for other camps in the Fifth Service Command outside of Kentucky. It was also not uncommon for groups of prisoners to be transferred between Service Commands as labor and housing needs dictated. O.A. Hawkins, the WMC Labor Clearance Supervisor for the region, announced that 3,000 POWs had been earmarked for agriculture work directed from any of the 11 currently active camps in the state and would be "moved according to seasonal occupations" and regional need.[70] The remaining 100 would be split between Fort Knox and Owensboro, to remain in "reserve" for industrial or factory work as needed.[71] All of the branch camps in central and northern Kentucky operated from Fort Knox, with the exception of Owensboro which was maintained by Breckinridge. Southwest Kentucky had limited access to POWs from Campbell as no branch camps existed to provide additional service to those areas and most of south central Kentucky fell too far from Knox or Campbell to gain access to any POW labor. Farmers and local officials in Warren, Hart, and Barren counties unsuccessfully lobbied for a branch camp in their region. The Fifth Service Command and WMC agreed that a need existed, but required those counties to provide preliminary contracts for 1,500 prisoners before they could establish a branch camp. These counties could not fulfill the request by the August 1 deadline and therefore narrowly missed access to POW labor.[72]

Central Kentucky farmers, however, had no trouble filling contracts and gained a new branch camp at Shelbyville in June 1945. Shelbyville housed 250 men who hired out in groups of five or ten and worked in all of the surrounding counties. Henry County farmers, who benefited from the Eminence camp in 1944, were among the first to file contracts with the Farm Bureau for the 1945 season.[73] Henry County officials tried to reactivate the Eminence Camp, but the WMC and War Department determined that other branch camps, especially Shelbyville and Frankfort, were sufficient for Henry County's needs.[74] Although the local branch camp was never reactivated, Henry County farmers appreciated the use of the men, who had gained experience and speed since the previous year, and felt that working them "was quite the right thing to do, since the United States was, of course, obligated to feed them whether they worked or not and it seemed only the right thing to do to make them work for their food and shelter."[75]

Construction of new branch camps continued in 1945. Prisoners were housed at the Lexington Armory in Lexington, and at another new branch camp in Frankfort, located on George Collin's farm, just outside of town. Prisoners of War housed at the Lexington Armory on Old Frankfort Pike began working on August 13, 1945, and 77 contracts had already been signed for all 258 men. Of this number, 150 men were allotted strictly for Fayette County farmers; the remainder could be hired by employers in other counties. J. Ed Parker, Fayette County Farm Bureau Agent, explained to area farmers that little time remained for area farmers to sign a contract. Like most other branch camps, farmers had to provide transportation, but the Army provided lunches.[76] POWs at the Frankfort camp, numbering about 250, began working Kentucky crops on August 9, 1945. Bruce Poundstone, State Supervisor of Farm Labor, stated that orders for these men already exceed the number available, but suggested that additional branch camps may be constructed if the demand was high enough.[77]

Farmers in Woodford County were strategically poised to gain maximum benefit from both the Frankfort and Lexington branch camps. During the fall harvest they hired a total of 245 POWs from Frankfort and another 25 from Lexington. Despite these large numbers, Woodford County farmers needed even more manpower.[78] Harrison County farmers gained 60 POWs from Lexington to harvest their tobacco crop, but this small number did not solve their labor woes. Stanley Wilson, Harrison County Farm Bureau Agent, stated that while the POWs performed "generally satisfactory" they needed more men.[79] Scott County farmers contracted for 35 POWs in June, but by the end of August that number had jumped to 195. These men worked though September harvesting Scott County's grain, corn, and tobacco.[80]

Additional camps began housing POWs throughout August and September. The Paris branch camp held 225 on property owned by Mrs. J.T. Sharrard and was built in four days in August, 1945.[81] This camp hardly seemed large enough to fulfill the 350 applications for contracts filed by Bourbon County farmers.[82] The Boyle County Farm Bureau announced on August 16 that approximately 200 POWs would be available by mid-August and recommended early contracts to guarantee help.[83] The prisoners erected a tent city in Danville on August 17 and began working immediately on Boyle and surrounding county farms, including Garrard County which had contracts for 25 POWs.[84] R.O. Johnson, Garrard County agent, noted that some of the contracts had been signed a month in advance and that the war prisoners had proven their worth in Garrard by performing "2,385 man hours" that month.[85] By September 16, 1945, however, the season and the contracts ended and the POWs returned to their base camp leaving no remnants of their stay in Danville.

The Lexington Signal Depot at Avon, in Fayette County, also began housing POWs in 1945. They worked primarily on the military base at Avon while some worked under civilian contract. Lieutenant Colonel William A. Kelley, commanding officer at Avon, understood the local labor shortage. Once need on the base eased and civilian employees returned to a 40 hour work week, he began contracting POW labor to area farmers. He allotted 175 of the 250 Germans and Austrians at the Signal Depot to work in area farms. The number of men working off base averaged only about 35 at a time, partly because they could only be hired on a limited basis as contract work was primarily on Saturdays and other days as the work schedule at the Depot permitted. Depot guards and employees had already been volunteering their own time on Saturdays and Sundays to help area farmers. Once the Depot released the prisoners to work, contract duties fell to J. Ed Parker, Fayette County Farm Bureau Agent, and Clarence LeBus of the Farm Labor Committee, who announced that they operated under the same guidelines as at the Lexington Armory. High demand for POWs resulted in some contracts being denied. While POWs were hired out based on the earliest contracts, ideally all applicants received one full days work. Although, some employers signed contracts for three consecutive days for up to ten men at a time; others employed five men for six consecutive days.[86]

Bill Columbia, 16 years old at the time, recalled his family hiring POWs from Avon to work on their Winchester farm in Clark County. He remembered the truck arriving with two U.S. guards and about fifteen German POWs to help his family sucker their tobacco crop. He felt that they were "pretty fair workers, I don't know that they ever caused any problems."[87] Although the military kept the POWs segregated from the other farm workers, Columbia never looked at them as different, dangerous, or the enemy. He recalled that "I never gave it too much thought; they were just like the other workers out there on the farm." He added that although the Germans helped only one season, they filled an important labor gap as "there wasn't too many people to get to work on the farm [since] most of the boys were in the military." Once the POWs left Columbia's family performed these tasks without POW help. Having the POWs, even for a limited time, proved helpful, but as Columbia admitted his family was happy when labor conditions returned to normal after the war.[88]

The end of hostilities further reduced the workload at the Signal Depot, resulting in the adverse effect of releasing 440 of the 2,200 government employees. Kelley pointed out that the reduction directly correlated with the end of the war and had nothing to do with using German prisoners.[89]

While POW labor helped in Central Kentucky, the labor crisis still existed. J. Ed Parker, Jr., County Agent urged that "workers in other industries who have spare time to register at his office to aid in the burley harvest." Kentucky Farm Bureau agents' efforts to transport workers from Eastern Kentucky counties also failed. The WMC certified that the region needed more help and prisoner labor seemed the only answer. The War Department agreed and released an additional 150 POWs from Fort Knox to the Lexington Armory in late August 1945.[90] By early September, Central Kentucky farmers boasted that although the weight of the crop was lighter than the previous year, the quality certainly exceeded it. If not for the POWs much of this bounty would have been lost. Prospects for farmers brightened for the first time since the war began because POW labor helped house the peak of their crop on time.[91]

Of all the stories concerning POW labor in Kentucky, none seems more remarkable than the tale of Smith Broadbent, Jr.'s use of German and Austrian labor in Trigg County. Everyone within three counties seemed to know about Smith using these men on his farm. Myron Pool, a Christian County farmer, recalled that Broadbent "had a choice bunch of prisoners and they could do almost any kind of work."[92] Margaret Rudd, of Eddyville, a home supervisor with the Farm Security Administration, worked Lyon, Christian, and Trigg Counties and remembered Smith's POWs. She said, "We all knew that they were in the area" and "that they worked at Broadbent's."[93] Monroe McGhee, a Trigg County farmer living in Buffalo, remembered that the Broadbent's had a large scale operation there and needed the POWs to help bring in their crops.[94]

Broadbent had one of the largest farms in the county, with approximately 3,000 acres, and eventually hired forty POWs from Camp Campbell in 1944. Smith, Jr. recalled that he used all forty in his tobacco crop but during the corn harvest had only asked for twenty of the men to return. He stated that "as it happened, the 20 men we requested for permanent work were all Austrians."[95] When the long-term contract ended on December 7, 1945, he arranged for the men to attend a Christmas dinner at his home. During the evening a POW named Sageder performed "Silent Night" on the family piano while the others sang carols. Later a POW "dressed in a Santa suit" and they all exchanged gifts. Afterwards they "all went to Mt. Zion Methodist Church for a special Christmas service."[96] The friendship that the Broadbents developed with the POWs lasted a lifetime. They continued to communicate with each other through letters, pictures, and postcards, and twenty-five years later the Broadbents visited them in Austria.[97]

While few stories matched the Broadbent's, most employers appreciated the Germans and the work they performed. The difficulty in getting the program started seemed to be worth it once underway. The government took on a daunting task when it instituted the labor program and therefore it started slowly. The only parallel at the time was the even larger task of housing and handling the POWs. Concerns for security, full employment, and productivity all derived from the early planning for this program. It had obvious benefits for local employers; farmers had access to men to harvest crops that otherwise would have wasted in the fields. Local and state agencies brokered deals that helped save their region's economy. The U.S. government had much to gain from this program as well. Besides the factors stated above much of the profit from the POW labor went to the Department of the Treasury. Housing, clothing and feeding these men drained the economy and their labor became means of providing for their upkeep. Most of the POWs enjoyed the opportunity to work. It allowed them to leave the mundane day to day of camp life, where they could interact with civilians, catch at least fleeting glimpses of towns and equally important, see girls. POWs who worked had an opportunity to earn extra pay which could either be spent as canteen coupons at the POW operated store or saved to be paid in cash upon reparation. Another side existed to this seemingly win-win situation, however, that must be examined before any true cost-benefit analysis can be conducted. Problems existed that plagued the labor program from its onset. These problems stemmed from union and employer grievances to difficulties created by the POWs themselves who often refused to work or escaped from their labor details.

Chapter 4
Sowing the Seeds of Democracy: The Trials and Tribulations of the POW Labor Program

I hold it, that a little rebellion, now and then, is a good thing, and as necessary in the political world as storms in the physical.
-Thomas Jefferson in a Letter to Madison[1]

$\mathcal{T}$he implementation and success of the POW labor program was beset by problems from its very onset. People living near the camps feared for the safety of their families in case of a POW escape, and some complained about proposed POW camps or work sites located too close for comfort within their communities. Union arguments, civilian protests, and work stoppages all threatened the labor program. At times local residents joined workers and unions in protesting aspects of the POW program. None of these democratic complaints were lost on the prisoners who read the papers, overheard the local problems, and absorbed these basic lessons in democracy and the

American labor system. The POWs practiced their own "democratic protest" when they mimicked the protest of American labor, including creating work slowdowns and strikes. As this chapter demonstrates, many factors slowed down the utilization of the prisoner laborers and threatened the success of the POW labor program. Yet, American officials ultimately surmounted these obstacles to create the most successful prisoner of war labor program in U.S. history

Prisoners of war provided much needed labor for Kentucky's farms, but did not alleviate the need for other workers to fill this gap. This required the government to use emergency measures including importing foreign workers and giving deferments to men employed in essential industries. Many Kentuckians found the labor shortage appalling, and some preferred to lay blame on government bureaucracy and mismanagement of resources.

Leigh Harris of the *Henderson Gleaner* voiced this opinion loudly in his editorials. The Hopkinsville *New Era* reprinted his article of protest which stated his feeling that "the Washington idea seems to be that the farmer whittles on the cracker box at the village grocery until some pleasant morning he knocks the ashes from his corn cob pipe and says, 'I believe I'll plant a crop'."[2] Harris blamed the government for "the red tape which ham strung federal cooperation."[3] As for the German POWs, he stated "they are good workers" but the small farmer could not meet the "impossible conditions" set forth by the government to utilize them."[4] This point could not be disputed. Smaller farmers typically could not meet the requirements of guaranteeing work for at least ten men at a time, providing transportation, and paying the contract in full upfront. Unless several farmers could enter into a joint contract, they had to forgo the extra help.

Hiring war prisoners presented other problems. Civilians and returning veterans feared being displaced by this "cheaper" labor, and unions took up the cause of the American worker. Unions accused the government of employing POWs to take away American jobs and suppress wages. The government argued that many civilians used the labor crisis as leverage in demanding exorbitant wages. The government ensured that civilians did not lose jobs; no POWs could be contracted until the War Manpower Commission (WMC) investigated and determined that not enough civilians could be employed.[5]

Union protests caused the War Department constant grief. The Provost Marshal General's Office (PMGO) and the Army Service Forces (ASF) felt that unions impeded POW employment at nearly every turn. They argued that the unions applied "great pressure . . . on members of Congress" and they constantly flooded the PMGO with "letters of complaint" sent "directly or through senators and congressmen."[6] Seemingly nothing could be done to please the unions. The ASF and the PMGO attempted to communicate with them prior to hiring and incorporated the aid of the Industrial Personnel Division and the WMC to certify labor needs only after consulting with local communities. The PMGO stated that it was "difficult to demonstrate to American labor [unions] that the use of prisoners of war to alleviate shortages of manpower was a contribution to the successful pursuit of the war and, for that matter, to the well-being of their own families."[7]

Many Kentucky farmers became accustomed to using POW labor and by the winter of 1944 signed contracts employing them in stripping tobacco. Although their use in tobacco warehouses and redryers had been debated, many employers welcomed the idea. Even in this new industry Christian County remained one of the most progressive areas in the hiring of POW labor. The Farm Bureau entered into a new and impressive contract that would expire on April 4, 1945, the contract allowed county farmers and tobacco warehouses to hire up to 100 men per day.[8]

Local unions in central Kentucky impeded similar contracts. By November 1944, Fayette County farmers, redrying plant owners, and the U.S. Employment Office, realized that the acute labor shortage experienced on tobacco farms in the fall would spill over into the redrying plants during the winter. As soon as the WMC certified the need for POWs in this industry, employers announced that they intended to hire as many as 200 to work in the ten area redrying plants. The Lexington Central Labor Union protested the move and drafted an official letter to H.H. Mayse, manager of the Lexington division of the U.S. Employment Service on December 2.[9]

Despite these union protests, the Lexington Tobacco Board of Trade searched for suitable POW housing and the Fifth Service Command inspected the proposed sites on January 13, 1945. They approved an underused building at the Lafayette School, measuring 250' x 56' and formerly used by the Lexington Signal Depot, to house the 200 men. Colonel D.Y. Dunn, school superintendent, explained the possible use to reporters on Tuesday, January 16, 1945. He deflected community concerns by adding that the building, while on school property, was near the sports field and some distance from the main campus and that "no definite action had been taken to lease the building."[10] Most residents remained unaware of the event until the morning paper arrived and a number of them started to protest. Dunn echoed agreement with the protestors stating that "the proposed use of the school building is outside our school program and we don't want to become involved in any controversy."[11]

The clamor grew until over 50 residents joined the protest, some threatening legal action. One resident stated that he had no problem with using the POWs, but that the residents "do resent the fact that warehouses and the United States Employment Service have tried to railroad the proposal through by exerting pressure on the school board without the public's knowledge." He added that they also opposed the use of "school property for housing war prisoners."[12] Lonnie Webster, President of the Lexington Central Labor Union, claimed at an emergency board meeting to have received "numerous requests from residents" and "parents . . . asking [the Union] take action to stop the move."[13]

Realizing this pressure, Dunn announced that "the [school] board is willing to co-operate [with the establishment of the camp] only in the case of an extreme emergency."[14] That emergency, however, had been looming since November. The Lexington *Herald* ran side by side articles on January 17. One discussed the potential for the entire 1944 crop to be wasted on the warehouse and factory floors, the other protesting the Lafayette site.[15] Herman Robinson, the Secretary of the Tobacco Board of Trade, declared that the tobacco industry had reached a crisis stage and if labor could not be found then a sales holiday was the "only resort to divert labor to the redryers and clean up the processing of sold leaf."[16] Warehouse and plant operators in the area had already been operating with only 50 to 60 percent staff and some on only one shift. Kentucky faced losing one of their largest crops. [17]

On January 18 the Lexington Tobacco Board of Trade announced that the Lafayette school would no longer be considered. Some local farmers and redryer operators agreed that government pressure tactics had been applied to the school board. The Lexington *Herald* argued that "pursuing the same policy of secretiveness which they have followed since beginning efforts to obtain war prisoners early in December, tobacco officials last night [January 17] declined to comment on progress made in conferences yesterday."[18] L.J. Gorin, a member of the Lexington Tobacco Board of Trade assured members of the community that they did not use "pressure" on the board of education. He explained that the original location was a site at Winchester Pike-not on school property. Military inspectors learned that the school had a "collapsible barracks" and opened a dialogue with Colonel Dunn transporting it for use. According to Gorin, who accompanied the inspectors, Dunn instead offered the alternate building on the campus and then had the school board draw up and sign a contract. Gorin concluded that they were now in a hopeless situation as the community protest, threatened litigation, and reversal by the school board, had basically cancelled the lease contract.[19] In his own press release Dunn stated that "the proposal had been made subject to final approval by the board of education and that the withdrawal had been made before the proposed contract had been signed by representatives of the tobacco industry."[20]

H.C. Robinson, Secretary of the Lexington Tobacco Board of Trade, lamented the situation. He argued that every effort had been made as early as September to gain the cooperation of the community and the unions and to prepare them for this labor crisis. On the 19th he announced that they have given up all attempts to hire POWs in redrying plants, but that this decision had nothing to do with union protests.[21]

Union problems also arose over employment of Breckinridge POWs at the Owensboro branch camp. The Germans had been working in industrial plants when the Owensboro Central Labor Union filed a grievance stating that competing plants were hiring the men. The Union's concerns did not fall on deaf ears. Colonel R.L. Shoemaker, Camp Commander at Breckinridge, along with Lieutenant Colonel H.E. Johnson, the POW Camp Commander, and representatives of the WMC, feeling pressure from civilian and union groups, announced the military policy in hiring out POW laborers by assuring concerned parities that "no discharged veterans or other workers are deprived of employment due to the utilization of PW labor." [22] B.J. Killigan, district manager of the WMC, stated that POW employment began "after all efforts to locate civilian farm hands were futile."[23] Shoemaker ensured that the military would "pull a prisoner from any job the moment the investigation discloses that other labor is available."

The POWs caused problems of their own that impeded production on Kentucky's farms. Myron Pool, a Christian County farmer, employed German and Austrian POWs to work his tobacco and corn crop. Pool felt that "most of them did very well," although he recalled several less than ideal situations. One time after he explained how to pull and cut corn the men ignored him and began pulling corn from the stalk. One POW took the ears "one at a time in his hand and [laid them] over in a pretty pile." Pool recalled being aggravated and stated, "That way you did not get much done." Later when throwing the corn on the wagon another POW on the down row, the row directly behind the wagon, fell behind and Pool helped him until a few minutes later when the POW "hit me in the head with one of the ears of corn." The guard who "was [typically] hunting squirrels in the woods" told Pool that he would have the man reprimanded, but Pool told him not too, "I did not think it was on purpose."[24]

Pool also used the men in tobacco. It was another new experience for these war veterans. "We couldn't get the prisoners to climb up in the barn," Pool recalled, "they were afraid of heights." When they eventually climbed into the barn they "tied themselves to the tier poles with their belts." Pool stated that "you can see that with some prisoners you did not get much done." Communication proved difficult as well, especially with the guard not always being available. Pool said that he and the other farm help "would make motions and stuff, and maybe one in the bunch could understand a little and he would explain it." One time he brought the men water and a prisoner asked him "what went quack quack?" Pool said "ducks." The

POW replied "water is for ducks, we want schnapps." The worst instance that Pool knew of involved his neighbor whose "prisoners agreed to work on Sunday," but once there "they refused to work, so they had to walk six miles back to Fort Campbell." He remembered that as "the only time I saw them not want to work." Pool concluded that "as a whole they were a lot of help at that time, that is if you had a lot of patience, I think if you got to know them they were more helpful and dependable."[25]

The relatively mild problems experienced by Myron Pool are examples of POW misbehavior on farms. Sometimes the POWs demonstrated complete work stoppages and created other problems within the camps. An explosion in the laundry at Camp Campbell led to a temporary work stoppage. Although the subsequent investigation found no injuries, authorities discovered that a live cartridge "believed to have been inadvertently left in a suit pocket" caused the explosion.[26] That the POWs possessed a cartridge caused alarm, but other difficulties at the camp that week placed the war prisoners under greater scrutiny. One of the POW spokesmen at Campbell refused to carry out a direct order given by Lieutenant Colonel Byrd, Commander of the Campbell POW Camp. Byrd gave the man a stint in solitary confinement. Guards at Campbell sent six other men to share his fate that week, one for spreading unrest, and the others for being uncooperative. This situation did not sit well with the rest of the Axis men at Campbell. Once they learned of the plight of their comrades, 314 POWs went on strike. The strike ironically began on June 5, 1944, the day before the D-Day invasion, and shut down most POW productivity. Byrd gave the maximum punishment allowed by War Department regulations and all 314 strikers received a bread and water diet and barracks confinement. This punishment translated into 18 ounces of bread a day for up to fourteen days and unlimited water. Other punishments, usually instituted before and then accompanying the bread and water "no work, no eat" policy included loss of privileges and withholding of pay.[27] Most of the men reconsidered on June 6. By June 7 the resolve of the others had evaporated and they returned to work.[28] Due to the size of the problem, outside authorities had to inspect the camp. These investigations resulted in Camp Campbell being deemed a properly operated facility and Byrd receiving a commendation from "the provost marshal, the Swiss legation, and the Department of State for 'excellent supervision' in accord with the Geneva Convention."[29]

The amount of food provided to the POWs in general also became a major issue involving not only the prisoners, but also farmers, civilians, and the military. The Geneva Convention required that POWs be fed and housed equivalent to U.S. servicemen. POWs often had food in quantity and quality greater than the civilian population who lived under a rationing system. Prisoners received about 2,000 calories, but sometimes this soared as high as 3,000 or more, per day. The situation regarding the food that prisoners consumed came under scrutiny almost immediately. In 1943 one writer to the *Cadiz Record* confessed to "finding extremely repugnant the thought that at this moment some arrogant, unregenerate Prussian soldier in Texas is eating beefsteak when some of our friends in other parts of the country write that they have not been able to purchase an ounce of beef for at least four weeks."[30] The writer continued that this is all part of upholding our end of the Geneva Convention, whereby "we are at liberty to assume that our soldiers are eating beefsteak . . . though doubtful."[31] J. Earle Bell toured Breckinridge in 1945 and assured readers of the Union County *Advocate* that the POW menus "did not contain the steaks and butter heard so much about, but indicated that the prisoners are well fed."[32]

Concern over feeding POWs gained increased attention in both Kentucky and the national press. Columnist Drew Pearson helped focus public indignation in his February article in the Sunday *Herald-Leader*. Pearson bluntly stated that "German prisoners of war, many of them arrogant, insolent, and considered beyond political rehabilitation, get rationed foods denied civilians, and in some cases receive scarce foods requiring four times the food stamps now allowed American civilians."[33] A recounting by Pearson of some of the typical weekly menu items, including "turkey ala king, veal, bacon, and pork chops," helped rouse the anger of an already skeptical Kentucky audience. He juxtaposed that "meanwhile, American boys held by the Germans complain that were it not for Red Cross packages provided them by relatives they would be hungry constantly."[34]

The chorus of Americans across the nation protesting POW rations was joined by reporters and major news figures. Walter Winchell reported similar stories on the evening news and reports by Pearson, Winchell, and others helped crystallize the situation in the minds of Kentuckians like Mrs. H.C.W. who argued against the "grand" treatment German POWs get while "our boys are being tortured and starved and robbed of all their valuables."[35] She stated that continued good treatment given POWs will only make them want to "stay over here and soon ruin our once grand country. I believe we should treat them just as they are treating our boys."[36]

The U.S. War Department, State Department, legal scholars, and interested citizens knew and understood the Geneva stipulations. So too did the Swiss Legation and the International Red Cross, both tasked with inspecting and reporting back to the Third Reich on conditions in U.S. operated camps. The POWs also knew their rights and the U.S. obligations under the treaty. Failure to follow them could result in protests, strikes, and complaints issued to the Red Cross investigators. Yet, even with the legality constantly being explained over the course of the POW labor program, the situation still drew ire from Kentuckians going without.

The food provided to American POWs in Germany, it should be noted, never equaled that provided to active duty U.S. servicemen or German POWs in U.S. captivity. Americans held by the Germans often had to eat food greatly reduced in quality and quantity, roots and twigs, watery soup or stew with bits of horses or meat typically uneaten in the U.S. American soldiers dubbed these meals, composed of substandard, odd, and scavenged material, the "Hitler Diet." German soldiers at the front, however, not to mention the average German citizen, never had a diet with a caloric equivalent to that given to their American counterparts. Each year of the war brought increasing difficulty to the war strapped nation, which suffered from a shortage of raw materials and low farm production due both to the Allied naval blockade and the drafting of their young men from the farm fields to the battle fronts. This hampered the ability of the Third Reich to provide adequate rations to its POWs. It could be argued, however, that they upheld the Geneva Convention by providing the same limited caloric value as being given Wehrmacht troops.[37]

The issue of feeding U.S. held prisoners became emotionally charged and each side seemed to have some validity. The U.S. government argued that fulfilling its treaty obligation not only kept U.S. honor intact, it also ideally provided better treatment for American forces held in enemy POW camps. Some members of the government looked at the Cold War looming and also saw repairing postwar relations with a democratically aligned Germany as an added benefit of this proper treatment. Disseminating this to the soldiers level meant that treating prisoners properly, however distasteful, was part of doing one's duty. As former POW Howard Tromp stated, "it was easy for some to see all the Germans as Nazis, and blame them, even though that was not the case."[38] Many of the farmers, guards, and camp officials, who worked with these men, saw the prisoners on a more personal level. They were just boys, like American youths, serving their country. The POWs also performed a labor service and getting the most out of their employment required a certain level of food and good treatment.

In March 1945 the menu for the POWs drastically changed for the first time. War Department officials stated that the change would only affect the food types and not the caloric amount. The War Department claimed that the POWs did not like the types of American foods provided and preferred German food prepared in their traditional manner. Much of the food on the previous camp menus had been rationed in the U.S. and the POWs apparently "refused" to eat much of it and let the food go to waste. POWs now received food "not usually consumed in any quantity by Americans, such as pig knuckles, fat back, and so forth."[39]

The new menus reflected vastly different changes than what the military cited. The Louisville *Times* printed the revised menu and noted that it barely resembled those previously discussed. POWs, for instance, would be allowed 25 pounds of salad in exchange for the 45 pounds of beef that they typically would have had. This also included a reduction of sugar by four pounds with no apparent substitution. They were allowed 92 pounds of potatoes, up from 74, but had to substitute pineapple, which they reportedly enjoyed, for prunes. Fifth Service Command Headquarters included a press release stating that "the use of critical and high ration value food will be kept at a minimum. Non-rationed fresh foods will be used as extensively as possible in feeding prisoners." It also stated that the POWs would receive 2,500 calories per day and that a fixed ten day menu would be used for the duration of imprisonment.[40]

The POWs realized that this new menu changed not only the types of food given, but significantly decreased the caloric amount given. For most POWs in the U.S. the meat allowance did not exceed four ounces per day. Former POW Howard Tromp recalled getting a reduction in the amount of food being allowed after V-E Day (May 8, 1945), but was never sure exactly why. POW menus received the first major reduction during the spring of 1945. Civilians and prisoners alike felt that this had to do with the victory in Europe and an ensuing lifting of U.S. obligations under the Geneva Convention. Others felt that it had more to do with the discovery of death camps in Europe and the outrage of U.S. military and civilians.[41]

While the POWs might resort to the means of work stoppages and slow downs to protest, the results only ended in confinement and a bread and water diet, a further reduction in food. Kentucky farmers, however, came to the aid of the POWs. Many farmers had been accustomed to preparing meals for their POW farmhands just as they did for the civilian workers. The military constantly battled with farmers over providing these types of "favors." When farmers learned of the caloric restriction they took action. Patricia Ellis recalled her mother's dissatisfaction with the fact that the military only sent the POW farm workers sandwiches for lunch. Her mother and two other women cooked them lunches while Patricia brought the food and drinks to them. She recalled that while bringing them their food she was "so scared of them, they didn't speak English and they laughed and said things in German when I gave them their food. If they had been planning on killing us I wouldn't have even known the difference."[42] Edgar Radford said his family knew that "it was against the rules to feed them, but it was alright with the guards," so his "mother always fixed sandwiches for them."[43]

R.H. Proctor, Assistant Secretary of the Kentucky Farm Bureau, protested loudly about the caloric decrease by firing off complaints to Senators, Congressmen, and the Associated Press which ran articles in dozens of newspapers that called the situation "unsatisfactory." He argued "that it was with shocking dismay that we learned today that prisoners of war doing farm labor in Kentucky are being fed thin soup rations that contain far below the nourishment required for farm work. They are fed only half a canteen of soupy mixture and one to two slices of bread three times a day."[44]

Proctor then related how useful these men had been and that the food situation needed to be rectified. "These prisoners are contributing a large measure of relief to a critical farm labor shortage, but being fed only such rations as they are receiving, they are becoming exhausted by mid-afternoon and the effectiveness to the relief of the farm labor shortage is decreased by this condition. In the light of the fact that there is no other labor available, we beg that you with all haste do everything possible to remedy this situation."[45]

W.D. Talbert, Christian County Farm Agent, stated that area farmers had noted the situation and agreed with Proctor that afternoon work slowdowns seemed to correlate with the reduction in food. West Kentucky farmers complained that "the prisoners were not . . . working so well as they did before the capitulation of Germany . . ."[46] Talbert assured citizens that advocating an increase in POW rations did not "mean that the farmers are leaning toward the Germans, but that they are concerned purely where lesser amount of work is obtained because of improper nutrition."[47]

The War Department and Fifth Service Command Headquarters retaliated by publishing the POW menus. They reiterated that non-working POWs received at least 2,500 calories per day, those engaged in moderate labor 3,000 calories, and those in farm labor 3,500 per day.[48] The military claimed that farmers felt that the POWs needed the same "Kentucky Breakfast" to which they had been accustomed.[49] The military assured civilians that although the POWs received fewer calories than their Kentucky farm employer, they still received adequate nutrition and caloric intake on par with American soldiers. They wanted the farmers to understand this clear difference. With these statements the War Department felt that they had finally addressed the complaints by the Kentucky Farm Bureau and its constituents. After a "thorough investigation" on June 18, the Farm Bureau withdrew its complaints. J.E. Stanford, Executive Secretary, stated that they had been "convinced . . . that the overwhelming majority of farmers using German prisoner-of-war labor [now] believe these prisoners are fed sufficiently to enable them to do a full day's work."[50]

Even the retraction by the Farm Bureau and the reassurance by the military did not dissuade all Kentuckians. Farmers continued to provide extra rations to their POW farm hands and others continued to protest to newspapers and local farm authorities. A June editorial to the Louisville *Times* argued that "men are animals. German prisoners of war, regardless of whether one wishes to be humane, must be fed rightly, when at work and when idle, if they are to be good workmen."[51]

By the end of June additional changes had been made in POW menus. The War Department echoed its earlier statement that POWs continued to receive adequate daily calories and the new menu reflected a greater portion of meat, eggs, cheese and potatoes. The War Department pointed out that although the "quality of meat remains the same; only the poorer cuts are being authorized."[52] The military never admitted to making these changes because of continued pressure, but the *Courier-Journal* correlated the new announcement with the ending of protests. A Fort Knox public relations officer stated that the change had been implemented simply because POWs doing farm labor could not get the hot lunches served others at camp. He admitted that POWs employed on farms ate lunches of a decreased caloric amount than their German counterparts working on base. He was careful to add, however, that this lunchtime caloric deficiency was made good to farm-working POWs by increased meal sizes at breakfast and dinner.[53]

Safety complications also hindered the complete success of the labor program. Many of the farmers picking up POWs had never been on a military base before and had no real knowledge of military regulations. Others understood how rigidly the speed limit and other driving laws were enforced by the Military Police (MP). MPs constantly wrote tickets to farmers and contractors who repeatedly broke the law. The traffic problems peaked in November 1944 at Camp Campbell when the numbers of traffic accidents and fatalities forced camp authorities to post notices in the local newspapers. Military officials also requested Kentucky and Tennessee police to increase patrols on Highway 41, the major thoroughfare that connected the base with the two states.[54] Byrd finally responded to increased infractions by issuing a warning to the Christian County Farm Bureau that if these willful violations of camp safety rules continued it would constitute a breach of contract and result in immediate termination of POW usage for area farmers.[55] Byrd's threat was not idle as at least one farmer found out when stopped on post for a traffic violation and had "his prisoners taken away" and POW "labor denied him for a week."[56] The Christian County Farm Bureau, which had been handling contracts as a free service for area farmers, threatened to withdraw its assistance if farmers could not obey camp rules and cooperate with military authorities.[57]

Job safety became another concern for officials. The military, the employers, and the POWs, all understood that most of the work would be new to the prisoners. They employed training methods and programs to overcome many of these problems. The military offered the use of POW officers as supervisors and translators to large groups, when available, free of charge. Camp officials explained the rules of proper usage and what to expect from the POWs. Finally, the ASF and PMGO prepared handbooks and articles concerning types of work permitted by the Geneva Convention and how to safely and properly utilize the POWs.

Two Army Service Forces Manuals proved particularly helpful. The first handbook, "Safe Work Practices for Prisoners of War (German)," or manual

(M805), was broken into sixteen sections and printed in English side by side with German. It covered nearly every situation that the military envisioned POWs and employers encountering. Some of the rules, like wearing goggles when working near machinery, or not playing around equipment, seemed counterintuitive but the military sincerely desired that no one be injured.[58] A second manual "Handbook for Work Supervisors of Prisoner of War Labor," issued in 1945, emphasized that the employer had the same responsibility for POW safety on the job as for civilian workers. The military informed supervisors that a POW could "protest against doing unhealthful or dangerous work." The manual listed examples of this as using "high-speed cutting instruments or explosives, climbing to dangerous heights," and "being exposed to risk of injury from falling bodies or bodies in swift motion not under full control." [59]

Even with these precautions in place accidents happened. Two POWs received injuries in a car wreck while being transported to the farm of J.C. Dunavent from the Eminence branch camp. One broke his leg and the other broke his arm.[60] In another instance five men were hit by lightening while working in a Scott County tobacco barn. The blast killed Orville W. Thomas, a civilian who was working the tier nearest the roof, and injured four POWs.[61] Accidents and injuries were no more or less common for POWs than for civilian workers and those injured on the job received injury benefits like U.S. civilians or military personnel. They gained workers compensation correlating with the injury and time off; minor injuries might receive one day off with pay, while POWs suffering major injuries, such as loss of limbs, were paid for the duration of their captivity.[62] The amount of pay received also varied depending on geographic location and type of injury, but ranged from half salary to full salary. When a POW was injured the employer had to write a statement to accompany the guard report of the accident. The PMGO scrutinized many of the minor accidents with follow-up investigations after discovering that "many prisoners deliberately incurred minor injuries [to] gain a few days of rest on half pay."[63]

Dozens of men died during their stay in captivity. Some of these deaths occurred from wounds suffered in combat, natural causes, or being killed in an escape attempt. Others resulted from work related accidents. If the cause of an accidental death seemed obvious a detailed report had to be written by the guard and sent to the camp commander. The commander then forwarded a typed report to the Fifth Service command. From there it went to the ASF and PMGO headquarters to be disseminated to the Swiss and then relayed to German authorities. If, however, the U.S. sentenced POWs to hard labor, "real" prison, shot them in an escape, or executed them; the situation was thoroughly investigated by internal sources, including the War and State Departments, and might be scrutinized by the neutral protection power. The death of an enemy national remained a sensitive topic and the threat of retaliation always seemed possible.[64] There were a total of 477 deaths among German POWs in the U.S., of these 212 were accidental and 265 were from natural causes. This number does not include the 56 POWs killed in escape attempts and may not include at least 5 who received the death penalty at Fort Leavenworth.[65]

Fifteen men died at Fort Knox and Camp Breckinridge and all were buried in the Fort Knox cemetery. Five prisoners died at Campbell and were buried in a private cemetery on post.

Concern over wages was a more common obstacle for full employment of the POWs than work related accidents or deaths. The military established local Wage Boards for the communities that the POWs worked. The War Department wanted POW labor to perform as well as civilian labor and expected that they would be paid the same too. The predicament that the military encountered was that area farmers, who employed the POWs, also sat on these Wage Boards and had a penchant for lowering the wage rates. These dishonest activities not only caused numerous problems throughout the program, but they lent credibility to the arguments of unions and civilians that the military used cheaper prisoner labor to squeeze them out of jobs. To address this the military monitored contracts more closely, investigated complaints, and if they discovered fraud, reset wages and issued new contracts. The War Department did not cite individual cases, but stated that they were "frequent" in agriculture, but uncommon in industrial work.[66]

The pay issue also caused difficulty for some of the POWs. The standard POW wage was 80 cents per day for enlisted men, more for officers, and 10 cents a day for non-workers, paid in canteen coupons redeemable at the camp store. By Convention all enlisted men had to work and officers could volunteer as supervisors at wages set according to rank that topped out at about $40 a month. One quandary concerned lack of verification of officer or enlisted status. This basic information was contained in the *Soldbuch*, a personal record issued to all members of the German military, but souvenir hunters confiscated them upon capture and few prisoners had them by the time they reached in Kentucky. Hasty field promotions, where men received promotions to officer status before capture and before authorities in Berlin could process the new rank, only exacerbated the situation. Few non-officers claimed officer status to get higher wages, to get out of work, or for more privileges. Rather it was the officers who had no verification and were forced to work manual labor for less pay who complained. Germans protested through camp channels to the State Department or the Swiss legation which passed these on to the German government. The Third Reich eventually verified their ranks, but the process often took months.[67]

One of the most difficult aspects of employing POW labor concerned getting access. Only three base camps existed in Kentucky and a great need had to be demonstrated before a branch camp could be established. South Central Kentuckians realized that getting a branch camp required much planning and early contract commitments and their attempt failed. The Daviess Countians prepared to fight for a branch camp in the winter of 1943-1944 and determined not to fail like their counterparts in Warren and Barren Counties. R. Murray Hagan, W.J. Mitchell, and T.R. Hannister, the representatives of the Davies County Farm Bureau Labor Committee, wrote to Major D.M. McLeod at Fifth Service Command Headquarters on December 20, 1943, informing him that "within a radius of twenty miles of Owensboro, Kentucky,

(County seat of Daviess County) is one of the most productive farming sections in the state."[68] They lamented that many farm hands have taken industry jobs and received wages "so high that no farmer can compete."[69] Having employed POWs from Breckinridge in 1943, Daviess County farmers understood the benefit of POW labor, but they had to transport the men from Breckinridge, a fifty mile trip each way. They argued that this restriction proved stifling for time, gas, and amount of labor used and concluded that a branch camp at Owensboro would remedy these problems. The Daviess County men also provided research documenting that the U.S. Employment Service recommended 1,200 positions, but they only asked for 500 POWs. They also provided a communication between Kentucky Senator Alben W. Barkely and Allen Gullion, the PMG, who left the decision to the Fifth Service Command. They gave copies of the preliminary reports of the WMC Representative who recommended the use of POWs in Owensboro. The case seemed airtight and Daviess Countians must have certainly expected a speedy approval and construction of a branch camp.

On January 5, 1944, R. Murray Hagan and the "newly" dubbed Prisoner-of-War Committee of the Daviess County Farm Bureau drafted a second letter to the Fifth Service Command.[70] The committee addressed a valid argument, however, that transporting the men such great distances had the possibility that the weather differed at one place or the other. If the weather was poor at the camp then the farmer could not pick the men up even though back at the farm the weather was fine, or if the weather was poor when they returned to the farm the POWs could not work.[71]

The Daviess Countians received a curt reply on January 15 from the Fifth Service Command that they needed to address the issue to the U.S. Employment Service. B.J. Killian, the manager of the U.S. Employment Service at Owensboro fired off a retort on January 21, "I wish to state that there is now, there has been for some months, and will continue to be in the future a need for such a camp at Owensboro. Please consider this as a formal application for such a camp . . ."[72] Killian reminded the Fifth Service Command of the failed 1943 attempt to establish a branch camp at Owensboro and that at that time "there was not a sufficient number of unemployed prisoners available to meet our requests."[73] He then notified them that a recently vacated Civilian Conservation Corps camp nearby could house up to 300 men. Killian even placed a February 15 deadline on the Fifth Service Command to respond, ostensibly as the farmers needed to know what help to expect before planting the year's crops.

The Davies County farm committee followed this up with a third letter on February 7 asking the Fifth Service Command to notify them if they were unable to get a branch camp since the "food production for 1944 will be curtailed."[74] That same day Robert C. Goodwin, Regional Director of the WMC, wrote to R.L. Shaw, Acting Chief of the Division of Placement for the Fifth Region of the WMC, recommending a branch camp at Owensboro and commenting that Daviess County employers "are certain that near year-round employment could be given to prisoners if a sub-camp could be located in the immediate vicinity of

Owensboro."[75] Shaw replied that Owensboro would not get a branch camp and that the POWs at Breckinridge were already "employed on work of equal or higher priorities."[76]

These farmers did not dwell on the rejection. Instead they did what they had been doing all along, and getting quite good at, they sent another letter on the 19th asking if the War Department or WMC had "entertained the possibility of requesting the transfer of additional prisoners from prisoner-of-war camps other than Camp Breckinridge." They continued that "we did not intend to create the impression that we were recommending that the prisoners for the Owensboro Camp be supplied from Camp Breckinridge or any other specific camp."[77] The official correspondence at this point ended, but their persistence eventually paid off with the creation of a branch camp later that year at Owensboro.

Transferring POWs out of Kentucky to work at camps in other states caused a great deal of worry for Kentuckians. The first notice came with an announcement in the summer of 1944 that a majority of the POWs at Camps Campbell and Breckinridge would be moved and the POW camps potentially closed in order to service Ohio and Indiana camps that needed labor.[78] While the Fifth Service Command certainly had the right to transfer men and similar transfers occurred across the U.S. in order to match available manpower with local labor needs, this decision rankled Kentuckians.

Numerous west Kentucky farmers had existing contracts for the prisoners from Campbell and argued that the proposed move was an underhanded blow against regional farmers who "had based crop schedules on the contracts." The Fifth Service Command rooted their decision on a compilation of reports and studies. Robert C. Goodwin recommended the transfer after discussing it with other labor leaders who agreed that Kentucky had not fully utilized POW labor. Goodwin argued that areas like Hopkinsville had contracts for 300 men, but "less than 50 prisoners daily had been used for the first three months of 1944 and slightly over 100 since that time." Goodwin's draconian measures would have reduced Campbell to a skeleton crew of only 100 POWs and Breckinridge to 150, until October when another 100 would go to Camp Perry, Ohio.[79]

Goodwin told the press that he recommended the move due to the "less than full utilization of prisoners-of-war at the two Kentucky" camps and the "labor shortages expected" in Ohio "where the utilization of prisoners-of-war has been extremely satisfactory."[80] He added that "we anticipate . . . controversial questions [and] considerable protest by some of the agricultural groups in Kentucky." He contended that the farmers and labor groups' arguments were "rather weak" because records proved Kentucky POWs "being idle a considerable amount of the time." He added that "it appears that the Extension Service wishes to be assured that there is a pool of labor which can be drawn upon in the event it gets into labor difficulties." [81] Yet, Kentuckians would argue that this announcement, publicly made on June 3, was made well before state farmers would know exactly how many workers they would need, but knew they would need to rely on large numbers of POWs due to the shortage of free labor. Despite that it was a month or more before the tobacco season was underway and several months before corn would be harvested many farmers had already been preparing advance contracts even before Goodwin recommended the transfer. Goodwin was correct about one thing, Kentuckians protested quite loudly. They successfully lobbied against what the Farm Bureau called a "Yankee raid on our essential farm labor" and the Fifth Service Command dropped plans to transfer the POWs.[82]

The end of the war in Europe in May and against Japan in August both renewed alarm. Farmers across Kentucky believed that this would also mean the end of their contracts. The victory over Germany, as far as it concerned the harvest season, seemed to threaten the summer and fall crops. The War Department and PMGO informed county agencies, however, that while preparations were being made to repatriate the POWs, it would be a long and slow process and those contracts for 1945 were not in jeopardy.[83] The realization that 1945 would be the last harvest in which POWs played a significant role began to sink in after the War Department announced that as of May 10 German POWs would no longer be shipped to the U.S. and preparations were being made to repatriate those now in the country.[84]

By the fall of 1945 farmers awaited the impending closing of nearby camps. Lieutenant Colonel Harley E. Johnson, Commander of the Breckinridge POW Camp, assured area employers in August that there were no definite plans yet to close the camp down. He reiterated a War Department announcement that "PWs would not go home until they are no longer needed for farm labor . . ." and also once "necessary shipping space is available."[85] September marked the end of POW employment in Boyle County. John C. Brown, County Agent, informed residents that the Danville camp would be closing by the end of the month as the POWs returned to Fort Knox.[86] A similar announcement was made by Dan Goodman, the Fayette County Farm Labor Assistant, who stated that half of the POWs at the Lexington Armory would be sent back by September 15 and the rest by October 15.[87] On September 9th, Graham Young, County Agent in Bourbon, added the Paris branch camp to the number that would be closing that fall.[88] The Owensboro camp closed in October and Lieutenant Burdette Barnhill, Commander, accompanied the POWs and guards back to Breckinridge.[89] By early winter of 1946 all of Kentucky's branch camps had closed and POW labor was no longer available for civilian contract.[90]

With the closing down of the labor program the state could finally make some estimation of the benefit of POW labor. Farm Bureau receipts, camp records, and newspaper reports noted that the POWs literally saved thousands of crops each year from 1943 through 1945 that otherwise would have wasted in the fields. Farmers generally got along fairly well with these men and found them to be good workers. The War Department and the War Manpower Commission were the largest of several cooperating agencies designed to ensure full and fair employment of the POWs. They tried to allocate them to the areas where the labor shortage was the worst and where they were least likely to displace civilians. These agencies, while trying to fulfill their obligations, often ended up muddling things or working at cross purposes as demonstrated with the difficulties in creating branch camps and moving labor from Kentucky while both contracts and need existed for POWs. Even with the ruckus raised by the labor unions and the difficulties of canceling contracts, moving men, and not allocating enough men, which the farmers blamed on the government, the program seemed to be successful.

Chapter 5
Werewolves in the Eagles Nest: Nazis and Anti-Nazis at Camp Campbell

Of course, we live in a community, and there should be a spirit of mutual understanding. Actually, it is a madhouse rather than that. Austrians, Yugoslavians, French and the like, as well as Germans, are whirling around . . . inside the fences . . . And they all feel oppressed—by the Americans.
-Friedrich W. Schiltz, anti-Nazi at Camp Campbell

Werewolf: Middle English, from Old English werwulf (akin to Old High German werwolf werewolf), from wer man + wulf wolf: a person transformed into a wolf or capable of assuming a wolf's form.
-Merriman-Webster

Werewolf: An organization of guerilla fighters set up in the closing days of World War II, who looked upon themselves as a paramilitary auxiliary of the Wehrmacht. . . they hoped to fight behind the Allied lines to create diversions. . . and, if captured, to claim the rights of prisoners of war. [1]
-Louis Snyder, *Encyclopedia of the Third Reich*

Nazi power behind barbed-wire remained as strong, if not stronger, than in the Third Reich. The Nazis wielded the heavy club of discipline and order and sent it crashing down on those who displayed even the slightest hint of defeatism, disloyalty, or collaboration with American personnel. With brutal efficiency Nazi soldiers controlled their fellows with threats, beatings, and promises that penalties would be extended to families of wrong doers in Germany. Dozens of POWs received late-night visits from the "Holy Ghost", the code word for a fatal beating delivered as subtly and brutally as wrapping the victim in a bed sheet and pummeling him with bed slats. In other cases a kangaroo court or midnight tribunal consisting of an assemblage of many POWs passed and carried out the sentence. Simple slips of the tongue, translating American news of German defeats, or speaking to guards could place a man on the list of suspicious POWs. The Nazis seemed to know everything taking place within the camps. A spy network listened to conversations, read mail, and constantly probed for weak links in the fascist chain. The other Germans knew that Nazi officers kept a watch on them and documented their movements in records that might very well turn into death certificates. Trapped within the confines of the camp and in close quarters with men intent on keeping German discipline and Nazi order operational, some men feigned allegiance, while others gambled their lives in escape attempts.

These Nazi activities continued unabated during the early period of the housing program. Eventually, after numerous inspections and multiple cases of beatings, murder, and pleas for help, the Army Service

Forces (ASF) and Provost Marshal General's Office (PMGO) realized the full extent of the problem. Officials finally agreed to screen and segregate the men based on their degree of fascist belief. Hard-core Nazis and ardent anti-Nazis, would be separated from the general population of POWs and placed into specially designated camps. The term anti-Nazi describes anyone in a German uniform not adhering to the fascist line. Attempts had already been underway to house Navy personnel away from other branches of the Wehrmacht, but they too had to be screened for extreme political beliefs. The screening process relied on scurrilous information and obviously lacked accuracy. Most men did not have their *Soldbuch*, a copy of their military service record. Without access to these official documents, military officials had to base their decisions on what other POWs claimed about the individual, the camp commander's comments about the POW's actions since arrival in the camp, and information from an interview with the POW. This did not create much of a problem with the anti-Nazi POWs, who were more than happy to express to U.S. officials their hatred of the Nazi regime. This was equally true with Nazi POWs who proudly admitted their party affiliation. Many of the fascist men, however, feared separation from their fellows and suspected potential U.S. retaliation for Germany's part in the war and thus kept their party membership a closely guarded secret. Some of this group also felt that the Fuhrer's cause would be better served if they lied to be classified as anti-Nazi so that they could accompany that group and continue to spy and report on their activities. They felt that recording their collaboration with the Americans would provide important information during their treason trial after Germany won the war. These methods left much to be desired and led to many men being segregated on the whims of individual camp commanders rather than on political ideology. For many POWs the often ineffectual process moved along at a grueling pace that allowed the Nazi element to continue their reign of terror for several more months.

Segregating prisoners and dealing with Nazi control and violence within the prisoner camps created the greatest problem that the U.S. faced in the entire POW program. Ultimately several camps had to be re-designated to house these newly screened POWs. The official War Department language used to classify the Kriegsmarine, German Naval personnel, however, proved confusing for those tasked with screening and segregating them. Rather than simply call the camps Nazi, anti-Nazi, or no affiliation as they did for the other camps, the Kriegsmarine "not classified as Anti-Nazi" went to Camp Papago Park, Arizona, while the remainder stayed in their current camps. This simple grouping, designed to solve a problem, created many new ones and haunted the ASF and PMGO. This was especially true when officials at Papago Park proved inept and POWs caused numerous problems including orchestrating the greatest escape in the U.S.[2]

As for the other members of the Wehrmacht their separation proved equally difficult. The worst offenders went to Camp Alva, Oklahoma, reserved for Nazis.[3] Those on the other end of the spectrum, the anti-Nazis, went to one of four "safe-havens": Camp Devens, Massachusetts; Camp McCain, Mississippi; Camp Ruston, Louisiana; or Camp Campbell,

Kentucky. Campbell held the largest number of anti-Nazis, many of whom had been very cooperative with U.S. officials in gathering intelligence on the Third Reich and the Wehrmacht. Officials hoped that by placing these men safely away from the Nazi element they could continue this symbiotic relationship. They soon realized that this separation caused additional problems. The anti-Nazis group was a catch all of all non-Nazi POWs and the group at Campbell proved to be a fractious and uncooperative lot. To make matters worse Werewolves, Nazis in the anti-Nazi guise, infiltrated Campbell, causing difficulties for both Germans and Americans.

The problem of Nazi domination of the camps was as violent as it was thorough and it had reached epic proportions prior to U.S. officials stepping in. Heavily indoctrinated men captured from the battles in North Africa brought with them their unswerving faith in Hitler and victory, confidence gained in earlier battles, and youthful defiance. Their officers, by virtue of precedence, established a regime in exile within the camps. Yet, the Nazi element was relatively small, especially for the control it exerted. Many of the problems encountered during the POW program had been erroneously attributed to Nazi activity and in reality was the work of boredom, pride, and ego. These activities included defying the guards, displaying Nazi paraphernalia, and refusing to work. Murder and beatings, of course, remained the purview of the Nazis. The Nazi minority ruled within the camps and held responsibility for many executions and an untold number of forced suicides. One historian placed the number of Nazi related murders in U.S. camps at around 300. The number of men that escaped the camps out of fear of the Nazi presence can never be calculated, mostly because few of these men dared give that as their reason. Along the same lines, the number of POWs requesting transfer for fear of being victimized could be told through official records only with extreme difficulty, assuming that all of these records exist.

A few of the most well-known cases of murder within the camps surround men like Corporal Johann Kunze, who met his fate at the hands of his fellows during a midnight tribunal in the mess hall at Camp Gruber, Oklahoma, on November 4, 1943.[4] The murder of Hugo Krauss at Camp Hearne, Texas, on December 17, 1943 presented another case.[5] Heino Erichsen served time at Fort Knox and at Camp Hearne. He personally knew Krauss and speculated on the crimes that brought him a visit from the "Holy Ghost." Erichsen recalled that Krauss' parents had previously become U.S. citizens. They visited him in the camp and often brought him gifts, and in Erichsen's mind this made the Nazis suspicious of him.[6] Authorities eventually apprehended and tried the murderers of both men. The POWs involved in the murder of Kunze went to a trial presided over by Leon Jaworski of later Watergate fame. They all received the death penalty carried out by hanging at Fort Leavenworth. Those who murdered Krauss received prison sentences. Although permitted by the Geneva Convention, a court martial of enemy soldiers was a truly delicate matter, especially in serious cases where the death penalty and executions resulted. These investigations and trials operated under international scrutiny and therefore special effort had been made to ensure thoroughness and accuracy. These two trials represent only a fraction of the murder cases within U.S. operated camps.[7] In most cases the investigators ended up without enough evidence as POWs refused to talk for fear of implicating themselves or of the Nazis finding out that they assisted U.S. officials. Most cases proceeded only through luck or on the rare occasion that cooperative POWs could be found. Cooperative men, of course, usually demanded transfer to avoid the Nazis.

Although they efficiently used threats, fear, and strong-arm tactics, murder proved the ultimate tool available to the Nazis. As early as February 1943, U.S. officials knew that camp Nazis had been censoring prisoners' mail and other reading material. An official Army statement noted that these tactics coupled with "intimidation and violence" forced "adherence to the National Socialist group in each of these camps."[8] The number of threats, beatings, and the "near" misses of POWs who narrowly escaped, was easily three times the number of actual murders or forced suicides within the camps. A prisoner speaking to a guard, having a visitor, or translating an English newspaper that painted the German military in a poor light, such as reading of a defeat, could all bring the Holy Ghost out. Nearly every memoir, interview, or conversation with a former German POW reveals that they knew of the penalty, or witnessed first hand the Nazi brutality. Howard Tromp, a former POW in Huntsville, Texas, for instance, befriended a guard and received visits from his aunt, a German who moved to New Jersey and became naturalized before the war. Both of these went "against" the unwritten Nazi rules. Tromp, for unrelated reasons, received a transfer, along with some other POW laborers, to the Las Cruces, New Mexico camp. The night before his transfer his bunk mate leaned over and calmly told him that he was lucky to be leaving as his name was on the list. Over sixty years later he vividly recalls that comment. Although he did not know exactly why, he clearly understood that the Nazis had intended to murder him. [9]

Even in Kentucky, where Campbell became a "safe-haven," POWs were not safe from the Nazis. Heino Erichsen recalled that "after the Allied invasion of Normandy in June 1944, large contingents of POWs began to arrive in the United States. Many ended up at Fort Knox. A lot of them were diehard Nazis. Worse than that, German Waffen SS, Hitler's special forces captured in France, arrived, too. The SS were always ready to instigate a fight over allegiance-with no holds barred."[10] Investigations at Knox revealed prisoners with Nazi allegiance that caused serious problems for fellow prisoners. Sergeant Hans Cordts, the spokesman at Knox, was court-martialed for organizing, participating in, or associating himself with those who perpetrated several beatings of other prisoners.[11] Private First Class Wilhelm Klocke used his unique position as interpreter for Cordts to "misrepresent conditions in the compound." While at Knox he was involved in "an altercation" and prior to his arrival published an "anonymous" paper at his previous camp "for which he was punished."[12] A follow up report determined that "between the two of them, they were largely responsible for recent unrest and disturbances" at Knox, that resulted in the "shooting of seven" men. Ernst Schlotter and Friedrich Wolf, who died, were included in this number. Unfortunately, the Fifth Service Command allotment for sending men to Alva, Oklahoma, the camp for hardcore Nazis, had already been reached. Camp Clark, Missouri, served as a secondary camp to hold Nazi POWs, but it too was at maximum capacity. This forced officials at Knox to detain them and keep them from causing more trouble in the compounds while the Fifth Service Command searched for suitable locations for them.[13]

The Nazis working in camp mail rooms used the lack of American supervision and trusting U.S. guards to effectively infiltrate the prisoner postal system and screen and monitor the letters and packages that other Germans were sending and receiving. Once discovered this led to many camps issuing orders similar to those enacted in January 1944 at Breckinridge. Pursuant to the new order all boxes for outgoing mail would be located at central locations, padlocked, and have slots only large enough for letters and post cards. Only American officials had access to the keys and all incoming mail would be handled by the guards and select prisoners. These measures, however, proved ineffective to curb all the methods of sabotage by the Nazis and typically led to other means of infiltration.[14]

POWs at Breckinridge had problems as well. After the formation of the anti-Nazi company "battles" within the camp were incessantly fought with the Nazis and other "good" Germans within that camp. Eventually the spokesman of the camp brokered a deal whereby the Germans would all cooperate "impartially." However, the anti-Nazis discovered many discrepancies with this new policy. In one instance requests by the anti-Nazis for materials and religious pieces had been denied or never submitted because they "could not keep apart church and politics." At the same time, however, one of the Nazis attempted to persuade the men in his barracks to quit attending mass. As new men arrived in the camps and were formed up into companies, "good" Germans already at Breckinridge warned them of the "company of criminals, traitors and Non-Germans" housed there.[15]

Lieutenant Colonel Einer W. Chester knew of the friction that existed behind the wire at Breckinridge. As Camp Commander he addressed the POWs in charge in a futile attempt to get them to put ideological differences aside. Particularly he attacked the Nazi group who insulted and threatened their fellows. He explained to the POWs that he knew that some of them sang German songs of Nazi origin or in other ways insulted the U.S. or its Allies. He instructed them to stop these activities. He bluntly told the POWs that "it is not the purpose of the American Government to force Prisoners of War to accept the Democratic Ideology, nor is the American Government concerned in your political ideals except those that cause disunity or which may be prejudicial to good order and discipline." He further added that "it is my wish that all Internees having problems of any nature feel that they have open access to the Company Commanders at any time, and you may rest assured that your problems will be treated confidentially and will receive due consideration."[16] This final statement, by all accounts of former POWs and officers at Breckinridge, rang true. These men claimed to have a good relationship with Chester, who exhibited patience and understood their needs. This situation changed when Chester's replacement arrived in 1944.

In 1944, the anti-Nazis at Breckinridge wrote a brief history of the problems within the camp to give to U.S. officials as evidence of the difficulties they faced and the crimes perpetrated against them. Their history began when the first 500 POWs arrived from North Africa on May 10, 1943. During this period "a good deal of them-not at all the majority but a rather influential part-were decided enemies of Hitlerism." During this time the Nazi portion within the camp was rendered temporarily powerless due to "the great shock" of being defeated and captured. Eventually the shock wore off, according to the authors, as the Nazis learned

> that they were treated humanely and politely and not at all the way they used to treat their prisoners; they had more to eat then their whole family at home; they had every comfort. They took the American kindness for weakness and they became bold again. Their first attempts to start their propaganda, was to spread lies about the battlefronts. [17]

Eventually, the Nazis established their dominance within the camp. This was due largely to the fact that the Nazis represented a united front, were the established authority in the German military, and were willing to resort to violence. The anti-Nazis on the other hand, came from traditionally divisive backgrounds, and some defected from the group. Yet, those who held fast to their anti-Nazi beliefs represented a not inconsiderable minority of just over 180.[18]

To rectify these problems the Camp Commander at Breckinridge separated the men into their own anti-Nazi "company." Friction still existed that included threats of large scale "riots" and some talk of mass violence between Nazis and anti-Nazis. The problems escalated when the new camp commander regrouped these men under the same POW authority. This meant that the anti-Nazis, who escaped from Nazi power and had been afforded some protection by the guards, found themselves again within the clutches of Nazi leadership. The anti-Nazis at Breckinridge only escaped this fate when they transferred to Camp Campbell, Kentucky, and Fort Devens, Massachusetts.[19]

Critics, including historians, researchers, and especially those involved with the program, blame the U.S. for not screening and separating the Germans before sending them to the camps. Former POW Heino Erichsen commented that "the Americans' idea of processing looked like the perfect place for a European criminal to create a new identity. I worried that they would not try to sort out the Nazis from the rest of us."[20]

Occupied with fighting the war, Allied soldiers only captured and disarmed prisoners and sent them on to their holding camps. The ASF and PMGO busied themselves with building camps and processing the men. Most felt that separating men in German uniforms from those in Italian uniforms seemed sufficient. The concept of an anti-Nazi or non-Nazi seemed foreign to most soldiers and officials. Certainly, the GI in the field had bigger concerns. So, until the impetus for change came from within the camps, things progressed as "normal." Erichsen noted that "rabid Nazis slipped by unnoticed until they maimed or killed fellow POWs whom they considered anti-Nazi or disloyal to the party."[21]

By February 1943, Allen Gullion, the PMGO, Blackshear M. Bryan, the Assistant PMGO, and J.A. Ulio, the Adjutant General, agreed that stemming the "rising tide" of Nazi violence required "complete and effective segregation." [22] Despite this concurrence by the chiefs of these agencies no policy on this reached the camps and therefore little changed. Bryan directed the service and camp commanders to begin a complete screening and segregation of prisoners beginning on February 18, 1943. Bryan's directive, however, only identified broad categories of political ideology with no procedures for camp commanders to make a proper determination into which category the men belonged.

Bryan's order classified the men as Nazis and others. Navy men needed to be kept separate from the other Wehrmacht troops because the U.S. Department of the Navy cooperated in housing and handling them, but the simple Nazi or not Nazi terminology also applied. U.S. officers could easily and quickly identify which men belonged to the Kriegsmarine, the German Navy, but experienced difficulty identifying which ones were Nazis. By the time Nazi violence within the camps came to light, the situation reached emergency levels. Unfortunately, forgoing a further delay to complete the segregation process seemed impossible since U.S. camp officials had to interview the Germans, examine their military records, and evaluate them to determine their degree of Nazification. Future orders that described many Nazis as having swastika tattoos helped physically detect Nazis, and later military records and other POWs helped point to other Nazis.[23] As 1943 drew to a close the U.S made no real gains, but by early 1944 the screening process began to make real headway.

Screening reports discovered in March, 1944, that only about fifteen percent of the men in any POW camp were actually fervent Nazis. They realized that these Nazis cajoled the rest of the men. U.S. officials labeled up to fifty percent of the remainder as simple "opportunists," those who gave lip service to the Nazi regime and toed the line, with a strikingly small five percent actually holding clear political beliefs opposed to fascism, but generally keeping their mouths shut.[24] While officials knew of the anti-Nazis they seemingly had not realized that such a large number of POWs fell into this "new" third category.

Despite the pressing "emergency," results from the screenings began coming in thirteen months after the PMGO directed the efforts of the service and camp commanders. The War Department implemented change, but the process took precious time. Colonel R.G. Jacobs, the Executive Officer at G-2, added more dismal news in March 1944, when he informed officials that the process of complete screening and segregation would take an additional four months to complete. This program plodded along until the late-summer of 1944 when it seemed that all the POWs now occupied camps properly designated for their political ideology.[25]

The military difficulties in segregating the Nazis resulted from a mixture of ignorance, bureaucracy, and a desire on the part of some U.S. camp commanders to keep their Nazis, who as a group seemed generally cooperative with U.S. authorities. Friederich W. Schiltz, former Campbell POW and anti-Nazi, described this lamentable situation. According to Shiltz, Nazis gained a "renowned" and "complete obedience, formulated by Prussia and afterwards taken over by the Third Reich." [26] He argued that the government "considered [this discipline] as one of the pillars of the state, but its detrimental effect upon a decent inside and towards the neighboring states is proven." [27] Shiltz felt that U.S. officers and guards appreciated this unquestioning efficiency, since "a snappy behavior looks nice," and is "machine-like. You feel it is like a good running motor, smooth and dependable." He wanted U.S. authorities to understand that "it is all façade. There is no thinking behind it. You must not think, otherwise it wouldn't function that well and rapidly. It takes no intelligence. It culminates in the Nazi sentence 'Fuehrer, fefiehl, wir folgen dir.' (Fuehrer, give the order, we obey and follow.) This is a flock of sheep, conducted by a shepard." [28]

Clearly the Nazis needed to be sent to a separate camp, closely monitored, and kept away from other POWs. Camp Alva, Oklahoma became that camp, but as later evidence demonstrated, not all men at this camp were Nazis, and not all Nazis went there. Some Nazis ran the camps efficiently and often cooperatively; this led to some U.S. officials and guards allowing certain men to "fall under the radar" when preparing transfers. On the other hand, camp commanders found this a brilliant opportunity to dump their "troublemakers" and it became an efficient way to be rid of repeat escapers or ringleaders of work strikes. The segregation of the Nazis from the main body of men, therefore, was a step in the right direction but not entirely successful. It stands to reason that the camps designed exclusively for anti-Nazis also had similar problems.

The anti-Nazi camps contained a mixture of men from varying backgrounds and political views. In their desperation for manpower the Third Reich actively recruited men from throughout Europe and Asia. Austrians, Poles, and Czechs, many of German descent, and driven by nationalism or Nazism, joined their brothers in arms. Soon after capture many of these foreigners desired to wean themselves from the Nazi fold as opportunism gave way to self-preservation. In other cases, foreigners were conscripted into the ranks against their will, or joined the Germans for reasons other than Nazism. Thousands of captured Soviet soldiers, for instance, had a choice between existence as POWs or joining the ranks of the German Army. Citizens and resistance fighters in the Ukraine, Georgia, Finland, and elsewhere, however, joined the Germans in hopes of gaining liberation from the Soviet yoke. Not all ethnic Germans were Nazis either and the disparity in political beliefs ran throughout the German troops. Many had been members of the German Socialist, Communist, or Catholic Parties. Former political prisoners or minor criminals made up the Penal Battalions that fought alongside German forces as early as the battles in North Africa. Many desired to surrender or be captured at the earliest opportunity rather than die for a cause in which they did not believe.[29]

Finding and separating these men became an important task as the U.S. military hoped to rehabilitate them to assist the American Military Occupation Government in spreading democracy and rebuilding post war Germany. Anti-Nazi status, however, did not make these men democrats and for many they were only allies of convenience. From a variety of political, social, ethnic, and criminal backgrounds, the anti-Nazis still made a divisive lot. The ASF and PMGO separated these men from the general population and placed them into the protective camps of Fort Devens and Camp Campbell.[30] POWs from these groups helped staff a later reeducation program that operated in four distinct camps in Rhode Island and Virginia. The men who went to the reeducation camps to study received early repatriation after the war ended in 1945. Most of the remaining POW population left the U.S. in 1946, but due to existing agreements worked in Allied European countries rebuilding and remained as POWs until 1947.

Army officials hoped to avoid a repeat of the situation at Camp McCain, Mississippi. The Third Reich learned that McCain exclusively held anti-Nazi prisoners and not only cut off aid being sent by Germany but added an implicit threat that these prisoners would be punished after repatriation. When the March 1944 directive advised camp commanders to begin screening POWs and arranging for the transfer of Nazi and anti-Nazis, Campbell already seemed to be the appropriate place for an anti-Nazi camp. The original POW camp had two fully functional POW compounds

119

capable of holding 1,000 men each, and a third was slated to be completed that year. These three compounds, XO, DD, and the newest one VW, unlike other camps, were not adjacent to each other. Most structures housed the POWs in compounds with adjoining barbed wire. This standard system decreased the cost of materials and personnel, while maximizing the coverage that towers, dogs, and guards provided and centralized the administration. At Campbell, however, one of the compounds sat nearly five miles from the other two. The German government refused to recognize or send care packages to Camp McCain because of its strictly anti-Nazi status, therefore U.S. officials disguised Campbell's true purpose by authorizing the XO Compound as a Nazi compound. Guards, POWs, and most of all, the Third Reich, would ideally be blissfully unaware of the distinction between DD and VW anti-Nazi compounds and the XO Nazi compound, all housed on the same post.[31]

The two compounds at Campbell provided space for up to 2,000 dedicated anti-Nazis, making Campbell the largest anti-Nazi camp in the U.S. The Fifth Service Command, headquartered in Ohio, operated all camps in Kentucky, Ohio, and Indiana. Camp Campbell received all of the Fifth Service Command's anti-Nazi POWs. Military officials, however, revised these rules and designated Campbell to house all anti-Nazis in not only the Fifth Service Command, but all service commands west of it. This meant that all POW camps from Missouri to California transported their anti-Nazis to Kentucky. The other service commands disagreed with this order when they realized not only the difficulty of such a transfer, but the potentially large numbers of men leaving their region. These POWs worked in agriculture and other industry and this sudden removal denied communities the labor on which they relied without any replacements. Several service commands refused to cooperate. The Seventh Service Command, for instance, protested and argued to instead house these men in branch camps designed for about 250 to 500 men and accomplish the same segregation without sacrificing access to their labor. Although Lieutenant Colonel Earl Edwards, the Assistant Director of the Prisoner of War Division, agreed, even he must have known that their proposal defeated the purpose. In this instance, however, perhaps logistics and economics won out over POW anonymity as long as security stayed intact.[32]

Lieutenant Colonel Carl B. Byrd, Commanding Officer of the Campbell POW Camp and the man tasked with preparing the DD Compound for the influx of hundreds of new arrivals and completing VW compound for the same purpose, set about this task with vigor. Just a few days after the Fifth Service Command issued the order, he requested to transfer seventy-five of his own POWs from the XO Compound over to the DD Compound as they represented "cooperative" anti-Nazis. He classified many of them as non-Germans and stated that they had "been giving valuable intelligence information and would be more willing to divulge further intelligence if they were assured of being transferred to a camp where they would not fear molestation." He further added that two of these men already had to be placed in special protective custody for fear of repercussions from their fellows for collaboration with U.S. officials.[33]

Major D.M. McLeod, Chief of the Prisoners of War Section, placed an addendum to Byrd's request as he sent it on to the Fifth Service Command asking approval for the request. He stated that even though the Fifth Service Command worried about Kentucky using more than the allotted space within the camp, making a lateral transfer of these men needed to be considered critically important. Although the Fifth Service Command already used its allotted space, which included 182 anti-Nazis, and left room for only 40 more men from that command, he urged that 77 more spots be provided to make transfers from XO Compound to DD Compound.[34] Even after Breckinridge sent over such a large group at once, continued transfers into that camp and future screenings soon turned up more anti-Nazis. Men like Richard Szymonik, whose entire anti-Nazi company moved to Campbell, stayed behind because he was in the hospital during the transfer. Others, like Alex P. Voglesberg had been stationed at the hospital as a ward man for nine months and wanted an outdoor job. As an anti-Nazi he ran afoul of certain members of the camp and therefore needed to be transferred to a camp like Campbell designed for anti-Nazis.[35]

POWs transferred from Breckinridge over to Campbell included those like Rudolf Tirk who once behind the wire joined the Free Austria Movement of his own volition in 1943. This organization accepted dozens of memberships from U.S. held POWs of Austrian origin. It informed new members that they should be proud of taking "the first opportunity to join the Friends of Austria, the United Nations, America and England." The organization explained that many "Austrians [have] freed themselves of this hateful yoke and have joined the United Nations." [36] They also added that "this attitude of our countrymen serves as a valuable support of our work for the liberation of Austria and the reestablishment of her independence." Hans Rott, the author of the letter from the Free Austria Movement, concluded with a warning for Tirk, "for the present we ask you to show by your conduct and behaviour in camp that the majority of the Austrians are not Nazis and were forced to become members of the German Army." In order to do this Rott suggested that Tirk and fellow Austrian anti-Nazis "keep the Austrian prisoners away from the Nazi and Fascists. Do your best to keep order among the Austrian prisoners and comply strictly with the orders of American officers and guards. The Americans must realize that the Austrians are their friends who were forced into the damned German uniform by a cruel fate."[37] Membership in such a group obviously carried with it anti-Nazi sentiments and certainly could not be revealed in a camp containing mixed ideologies.

POWs that joined these types of organizations needed to be monitored by the guards lest they become victims of Nazi terror. Yet, few U.S. officials realized that for some POW opportunists joining these groups allowed a clear affiliation as a non-German if not necessarily an anti-Nazi. Some Austrians feared being lumped in with the Germans and receiving whatever treatment awaited them within the camps or during post war American military occupation. A third group also joined these types of organizations, and the POWs, if not the guards, realized this fact. Nazis often pretended, playing the role they needed to, like wolves in sheeps clothing, in order to be transferred with the anti-Nazis and monitor the activities of their stockade brethren.

Numerous other problems and unforeseen circumstances plagued Camp Campbell immediately after Compounds DD and VW became active. First Lieutenant Walter Schoenstedt of the Special Programs Section inspected the compounds and despite the "segregation" process found the POWs to be generally uncooperative with American officials and having no *espirit de corps* among themselves. His report stated that "the smooth functioning of this camp is constantly being handicapped through the unpleasant mixture of several different types of Anti-Nazis, Nazis, non-Germans, run of the mill, and criminals. Although the great majority of the prisoners consider themselves Anti-Nazis, the camp, or even single compounds, cannot be described as such."[38] Some prisoners, like Friedrich W. Schiltz, POW of VW Compound, felt that American personnel failed to appreciate the plight of the anti-Nazis. He argued that they "overcame this mass-psychosis [Nazism] or mass-hysteria, as one might call it" by avowing an anti-Nazi stance. Schiltz contended that "we intend and plan the revival of the individual." Schiltz, as other POWs at Campbell, soon learned that the general circumstances of the camp hindered this hope for revival.[39]

Many of the so called anti-Nazis felt little comfort or safety in these newly designated camps. In March 1944, twelve Polish POWs from four different camps, all slated for transfer to Campbell, wrote a petition to Lieutenant Colonel Byrd and the War Department requesting a transfer to Camp McCoy, Wisconsin. These men argued that they were pressed into German service, have nothing in common with the Germans, and ultimately desired to join Polish forces. Six of the men who signed the petition resided at Breckinridge. Byrd forwarded the request, and the War Department agreed to send them to Camp McCoy, Wisconsin.[40]

In May 1944, Rudolf Schwanse appealed to the War Department. Schwanse claimed that he was a member of the anti-Nazi movement until Germany conquered his homeland of Czechoslovakia and forced him into service in 1940. He claimed that he deserted at the first opportunity and now only wanted to rejoin Free Czech forces to fight against the Nazis. Other Czechoslovakians held at Campbell expressed similar sentiments.[41] Josef Obermayer, writing to the Czechoslokavian Embassy from one of Camp Campbell's anti-Nazi compounds, stated that "my wishes are not security and rest, but to help [with] the liberation of Europe." Obermayer pleaded to be given the chance "to fight against the cruelties and bestialities of the Nazis."[42] In September 1944 a group of 238 Austrians held at Campbell joined the refrain of loyalty to the Allies and a desire to liberate Austria from its Nazi oppressors.[43]

French, Austrians, Poles, and Czechoslovakians, made up a large portion of the numerous non-German soldiers serving the Wehrmacht. After capture many of these Axis POWs went to the anti-Nazi Compounds at Camp Campbell. A group of five Frenchmen wrote the Free French Committee from Campbell in June 1944 claiming that after capture in 1940 the Germans forced them into service against the Allies on the Italian Front in 1943. Once in combat they argued that their "only desire was to desert" and "rejoin our French comrades of Alsace-Lorraine who left the compound before us and if circumstances permit, to serve Free France."[44] In November three German born Frenchmen, impressed after Germany invaded France, struck a similar refrain. Writing from Campbell's anti-Nazi compound in 1944 they asked the Free French Committee to grant them freedom from U.S. captivity to join their comrades in liberating France.[45] Eventually another petition came from Campbell, with the names of 30 Frenchmen attached, all claiming forced German military service on the Italian front. They detested being held captive in the same camps as their former German oppressors and asked to be allowed to leave the POWs camps in America to serve with the Free French forces liberating Europe.[46] Dozens of letters like these claiming Danish, Polish, Luxembourg, or other citizenship poured out of Campbell.

Other cases of "mistaken" ideology plagued the segregation process. Sergeant Wolfgang Mursa argued with his company leader at the Ashford General Hospital POW installation. In the heat of the moment the higher ranking German called Mursa a "Jew," leading to other prisoners threatening his safety. Once Mursa transferred to Campbell, the spokesman asked him to identify his ideology as either "Nazi or Anti-Nazi." Mursa told American officials that he was "a German soldier" with "political convictions opposed to the views of the other prisoners here. He then requested "a transfer to a regular prisoner of war camp."[47]

Private Eduard Pannek faced similar problems. He worked in the post laundry at Camp Maxey, Texas, where he had a confrontation with a fellow prisoner about the man's poor work ethic. When the man refused to work harder, Pannek complained to the supervisors. The other POWs saw Pannek leave to speak with the Americans and informed Pannek that they needed to speak with him after work. The men accused Pannek of treason and then beat him. The POW commander refused to see him. Fearing for his life, Pannek requested a transfer to another camp. He immediately protested his transfer to Campbell's anti-Nazi compounds on the grounds that "I am a German soldier and will remain as such until I am discharged or the war is over" and asked to be moved again, but preferred a camp for general prisoners, not one designated for only Nazis or anti-Nazis. [48]

The anti-Nazi compounds, located five miles apart, had one spokesman between them, Sergeant Georg Rupprecht, a Catholic priest. Camp officials found him to be generally cooperative, if only mildly effective. Rupprecht wrote to the PMGO through Camp Campbell authorities. In his letter he stated that as a "Catholic priest I have naturally always been opposed to the present National Socialists German Government and would therefore like to offer my cooperation to the Allied authorities as regards to post-war."[49] He moved to Campbell via a transfer from Camp McAlester, Oklahoma, after having a run in with camp Nazis. Despite Rupprecht's cooperative nature, First Lieutenant Walter Schoenstedt of the Special

Programs Section felt that he demonstrated a lack of leadership and control over his charges during his five month tenure as spokesman for both DD and VW Compound. Schoenstedt inspected the camps and POWs for how effectively the screening and segregation had been carried out. He bluntly stated that Rupprecht was "not strong enough, in a military sense, to run both compounds to the satisfaction of the camp commander."[50] Yet, few anti-Nazis had enough strength in numbers to control their comrades within these types of camps. Many men from these varied backgrounds did not always agree or get along before the Hitler regime. Socialists and Communists in Germany, for instance, have a greater history of violence than of cooperation. At Campbell, according to Schoenstedt, "the main difficulty of the Anti-Nazi compound is to be found in the fact that criminal elements have been mixed in with every company. This, the Anti-Nazis claim, is a discrimination against the majority whose reputation is being kept at a low artificially." He added that "strife and disunity between groups, awkward military attitude, weak leadership, and the civilian background of the prisoners (artists, doctors, writers, professors, actors, etc.) do much to prevent an understanding of the problems of those prisoners on the part of the American officers and the camp commander."[51]

Nazis behind barbed wire did more than just "terrorize" other POWs. Unlike the anti-Nazis they typically presented a solid front and brought with them their military discipline and order. Camp officials often appreciated that the Nazis governed themselves and followed the rules. Officials often maintained a "hands-off" policy in these deceptively well-ordered camps. This was also the reason that many of the problems in camps nationwide persisted so long in the first place. Camp Campbell was no different. American personnel seemed to prefer the smooth running XO Compound. Staff Sergeant Otto Guenther, the spokesperson for the Nazi compound, cooperated with Campbell officials, who in turn generally allowed the Germans to run their day to day operations behind the wire. Even Schoenstedt spotted the obvious façade, and that "the appearance of a 'smoothly run compound" was "very much to the satisfaction of the American personnel."[52] He commented that this allowed the Nazis and Americans at Campbell "to be backed by a stronger respect" while the "Anti-Nazis become a 'nuisance' and 'trouble makers' who write petitions and forget to act like soldiers." [53]

The men in the anti-Nazi compounds felt betrayed on several levels. They thought that American officials segregated them and then gave lip service to democracy and liberal ideas, while at the same time catering to the Nazis. They knew full well that the men at XO compound had been given preferential treatment by the guards and arguably the camp commander, Lieutenant Colonel Byrd, who due to "administrative difficulties" did not improve their situation. [54] At night the sounds of music from the Nazi orchestra, or laughter from Nazi theatre, wafted over the short distance into their compounds. The indignity had been made worse by the fact that the men at DD compound could barely assemble any type of band with their five musical instruments and at VW they didn't even have their own chapel, but shared it with a small office also holding their library and a classroom at alternating times, much less any type of theater props or musical instruments.[55]

As for achieving their roles as "nuisance makers" they fulfilled that through a method that most of the men in the anti-Nazi compounds could agree on, complaining. These men risked their lives to speak out against the Nazi regime either in Germany, in the camps, or both, and they refused to be lumped together and sit quietly with their feelings of indignation and abandonment. The men from compound DD drafted a letter intended for *The German American* in September 1944. They stated that they "lost the strength and power of the best sons of Anti-Nazi movement by the murder in American P.W. Camps . . ."[56] Because of their politics they offered support to the American government against the Nazi regime. They arrived at Campbell and willingly performed work, such as "loading of guns, military equipments, and weapons," prohibited by the Geneva Convention. Despite this cooperative attitude, they found their treatment "strange and unintelligible." The anti-Nazis claimed that "we never demanded an improvement of our condition in the contrary we declare we never want a difference in these things over against other P.W.'s," yet found "that the social conditions in our camps are far under the standard of the fascists camps."[57] Specifically these men said that "we are urged by the guards to work more", including Sunday labor, which was reserved for POWs as a day of rest, despite "our payments are not so punctual as in Nazi-Camps."[58] Fredrich W. Shiltz, an anti-Nazi from VW Compound wrote a letter to Major Mims, the Executive Officer of the POW Camp at

Campbell, stating that he regretted that in America "the general opinion considers them [the anti-Nazis] to be composed largely out of criminals and otherwise undesirable characters."[59]

In addition the anti-Nazis at Campbell never received the newspapers and books that they had requested. They thought that camp authorities either denied their requests or sent the material to other groups of POWs. These men argued that without this material they lacked the ability to create a library, pursue much in the way of intellectual diversion, or learn about other political systems, which they felt was one of the goals of their segregation. They did not know who ordered these shipments to be stopped or why the reading materials never arrived, but they were aware that the men in XO Compound had a well stocked library and access to daily newspapers, both in English and German.

Although these men may not have known it, they did have one champion of their cause, First Lieutenant Walters Schoenstedt of the Special Projects Branch. This Branch held most of the responsibility, under the PMGO and ASF, in creating, organizing, and monitoring POW political activity and reorientation, especially at the four reeducation camps.[60] Schoenstedt displayed keen insight when it came to understanding the psychology of the German POWs and their needs. He knew that their good treatment would lead ideally to greater cooperation between U.S. and German personnel that would continue after the war. He was also adept at distinguishing between Nazis and others. He realized that the anti-Nazi character, although widely varied, was an aberration to the German military and confused American GIs as well. According to him anti-Nazis "would look awkward in any uniform" and they should not be compared to the professional soldiers associated with the Nazi groups. He added that while "they are not always in a position to do as much in the laundry or in the tobacco field as the sturdy peasants from the XO compound . . . they will be able to do a job for the United States which might . . . turn out to be more important than any amount of lumber cut to proper size."[61]

The anti-Nazis provided intelligence on the Third Reich, its military, politics, and on other prisoners. After the war, the U.S. hoped that many of these former prisoners would assist the military government in running post war Germany. Scheonstedt informed members of the PMGO, ASF, and camp commanders, through his correspondence that he felt many of the POWs escaped to elude the steel grip of the Nazis and provided "the first expression of Anti-Nazi prisoners against Hitler's system."[62]

The greatest failure of the experiment in anti-Nazi and Nazi segregation at Campbell was the infiltration of Nazi elements into the anti-Nazi compounds. On June 3, 1944, Lieutenant Colonel Carl B. Byrd asserted that transfers to, from, and between the compounds at Campbell needed to be decentralized and streamlined. Major D.M. McLeod added on the 5th of June that "quite often prisoners of war shipped into this camp from outside the Service Command as anti-Nazis prove not to properly belong in this category. Also, occasionally prisoners in the Nazi compound are found that properly belong in the anti-Nazi compound."[63] When officers at Campbell read this statement they realized that they made some mistakes. No one could predict the seriousness of the problems to come.

U.S. officials began to discover numerous Nazi elements within the camps only three days after Major D.M. McLeod released his statement. In March 1944 thirteen POWs received transfer from Papago Park, Arizona, to Campbell's anti-Nazi compounds. By June 8, the hardcore Nazi ideology of two of these men brought them into conflict with the remainder of the compound. Officials placed Frank Justra and Karl Schlechtriemen in confinement pending transfer to a Nazi camp. Immediately after these troubles began five more men from the Papago group professed Nazi leanings and asked to be transferred.[64]

Sergeant Alois Antes received transfer from POW Camp Mexia, Texas, to Camp Campbell after having altercations with some of the Nazi POWs in that camp. During the interview with U.S. officials before the move, Antes evaded the question of his Nazi status. He expressed a strong Catholic leaning and "did not approve of the Cross [in the camp sanctuary] being draped with a Nazi flag." He also said that his problems stemmed from the fact that he "expressed himself too freely" and only later "realized his statements were definitely the wrong thing to say."[65] Despite the interviewing officials adding the caveat that "it is believed possible that Subject has been selected by Nazi group to be transferred as an 'infiltrator' to an anti-Nazi camp" he still received transfer.[66]

Antes, once at Campbell, immediately started trouble. He told camp authorities that "he was very much surprised and disgusted, humiliated and degraded, to find himself in an anti-Nazi Camp." Less than two weeks after arrival he refused a direct order by one of the American lieutenants to "stencil some clothing in the supply room." After a few days of bread and water confinement Antes finally became cooperative. Once back in the general population of the camp, however, he ran afoul of the anti-Nazis. The camp spokesman informed the guards that "he could not be responsible for [him] if he remained in that compound." The guards again took Antes into confinement, this time "for his own security."[67] Authorities at Campbell requested that Antes either be transferred back to Camp Mexia, Texas, or to Camp Alva, Oklahoma.

The first large scale Nazi infiltration at Campbell happened on June 8, 1944, with a transfer of 73 men from Fort Lewis, Washington. As with the preceding transfer from Papago Park, the ardent Nazi beliefs of two of these men, Kurt Bernich and Peter Schwierzck, forced their segregation from the men housed at Campbell. The next day, 28 other men from the Fort Lewis group refused to go to work, demanding transfer to a Nazi camp.[68]

Gefreiter Hans Stephan, who had been transferred to Campbell's anti-Nazi camp, became one of the most prolific perpetrators of false ideology. Hans, a Nazi, faked his anti-Nazi sentiments in order to gain access to this camp and came with a group of 13 other men from Camp Grant, Illinois. Once in the camp he went about his mission of "converting my comrades and bringing them back to 'Deutschtum nationalistic patriotism'." He told U.S. authorities "since everybody in this camp knows about my activities I feel that my life is endangered and I am asking the officials to be transferred at once."[69]

U.S. officials compiled a report on Stephan before agreeing to the transfer. Although he immediately volunteered for military service when Germany invaded Poland, he did not begin his active duty service until March, 1940. After capture he transferred to Camp Grant and then to Campbell. Once at Campbell he found the POWs transferred from Breckinridge to be among the worst types of anti-Nazis. According to Stephan these men were "chiefly Communistic agitators" who came mostly from the Penal and Rehabilitation groups including the 961st and 962nd Battalions and the 999ers. He continued that "after the war all members of these units will be tried for treason, and charges have been filed against them already in criminal courts." Stephan further stated that "the trouble with the Anti-Nazi camp is that the POWs think they were transferred to this camp so they can continue their political activities freely and do this without being subjected to serious threats."[70]

Lieutenant Colonel Carl B. Byrd compiled the official forms detailing the military action for Stephan. Byrd agreed to transfer Stephan back to Alva where he finally arrived in June 1944. Stephan left in full confidence that he finished his "mission" of compiling "a record of Anti-Nazis to be turned over to Nazi Officials in Germany after the war." Byrd expressed relief at removing this troublemaker from protective custody and from Campbell. Given the unrest Stephan caused during his brief stay and his overt Nazi leaning it came as a shock to both Campbell authorities and POWs when the man suddenly arrived back in the anti-

135

Nazi compound in October 1944. Byrd wrote to Fifth Service Command Headquarters that "it is not clear . . . why the prisoner of war camp at Alva returned him to Camp Campbell." He added that "of course he had to be immediately placed in protective custody as the other prisoners remembered him well from his previous stay at Campbell." Byrd asked that the prisoner be immediately transferred out of Campbell to another camp for Nazis.[71]

Wilhelm Schmitz, another member of the Camp Grant group, also requested transfer. Schmitz found himself at odds with the Nazi element at Camp Grant and therefore U.S. authorities labeled him as anti-Nazi and transferred him to one of Campbell's anti-Nazi compounds. Schmitz, a member of the Luftwaffe, told U.S. officials that "he does not agree with Nazi politics" and "especially opposes Nazi atrocities which he had witnessed in Lithuania and Russia."[72] Despite these feelings Schmitz found his new home even less welcoming. Within two months at Campbell he requested a transfer stating that "since I am a German soldier, I cannot agree with the Anti-German current noticeable here."[73] American officials that interviewed Schmitz noted that "he is convinced that these men here are all communists of the worst type. They deny being Germans and are looking forward to the communistic world revolution. Furthermore he thinks that 80% of the prisoners are traitors and ran over to the Allies not on account of their convictions but in order to cover up their past criminal activities."[74] Continuing his attacks on the men in the camp, Schmitz added that "he would perish mentally [if forced to stay in the compound] because he cannot make any friends with this type of people" and "cannot stand the continuous political arguments and discussions in the barracks." He finally explained that he would "prefer to live in a Nazi Camp, because 'the Nazis think as Germans'."[75] The army eventually transferred Schmitz to Camp Alva, Oklahoma. Army officials were troubled, however, when Stephan claimed that he reclaimed Schmitz for the Nazi cause and rescued him from within the anti-Nazi compound.

Schmitz's stay among the hardcore Nazis at Alva, Oklahoma did not go as he had hoped. Stephan informed his Nazi colleagues that Schmitz had been an anti-Nazi. This caused him problems in the camp and Schmitz asked the guards for protection. Schmitz learned of a pending transfer to move more Nazis from Grant to Alva and some of these were the men he originally had problems within that camp. He requested a new transfer and agreed to inform American authorities on all of the activities of Stephan in return for protection.[76]

On April 6, 1944, Lieutenant Colonel Byrd released a letter to the Provost Marshal General detailing some of the more egregious instances of foul-ups by those transferring men to Campbell. A transfer of fifteen men from Camp Grant, Illinois, led to problems when these men mixed into the same companies and barracks with a group of 182 ardent anti-Nazis from Breckinridge. These men expressed that they were not Nazis, but would rather mix with Nazis than the anti-Nazis. A simple transfer of companies seemed to fix the problem. Authorities from Camp Rosewell, New Mexico, transferred Alfred Klomann to the anti-Nazi compound. Klomann entered

137

the camp spouting Nazi slogans and claiming that he was a Nazi and a Gestapo agent. The duty officer immediately confined the man for his own safety. A similar thing happened when officials from Camp Aliceville, Alabama, sent Gerhard Horke to Campbell. Horke proudly admitted that he was a Nazi and a member of the SS. Both men received transfers to Camp Alva, Oklahoma. Yet, letters from Alva claimed that Horke was "definitely" an anti-Nazi.[77] Other mistakes included the transfer of four "violent Nazis" from Papago Park to Alva. In another instance, Fort Robinson, Nebraska, sent a severe mental case to Campbell. Private Gerhard Braune received mental care at Robinson and because of the severity of his condition had to be admitted "immediately to the Psychopathic Ward."[78] Byrd complained to the Provost Marshal that "prisoners are being received daily from various camps without Special Orders or records whatsoever. In many cases, telegrams received before the prisoners arrive, are the only records we have at the time of arrival. In several instances, telegrams have been sent with insufficient and inaccurate information as to the time and number of prisoners arriving. It is requested that this camp or this Service Command be notified as to the number of prisoners and time of scheduled arrival and that records be required to accompany the prisoners of war."[79]

Eventually the War Department issued orders to hopefully clear up some of the mess that occurred at Campbell. Lieutenant Colonel Earl Edwards, the Assistant Director of the Prisoner of War Division, understood that Campbell was designed to house not just anti-Nazis, but those "persecuted by fellow prisoners," but fell short of that goal. War Department officials decided that the names of every POW currently in one of Campbell's anti-Nazi camps and the reason for their transfer to that camp needed to be forwarded on to G-2 (Army intelligence) and to the Provost Marshal General. Further, all the men currently housed there needed to be screened a second time to determine their disposition. New regulations required the implementation of these safeguards each time an additional 100 men entered into the anti-Nazi compounds. Those housed in Campbell not meeting the specific requirements received transfer to appropriate camps. During the interim, War Department officials determined that those classified solely as anti-Nazi from other camps should be transferred to Fort Devens, Massachusetts.[80]

Even these top-down measures fell short during implementation. The case of Erwin Ebeling and Walter Brandtner illuminated just how deep the Nazi problem ran in the anti-Nazi camps. They requested transfer out of Camp Indianola, Nebraska, due to continued Nazi harassment, beatings, and even being sentenced to death. Ebeling and Brandtner thrived in Campbell until some of the Nazis from Indianola arrived. The newly arrived Nazis spied on the anti-Nazis, led protests against work orders, and caused disorder. They recognized Ebeling and Brandtner who revealed these "disguised" Nazis to the guards. In return for their service, Ebeling and Brandtner along with two other colleagues from Indianola received confinement without reason for 30 days. Prior to confinement other POWs in the camp accused all four of being "communists" by their fellow POWs and the confined men feared the fate that awaited them upon release. Ebeling claimed in a letter to the War Department that Colonel Byrd refused to meet with them and that the guards ignored their fears. He felt that his only recourse was to pen a letter directly to the War Department and then escape with Brandtner in order to mail the letter securely from outside of camp. He urged the officials to "please excuse this" action as it was "of the most urgent necessity" and assured that they would immediately "give themselves up again."[81] The two men escaped and the War Department received the letter, however, the action taken by U.S. officials is unknown. The men likely received transfer to Fort Devens, Massachusetts.[82] Campbell reached its full capacity in both of the anti-Nazi Compounds by October 1944, but given the transfers and re-screenings constantly being conducted, a healthy flow of men came in and out of Campbell.[83] Even as late as November 1944 petitions rolled in from numerous POWs who pledged loyalty to the Nazi Party but for some reason ended up in one of the anti-Nazi compounds at Campbell.[84]

Despite the many attempts by Nazi prisoners to sabotage the effectiveness of the Anti-Nazi camp, the experiment at Campbell did not fail. While Nazis and other unsavory elements successfully infiltrated the anti-Nazi camps, these dissidents lacked the ability to control the camps as effectively as in camps where Nazi POWs were the majority. Even the popular Nazi scare tactic of locating and punishing one's relatives back home fell through when they discovered that many anti-Nazis did not have relatives living in Germany or that their relatives had already suffered Nazi violence in concentration camps. Acting on information given by POW Sergeant Georg Rupprecht, spokesman for DD and VW compounds, the military located many of the "werewolves" within the anti-Nazi compounds and removed them. U.S. First Lieutenant Walter Schoenstedt of the Special Programs Section additionally recommended that some of the anti-Nazis be transferred between the compounds DD and VW and the "more radical be sent to Fort Devens."[85] He also ordered that these compounds receive the previously denied movies, books, and newspapers. Schoenstedt removed Rupprecht as spokesperson, replacing him with two sergeants. The new spokesmen, both anti-Nazis, professional military men, and transferred from other camps, would provide the anti-Nazis with the strong internal leadership needed. Each would be responsible for only one compound, Rupprecht represented both anti-Nazi compounds, and Schoenstedt hoped that they would instill needed order and ensure cooperation with Campbell guards and officials.[86] By the end of 1944 most problems at Campbell had been solved thanks to some far-sighted U.S. officials and cooperative prisoners.

Chapter 6
Holes in the Barbed Wire: Escapes and Escapees

"*It's* Easy to Bluff Americans" boasted a headline from the popular magazine *Collier's*, misquoting famed German POW escaper Reinhold Pabel.[1] Pabel disowned these words in his book, *Enemies Are Human*, but they may have belonged to any of the 2,222 POWs who escaped from U.S. camps. The POWs used numerous tactics to escape. Tools, utensils, careless slips of the tongue from civilian co-workers, tidbits of information cobbled together from other prisoners, and money garnered from guards and employers for POW crafted trinkets and medals, all proved useful for the future breaks through the barbed wire.

Prior to arrival in the U.S. most prisoners had no geographic concept of their points of disembarkation, permanent base camps, or the vastness of the American countryside. Positioning themselves geographically was one of the first tasks POWs busied themselves with once in their Kentucky camps. Where was Kentucky in relation to any major landmarks or, more importantly, escape routes? How near to Mexico were they? To one of the oceans? Could they make it to a major river and, if so, where would that take them? The precise distance by train from New York or Norfolk to Kentucky evaded them. They tried to count the stops, but the indirect route inland and numerous days spent on the trains kept even the most attentive guessing as to the mileage. Curious Americans surrounded the POWs and provided answers to their "academic" questions about U.S. geography. Many reporters and guards spotted the ruse for what it was. As one Kentucky reporter relayed "they wanted to know how far it was to New York. And they know they are near Louisville, but they have no conception as to where Louisville or Kentucky are."[2] The Germans practiced another trick even more skillfully, hiding the fact that many among them spoke English. They carefully guarded this secret and used it to eavesdrop on conversations, often gleaning important information.

Every good soldier had a duty to his country that if captured, he must try to escape. Bringing the German POWs into American backyards made many of the prisoners conscious of this oath. Officials from the War Department, the Army Service Forces (ASF), and the Provost Marshal General's Office (PMGO), remained aware of the potential for POWs to escape and cause sabotage and constantly maintained a vigilance to prevent opportunities for prisoners to escape. The U.S. designed camps under the often conflicting rubric of economic viability and security.

The layout of the POW camp and its inherent security became a deliberate deterrent for prisoner escapes. Usually constructed on flat land, the camp site was then cleared of trees, large rocks, and other obstacles. A double barbed wire fence, at least twelve feet high, with an additional three feet of wire hanging over, provided a second level of prevention. Guards and dogs patrolled the area between the fences. Towers standing at least six feet taller than the fencing allowed guards an unobstructed view of the camp, the area between the fences, and the land just outside of the camp. More importantly their position afforded them a clear line of fire and flood lighting illuminated the area at night, enabling security to be nearly as tight as during the day.[3]

Each POW base camp designed for 3,000 men, like Kentucky's base camps, Campbell, Breckinridge, and Knox, also housed Military Police Escort Companies (MPEC). These consisted of 132 men and three officers for every 1,000 POWs, totaling 405 men when the camps operated at full capacity. Camp guards received an additional nine weeks of training covering the rules of the Geneva Convention, self-defense, scouting, patrolling, and using their weapons to prevent escapes.[4]

Guard towers housed two sentries whose mounted machine guns were always half loaded with at least twenty rounds with an additional 180 rounds available. Each tower crew had a standard issue of ten grenades, a mounted machine gun, and their rifles. Corridor and Dead Space guards walked between the fences and guarded the Dead Line, beyond which a POW could be shot, and carried riot guns in addition to their normal weapons. Roving patrol guards mounted in jeeps had a vehicle mounted machine-gun with 1,000 rounds of ammunition. The Guard House stored all the additional weapons and ammunition, including an extra 150 grenades, doled out in case of emergency.[5]

POW camp guards have often been criticized as typically unfit for duty. Some were veterans of World War I, and others were prevented from active service by age, mental, emotional, or physical disabilities that hindered their military usefulness. This is a broad and often unfair generalization, and many fine soldiers pulled tours of duty as POW camp guards. I will present an alternative classification of U.S. camp guards. The first group, the so-called fraternizers, found common ground with the Germans. To these guards, the POWs looked like Americans. They loyally served their country; some spoke English, and a handful were even born in the U.S. The guards felt that the Germans were quite simply soldiers turned prisoners. The second and likely largest group of guards were just doing their jobs. They did not provide favors for or hold a grudge against the prisoners. A third type of guard hated the Germans and zealously undertook the job of handling these prisoners. Some of these guards included U.S. servicemen returning from overseas, who may have lost a friend in combat, or witnessed the horrors of war in Europe firsthand. The POWs quickly learned that they needed to be especially wary around them.

In addition to the guards and camp layout, procedures implemented by U.S. officials also hindered escape attempts. Frequent roll calls singled out missing prisoners. Surprise inspections often uncovered accumulations of U.S. money gained by trading with guards or civilians. Missing board slats and makeshift tools often led to unfinished escape tunnels, while sharpened objects or kitchen utensils posed as a means to cut the wire. Curfews, separate barracks, interior barbed wire, and gates kept the men in their "proper" place at night.[6]

Even with all the security measures in place, the fear of escaped POWs roaming the American countryside remained and for good reason. The U.S. could ill-afford to have enemy agents or prisoners running amuck, especially since the Germans had proven a potentially dangerous lot. U.S. officials learned important lessons regarding security from the experiences of their Allies. A riot at the Featherstone, New Zealand, POW camp left nearly 100 Japanese prisoners killed or wounded and one New Zealander killed and six wounded.[7]

The Australians failed to stop a mass escape from the Cowra POW camp in August 1944. Most of the 4,000 men housed at Cowra were Japanese who took a suicide pact and charged the fences with makeshift weapons and improvised clubs. Caught by surprise and overwhelmed by the sheer numbers of men many of the guards were wounded. Surprisingly only four guards were killed, but over 200 Japanese lay dead and about 100 were wounded during the escape attempt. The 359 men that escaped stood out in Australia the way that the Germans did not in the U.S., enabling authorities to swiftly arrest them, although many committed suicide rather than be recaptured.[8]

American arguments about the cultural difference regarding violent escapes by the Japanese on one hand and the generally non-violent attempts by Germans and Italians on the other could not explain the plot by SS and other Wehrmacht groups hatched at the POW camp at Devizes in England. These men plotted an escape to coincide with the German Ardennes invasion, hoping to capture British supply depots and tanks, sowing confusion and perhaps linking up with their comrades. The British discovered the plot and took measures to prevent it and dispersed the planners to different camps.

Many accounts exist concerning disloyal Americans in the U.S. aiding and abetting German saboteurs and escapers. Three Japanese-American women aided two POWs in an escape from Camp Trinidad, Colorado, by supplying them with money, clothes, and supplies.[9] Heinrich Haider, one of the POWs, an avowed anti-Nazi, stated that he spent two years in a concentration camp for urging Austrians to "rise up against Hitler" and that he intended to fight against Germany. The U.S. government acquitted the three girls who had faced the death penalty for treason.[10] Some Americans assumed that the dubious loyalty of these Japanese-American girls stemmed from their nationality. In another example, however, Kitty Case and Shirley Bruce, two "American" girls, helped two POWs escape from a canning work detail in Michigan.[11] Why did these "American" girls do this? Love perhaps? At Camp Hale, Colorado at least eight GIs and 5 WACs (Women's Auxiliary Corps) assisted in the escape of two German POWs.[12]

U.S. guards and officials understandably kept a close watch over the POWs. If a POW decided to test the camp defenses and the resolve of the guards, he entered a risky venture. When a POW decided he wanted to escape from the camp, he realized that the guard only had to shout "Halt" two or three times before shooting.[13] If the POW evaded the sentry and corridor guards, he had to cut or scale the first barbed wire fence and get into the corridor, the area between the two fences. At this point he had to be especially wary of guard dogs and the men in the watch towers.

The escapee therefore, while cutting through or scaling the second fence, had to dodge searchlights. Once through the second fence the man had to worry about guards conducting a random jeep patrol, roll-call or inspection, or discovering his absence before he made good his escape. If recaptured, the punishment included confinement, restriction to a bread and water diet, and loss of privileges. In order to improve their chances most of the POWs attempted this type of escape under the cover of darkness.

Even if the escapee proved successful, the POW became a marked man. The Federal Bureau of Investigations (FBI) joined the War Department in hunting the fugitive, and they performed this job zealously. The camp issued descriptions to all local and state police forces. Newspapers from several counties and often several states alerted the public. In Kentucky, descriptions of the escapers appeared on the front pages of newspapers the very next day and reports flooded the counties surrounding the camp. The Louisville *Courier-Journal*, the state flagship paper, often published these reports and occasionally these prisoners earned the dubious honor of being featured in the *New York Times*.[14]

FBI Director J. Edgar Hoover led the bureau's investigations of enemy aliens, saboteurs, and escaped prisoners of war. The FBI's early vigilance enabled the capture of eight trained German saboteurs who landed at Long Island in 1942 with the money, material, and intention to damage the infrastructure of the U.S.[15] They split into two groups, and some made it as far as Chicago, before two of them doubted their mission. They revealed their plans to the FBI, who arrested all eight before they conducted any sabotage. The six captured at large received death sentences, while the two informants received prison terms that were further reduced to allow their release in 1948. A second unrelated incident resulted in the capture and arrest of two German saboteurs who landed by submarine in Maine in 1944. These events justifiably increased fears of saboteurs and enemy aliens; six previously lived in the U.S. and two were naturalized citizens.[16]

Hoover announced in 1944 that among "those of foreign birth in our midst . . . a small minority [exists] who by their deeds or words exhibit a willingness to fight against instead of for America in a period of war."[17] He warned the American public that this threat loomed large and that preparations were underway "for the day when an attempt might be made to 'invade' America from within."[18] His words reverberated through the nation and preyed upon America's xenophobia. He constantly reminded Americans of the dangers of escaped POWs and cautioned that any collusion or cooperation with POWs carried a death sentence for treason. Although the most heinous crimes committed by prisoners at large were limited to stealing cars and food, trespassing, and property damage committed during the escape, he reminded citizens that "they *might* have committed crimes [and even though] we have not had acts of sabotage by the enemy, the fact remains that the menace is ever present" and "even one escaped prisoner at large, trained as he is in the techniques of destruction, is a danger to our internal security, our war production, and the lives and safety of our citizens."[19] While his dramatic warnings provided a necessary precaution, they also played directly into

149

pre-existing fears held by the majority of the American populace.

What if Hoover was correct and the POWs began escaping in larger numbers and became more violent and destructive? Considering the events in New Zealand, Australia, and England, could rural Kentucky locales like Union County be too careful? These international lessons hit closer to Kentucky than the distance across the oceans seemed to indicate. Statistics demonstrate the extent of this problem in the U.S. At its peak the U.S. held a total of about 425,000 Axis POWs. Breaking these numbers down by nationality shows approximately 371,000 Germans, about 50,000 Italians, and nearly 5,500 Japanese. Army records at the National Archives indicate that 2,222 Germans, 604 Italians, and only 1 Japanese prisoner successfully escaped. This means that the percentage of German escapes totaled about 0.6 percent of the Germans held in the U.S. In other words, less than one German in 100 actually escaped on average nationally. German prisoners in Kentucky accounted for sixty escapes, or 2.7 percent of the total, with more than the national average of escapes. None of these numbers take into account that some men repeatedly fled the camps. Although a total of 2,222 of the German POWs got away from the camps, many tried unsuccessfully and guards killed 56, with at least three of these in Kentucky.[20]

Kentucky also hosted the earliest actual escape by German POWs in the United States when three men escaped from a transport train on November 4, 1942. The train carried POWs and enemy aliens from Camp Meade, Missouri, to Camp Forrest, Tennessee, and made two stops between Nashville and Forrest.[21] Military officials counted all of the men at 10 p.m., but discovered them missing during the midnight roll call. The guards wondered whether the men jumped from the moving train or made it off at one of the stops, but deduced that they jumped somewhere in southern Tennessee between Nashville and Tullahoma. The FBI and state and local authorities joined the military in what became a three state manhunt for the fugitives.[22]

The escapees, however, wandered through Warren County, Kentucky, nowhere near southern Tennessee. They left the train not Wednesday night, as the authorities thought, but that afternoon when the train stopped near Bowling Green, Kentucky. They got off there after noticing the "half asleep" guards and spent the next two days wandering around Warren County.[23] Only one could speak English, and he became the spokesman and interpreter by inquiring of several residents along Richardsville Road their proximity to a store. Iva Simmons, who lived nearby, gave them some directions. About thirty minutes later she heard the announcement of the escape with descriptions of the men. She reported the encounter, but the men, although unaware of the sheriff's pursuit, made another getaway.[24]

After crossing at the Green River ferry they ran afoul of Granger Alford, a guard at Glenmore locks. Alford never realized that these "tough looking" drifters were hardened Germans veterans. He tried to run them off for trespassing on the ferry property and "stuck around" as R.C. Haney, the lock keeper, gave them water.[25] Unable to find shelter for the night they crossed the river again and started back towards

Bowling Green. After getting several phone calls the next morning the sheriff caught them as they wandered the road. Despite being armed with pocket knives, which they had owned before being interned, they offered no resistance. The sheriff's search turned up a little bit of money and one of them had a pocket full of corn.[26] The Germans sat in the county jail until Saturday when military and FBI officials arrived to question them and escort them to Camp Forrest. The event became big news in Warren County with three large stories in the local paper. Dozens of people came to the jail to see the "real-life" POWs who had been roving the Bowling Green countryside over the last two days.[27]

     With the exception of some creative planning on the part of POWs at Trinidad, Colorado, who dug a 150 foot tunnel, promptly discovered by authorities, the rest of 1942 and all of 1943 saw few escape attempts. This limited number correlated to the small numbers of POWs as only about 123,000 Germans were in the U.S. by December 1943. Once in America the men needed a period of adjustment to their new surroundings and routines before formulating any plans, and the fear of getting shot by guards or mauled by dogs loomed large enough to keep most German attempts to flee at bay.[28]

     The next two years, however, proved very different. Starting in January 1944 POWs began escaping by the dozens. Laxity of the guards, coupled with larger numbers of determined prisoners, led to increased attempts. POWs soon discovered that it was usually easier to escape from a work detail rather than from within the camp. The minute military officials learned of these escapes, the FBI, Kentucky State and local police, and news agencies received notification. The dragnet that occurred proved effective, typically leading to swift recapture. Few POWs lasted more than a day on the run. Most POWs lacked English language skills or knowledge of the area. Those that mingled with the civilian population often stood out, while others, bereft of the basic resources of food, shelter, or money, ended up turning themselves in. In fact, most of those who actually made it out of the camp were quickly recaptured.

Heinrich Poppe's experience proved typical among many escapers. He made a break from a work detail at Pembroke, Kentucky, on February 2, 1945. After spending the day hiding and not making any progress moving from the area, he surrendered the very next day.[29] When Gerd Roempke escaped from his Breckinridge work detail in February 1945, he thought he had defied the odds. He removed the PW on his uniform, but the stenciling left a faint "PW" outline on his clothes. Armed with some mastery of English and the foresight to travel only at night he stayed at large for several days until dumb luck ended his jaunt in Sturgis, Kentucky. Some youths recognized his faded Afrika Korps uniform and reported his presence to two Fort Campbell soldiers on leave. They apprehended him, bringing an end to a five state manhunt.[30]

Another duo suffered a similarly short excursion. Sergeant Herbert A. Retter, who gained a mastery of Japanese during his tour of duty with the German Pacific Fleet, and Private First Class Otto Hanschlager both escaped from Campbell by slipping through a hole in the wire. Their freedom ended accidentally when farmer Irwin Bracey discovered them

153

hiding in a hay bale in his barn.[31] Rolf Fitzner's escape from Campbell brought him to the Cumberland River where authorities found him hiding in some bushes. Fitzner, armed with a comb, butter knife, pocket full of pennies, and an unswerving belief that Hitler would win the war, surrendered without a fight.[32] Heinrich Schwellenbach escaped from Campbell, spent a couple of days at large, and then turned himself in.[33]

Helmut von Der Aue, a twenty-four year old German POW, had a pretty decent chance of defying the odds. On January 18, 1944, he made it through the wire at Breckinridge armed with a fluency in English and no trace of a German accent. He also fluently spoke French and Italian. Der Aue made a big mistake following the road. Kennard Smith, a school bus driver returning home, passed him that morning and immediately recognized him from the radio report. Smith rushed to pick up nearby farmer, Felix Thomas, who brought along his rifle. When the men confronted Der Aue, he just gave up.[34] Der Aue quickly became well-known to Union County officials for his continued exploits. Although he had the misfortune of getting caught by an attentive school bus driver in January 1944, he made a second attempt on April 3 that year boldly wearing his PW uniform as he sauntered off from Camp Breckinridge. His recapture and transfer to Mississippi only stoked his desire for freedom.[35]

Once in Mississippi, Der Aue, decided to make another attempt, this time aided by Mrs. Rogers. The two met while Der Aue worked on her farm in Boliver County, Mississippi. They fell in love and decided to get married, despite the fact that she already had a husband and a nine-year-old daughter. Authorities caught up with the couple in January 1946. Der Aue was held in Nashville while charges of aiding in the POW escape were brought against Mrs. Rogers.[36]

These types of escapes in Kentucky, sudden, daring, and short-lived, became typical of German escapes in the U.S. Even though most of these fugitives had been caught within days of their escapes, they still posed a potential danger to civilians and to the nation. Newspapers assisted the attempts of government and civilian agencies to recapture escapees by running sometimes sensational stories that excited individuals and often played upon their fears of the "Nazi on the loose." Reporters reminded readers of the fanatical Nazism of these dangerous enemies. Articles cautioned the public to "Watch Out For Escaped Nazi War Prisoners." Comments like the one from Hopkinsville Police Chief Walter Chambers to keep "doors and windows" locked "especially at night until the fugitive known to be here is caught" only added fuel to the fire.[37] Reporters at the Louisville *Courier-Journal* dubbed Guenther Schwriten with one of these unsavory titles after he escaped from Campbell in September 1944. Not only did this so-called "fanatical Nazi" speak only German, he also bore "a [*sinister*] scar above the right eye."[38] Fortunately, that very same day the *Kentucky New Era* announced Schwriten's recapture.[39]

Despite many overblown accounts of escape, many struck a nervous chord with an already edgy Kentucky populace. The facts that German spies had been caught, and that some Americans aided German POW escapes, made many Kentuckians suspicious and uneasy. Bluegrass residents often mistook stolen and damaged goods, vandalized property, and malfunctioning equipment, as signs of sabotage committed by escaped POWs, and perhaps the Americans that aided and harbored them.[40] People across Kentucky began seeing escaped German POWs. One citizen phoned police after witnessing three POWs changing clothes near his apartment building while an American guard watched. The police immediately notified camp authorities at Fort Knox and the Jeffersonville Quartermaster Depot just across the Ohio River from Louisville in nearby Indiana, but roll call at both locations accounted for all the men. Military Police investigating the report discovered that a U.S. captain and guards escorting a POW transfer stopped at the apartment complex where the captain lived to pick up magazines and books, but the POWs remained under guard and did not swap out clothes.[41]

Civilians across the country had been attentive in reporting sightings of escaped POWs and often aided in their recapture, but others obstructed pursuit. Some calls and eye-witness accounts had been pranks, others cases of mistaken identity. It became a dangerous game with potentially fatal consequences for American youths who painted PW on their clothes and wandered around near cities, worksites, and camps that housed prisoners. The Army warned that anyone being mistaken for a POW ran a very real risk of being shot by guards.[42]

Some POW escapees were daredevils. Several repeat offenders tempted fate by making as many as four successful breaks. It seemed that as soon as authorities returned recaptured prisoners they learned of new escapes. When Hermann Loescher and Walter

156

Scheiterle, escapees from Campbell, returned on June 13, 1944, authorities had just discovered that George Hornauf and Anton Scheffer had fled from Breckinridge. Their civilian occupations certainly did not prepare them for lives as fugitives. Hornauf, who spoke English, worked as a gardener; Scheffer worked on the railroad. They only lasted four days on the lam. Lack of success did not deter the duo from making a second escape in August, this time with eighteen year old Heinz Schober.[43]

The exploits of Hans Pfeilstuecker and Victor H. Prokop, two escapees from Camp Campbell, graced nearly a dozen Kentucky and Tennessee papers. In each report the spelling of Pfeilstuecker's first and last name changed. The pair made their first escape in July 1944. The manhunt began immediately after authorities discovered the two missing on the hot Saturday afternoon of July 1, and by the 3rd the newspapers had emblazoned their descriptions in the minds of west Kentuckians. For the POWs it truly was an Independence Day weekend, however, the irony may have been lost on them.[44]

Prokop's stint ended after about a week when, while still wearing his uniform, several men spotted him as he walked down the Julian Road in Christian County. The men who spotted him, afraid to confront him alone, gathered a posse at the Julian store. In the meantime, Prokop walked past the parked car of S.D. Freeman, occupied by Freeman's daughter, Barbara Ann, who recognized the PW on his uniform. Freeman and his daughter offered Prokop a ride and then informed him that he had been caught. He took Prokop to the Julian store, shocking the mob that had gathered

157

there. Prokop told authorities and those present, in good English, that he "was just bored with being in camp doing nothing and had escaped although he did not expect to keep his freedom long." He spent the last week "living on blackberries" and "looking around to see the country."[45]

With Prokop recaptured, Pfeilstuecker still remained at large as the two friends agreed to go their separate ways after escaping. Pfeilstuecker traveled into Trigg County where he inquired about work at the home of G.P. Thomas. Mrs. Thomas recognized the PW stamped all over his uniform and called Sheriff J. Charles Humphrey, who located the man hiding in some bushes near a cave. Pfeilstuecker did not resist arrest, but actually seemed elated by being taken back into captivity. He engaged the sheriff and others at the station in polite conversation explaining that as a school teacher he spoke English, French, and Spanish. He told the men that he admired Erwin Rommel, but despised Hitler. Armed only with an empty water bottle and a second bottle filled with water and blackberries, he stated what everyone already knew "the boys [escaped POWs] could do more damage here than over there [in Europe]." [46] He also told the men that he did not mind camp life, he just wanted "freedom" and if not for lack of food, "Charlie couldn't have caught me."[47]

The July 14, 1944 escape of Otto Zischke factors into this story as well. Otto's short lived escape allowed him to taste the fire of freedom not quenched by recapture. In November 1944 he joined with Pfeilstuecker as they both made second attempts. The men solved the dilemma of cutting the wire or digging under it by driving through the front gate in a stolen

Army jeep. They headed south into Nashville. After spending nearly a week at large they were recaptured. Pfeilstuecker, who now claimed to have been a civilian tailor rather than teacher, crafted them suits out of their PW overcoats.[48] The final chapter of this story occurred in March of 1945. Zischke, whose name also seemed to trouble reporters, decided that three times would be the charm as the 31 year old escaped through a hole in the wire. Willi Schaffner, a second-timer, who first escaped in December of 1944, joined Zischke on his "outing."[49]

While all escapes received public attention, some proved far more dramatic. Erwin Ebeling and Walter Brandner certainly caused a stir when they attempted to escape only to be chased throughout the camp. Surprisingly, however, the men lost the guards and the military declared them officially escaped and notified the FBI, who following protocol, notified state and local police, and the press.[50] The men made their way off base and tried to catch a freight train, not far from the L&N Railroad in Clarksville, when workers recognized them. They surrendered easily. Brandner told the police that they escaped because they had argued with Nazi POWs and feared for their safety.[51]

Four other prisoners at Camp Campbell made a 3 a.m. getaway in a stolen ambulance. Military policeman, Private First Class Maynard Walls, grew suspicious when he saw men filling the vehicle with water. A quick radio call to headquarters stating that no ambulance had left confirmed his suspicion and he followed the ambulance off post and into Clarksville. When he pulled them over he discovered the four escaped POWs and ordered them back to camp. Walls followed the ambulance back into camp and for his efforts received promotion to Corporal.[52]

At Fort Knox four repeat offenders did not know when to call it quits. Authorities became alarmed on February 15, 1945, when Fritz Jungman, Heinz Braunstorf, Erwin Biehl, and Werner Schwanbeck escaped. Unused to so many men escaping at one time, authorities desperately hoped to recapture them and end the mass escape. Fortunately, all four men stayed together and wore their blue denim uniforms with PW stamped on them and proved easy to find and recapture. In May, just four months later the quintet again escaped, this time in a stolen government vehicle. After visiting Horse Cave, they headed to Nashville where authorities recaptured them. Unlike their Campbell counterparts, and other escapees, the government came down hard on them. Each man received five year prison sentences for stealing the car. Why the government made examples of them when few other escaping prisoners had been punished so severely is unknown. Perhaps, it was a preventive measure, a warning for other POW wrong doers, or perhaps it had something to do with the war ending. It must be noted that the seemingly harsh penalty was within the tenets of the Geneva Convention and the law.[53]

Scant few prisoners enjoyed more than a week at large. Some of Kentucky's most successful escapees stayed on the run for a little over a week, but at least one held out for four months. Captain Wolfgang Hermann Hellfritsch escaped from Camp Crossville, Tennessee, on October 11, 1943. Tennessee and Kentucky authorities had been unable to locate him, until they discovered the Navy man working on a

Lexington farm in February 1944. Hellfritsch found employment as a farm hand at the Donerail horse nursery for sixteen days. When questioned about his activities and how he arrived in Fayette County he told agents that he hitchhiked, sometimes getting rides from the Kentucky State Police, and had spent most of the previous three months working on farms in Scott County.[54]

Heinz Eutin and Josef Saller both had short lived escapes, but what their freedom lacked in longevity, it made up for it with the attention garnered from the state presses. They escaped from Campbell on August 8, 1945. Eutin made it as far as Springfield, Tennessee, on his first escape in December 1944.[55] By the middle of the month the police still had not recaptured them, although they responded to several calls of attempted break-ins in Christian County that they assumed involved the men. Police nearly nabbed Eutin when they discovered that he had been holed up in the Belmont School and had been using the stoves to cook. When these "heavily armed" officers did spot him his ability to "run like a race horse" allowed him to get away.[56] Clarksville police finally ran down Saller on the 23rd, but the lithe Eutin still remained at large.[57] When they finally apprehended Eutin, it was on his terms. He enjoyed a meal at the Holt home in Lafayette, Kentucky, telling Mrs. Holt that he was "nearly starved." Mrs. Holt then fixed him some lunch, although she locked her house and left him on the porch. While Eutin ate the meal, handed to him out the window, Troy Holt and Joe Thompson arrived to apprehend him. Eutin who was "tired of hiding" agreed to go with the men to the police station.[58]

Escaping brought many risks, with getting injured, mauled by guard dogs, hunger, and exposure to the elements being common deterrents. Although prisoners attempting to escape were seldom killed, that was the ultimate price that they could pay. Josef Reitinger, a German POW from Camp Campbell, being transferred for medical reasons to Fort Benjamin Harrison, attempted to escape his guards, Sergeant Alva L. Kasse and Private First Class Roland Leathead, the medical attendant, at Clarksville's L&N Train Depot on January 24, 1945. The POW ran from the guards and Kasse pursued. Kasse paused after the German ignored orders to halt. He then fired two warning shots and then fired a third round which entered the POW's back instantly killing him. Newspaper reports did not issue the name of the German, but official records did, and Reitinger is one of the five buried at Camp Campbell's POW cemetery.[59]

In another incident, two POWs at Fort Knox were killed and five others wounded during a "disturbance." Private First Class Dewie Merritt fired upon the POWs after they refused to vacate the fence area. Merritt was taken for questioning by military police following the incident.[60] Heino Erichsen, a former prisoner of war at Fort Knox, recalled this event vividly. He disagreed with the *New York Times* article that the "guard prevented a mass escape!" Erichsen remembered that on that day some Nazis beat some other POWs and the guards made these men file out to find the culprits. Most of the POWs, according to Erichsen, had to stand between the fences only about eight feet from the tripwire or 'dead-zone' beyond which they could be shot. Erichsen, who was on work detail, did not witness the event, but heard that probably some of the men taunted the guards. One of the guards opened fire; despite the fact that another fence would have blocked any escape. The men killed, Ernst Schlotter and Friederich Wolf, were friends of Erichsen's. In his own book, *The Reluctant Warrior: Former German POW Finds Peace in Texas*, published in 2001, he defended his friends, stating that they never caused the Americans problems and did nothing "to deserve being shot." [61] Heino visited their graves at Fort Knox twice after he became a U.S. citizen. The Germans were buried with full military honors.

Given the defenses of the camp, the potential to be shot and killed, and the difficulty of remaining at large or making it out of the country, why did so many men tempt fate? Did they want to commit sabotage and destruction? Obviously not, none of the men in Kentucky or the total 2,222 escapees in the United States attempted to attack anyone or anything once outside of the camp. Some may have wanted to rejoin the German military, but this number must have been extraordinarily small. Not many of the men entertained the idea of returning to combat, suffering and rationing, when they lived in relative comfort and safety within Kentucky's camps. Considering the distance to Germany and the odds against making a successful trip back to Europe, even the few who may have wanted to make the trip surely soon discovered the futility of it. Making it to Mexico and freedom enticed some of these escapees who tried unsuccessfully to make the journey. Three men, however, members of the greatest group of Germans to ever escape in the U.S., left Camp Papago Park, Arizona and made it about fifty miles across the border into Mexico. The same problems that plagued escapees in the U.S. troubled them in Mexico. They lacked money and language skills, and stood out among the civilian population which prompted local authorities to swiftly arrest them. After some struggle, nearly leading to an international incident, U.S. authorities traveled to Mexico and returned the men back to camp.

Most men who escaped did it looking for adventure and certainly for freedom and as many of the POWs cited they hoped to find beer, women, and excitement. Some met girls while on work details and escaped from camp to rendevous with them. Even Karl Luft, Hans Richard Jonat, and Paul Hitzegrad, the first POWs to escape in Kentucky, claimed that they did it on a whim. One of the men suggested it while playing cards and then they just did it.[62]

The savvier among them also realized that the odds of making a break from the camp itself seemed nearly insurmountable. Work details, however, usually had less attentive guards, no barbed wire or dogs, and more opportunities to slip away. The drawback was that the prisoners returned to camp by specified times and the smaller number of men meant that the guard could usually look across the tobacco field, take a head count, and immediately realize that a man had gotten away. On the other hand, escapes from the main camp could go hours or perhaps even a day or two with help from others before authorities realized that someone escaped.

Most escapees remained at large for only a few hours or days, but that taste of freedom seemed to be all that they needed. Some had girlfriends or hoped to meet women. Few truly entertained the idea that they would be gone long, and only a handful of POWs in the U.S. remained at large for several months or years.

Chapter 7
Entertaining the Afrika Korps in Kentucky: Camp Life of German POWs

It is my desire, as spokesman of this camp, to thank you in the name of my fellow prisoners for your hearty Christmas greetings and for all the help and aid you have given us during these long years when we were far from home . . .
-POW Reinhard Schroeder to the Y.M.C.A.[1]

German POWs received a unique education in Kentucky camps. A skeptical observer might liken the list of entertainment and recreation activities to those provided in a liberal arts program of a high school or college. Monday through Friday, and some Saturdays, the prisoners worked until about five p.m. The rest of the weekday, until lights out, and the weekends belonged to them. Interested men attended one of the Physical Education classes or enrolled in Cinema, Music, Theater 101, or Introduction to American Democracy. Some POWs participated in Library Science, where they learned to catalog the hundreds of books received in the camp while others published their own newspaper. Camps, of course, offered Introduction to Christian Religion on Sunday. A lack of familiarity with the instructors never dissuaded the captive students, as teachers often came from among their own or one of their guards. Finally, if none of these offerings caught the man's eye, free time could be spent writing letters or milling about the camp.

The skeptical observer, however, failed to realize the importance of this "American Education." It kept the men occupied and hopefully away from mischief or escape endeavors. Ironically, the education within the camp provided a level of freedom unavailable to many in Nazi Germany, and largely unknown to the younger prisoners who grew up in the Third Reich. This system helped curb problems in the camp and gave the POWs an appreciation for America and democracy. The Geneva Convention required the holding power to allow recreation and diversion for the POWs. Even though the Bluegrass State did not house any of the four experimental reeducation camps designed to de-Nazify the POWs, education in Kentucky's classrooms impacted the Germans in positive ways.[2] The War Department and its subordinate agencies, the Office of the Provost Marshal General (PMGO) and the Army Service Forces (ASF), worked closely with the Red Cross and Young Men's Christian Association (YMCA) to provide one of the most comprehensive and democratic intellectual diversion programs ever offered to prisoners of war.

Although my argument that this intellectual diversion program actually operated as an education program may seem trite, in reality it functioned far more closely as a barometer to gauge educational and social growth, than at providing simple diversion. For most POWs keeping their bodies sharp and their reactions strong through sports activities became the first and most important step in their education process. The recreation room of the POW barracks included adequate space for indoor games, such as table tennis, a POW favorite. Outdoor areas, not always available but always sought after, allowed POWs to play faustball (fistball) and football (soccer), the favorite of German POWs across the nation.[3] POWs organized their own soccer teams to compete against each other. Sometimes the guards helped organize teams from different barracks to create friendly rivalries.

Lack of space and equipment proved only a temporary detriment for these sports activities. POWs, often aided by the guards, lobbied for outdoor recreation areas and when official space could not be found quickly enough, any open plot often worked just as well. The POWs had access to equipment from a variety of sources. The War Department allowed POWs to purchase their own from the camp canteens. The ASF and Provost Marshal General ensured that camp commanders stocked needed items as soccer balls and ping-pong paddles. Relief agencies donated new and slightly used equipment to the camps. The YMCA and the Red Cross provided the largest portion of all sports gear, among other items of use for other areas of the POW education program. Even with the donations and the German's ability to purchase equipment, the demand for equipment greatly exceeded what was available.

The ASF and PMGO maintained that the sports and recreation programs, along with the other intellectual diversion programs, kept the prisoners occupied and their morale high which prevented mischief and made the prisoners more pliable workers. Realizing the importance of these particular diversions, the military went above and beyond. In 1944 the ASF created an individual account with the sole purpose of allowing the military to purchase pre-assembled recreation kits for the camps. These packages included equipment for soccer, fistball, table tennis, and other activities that the POWs typically pursued. The great demand for these kits limited distribution to the rate of one kit for every 250 POWs, but "supply never seemed to match need."[4] Kits became lost in route or lasted less time than expected. Inspections by the military found that many orders went to the wrong camps, but these camps claimed not to have received extra equipment. At other camps the POWs never acquired the equipment because the guards hoarded it or it disappeared at some point between arrival at the camp and delivery to the prisoners.[5]

Prisoners, officials, and inspectors, commented on the wonderful recreation activities available at the camps. The prisoners loved soccer. Americans in the 1940s, like Americans in the 21st century, knew about soccer, but preferred baseball and football. On the other hand the POWs never truly understood or appreciated American football. Heino Erichsen, a former POW at Knox, recalled "we played soccer, too. Soccer was unknown to Americans back then. Our nervous young guards stared in distaste as we bounced the ball off our feet and heads."[6] The POW insistence on constantly playing soccer allowed the guards and camp officials to learn the rules of the sport.

Former POW Egon Hessenthaler also at Knox described a nighttime soccer game:

The summer months of 1945 were very hot at Fort Knox. One could barely think about sleeping. It was just unbearable. One evening, it was around 2300 when someone had an idea to play soccer. Of course, since it was already dark and the camp was only scantily lighted, we requested the guards to turn on a few of their headlights because we wanted to play soccer. What we thought to be impossible came true. The head lights came on, and we played our game to a lively participation of the guards. We hit the showers afterwards and the head lights went out again.[7]

When lacking necessary equipment, the POWs improvised. The prisoners at Fort Knox found ways around the lack of paint to mark their soccer fields. According to former POW Egon Hessenthaler "the kitchen gave out a sack of flour and a sack of powdered sugar to us and with that we marked our field. Because flour and sugar didn't last very long, we had to repeat the process over and over again."[8]

Paul Schnyder, a delegate of the International Committee of the Red Cross, described the recreation at Knox as "excellent" during a visit in April 1946. Reports of sports activities at Knox paralleled that of Campbell and Breckinridge.[9] At Camp Campbell the men at XO Compound, the "Nazi" group, had bigger and better recreation areas and access to equipment than their "anti-Nazi" counterparts at VW and DD Compounds. The men at XO, generally unhampered by space restrictions, played indoor table-tennis or used a large field to play soccer or fistball.[10]

When not outdoors, the POWs enjoyed watching movies and listening to the radio. Some prisoners took advantage of the good will of their captors by modifying their receivers to pick up and send short-wave. Camp inspectors grew wise to this tactic and kept a close eye out for modifications, but ·never denied the men the privilege of having the radios. After the war ended so too did the rationale of confiscating receivers and camp officials became less vigilant. Even the ostensibly harmless activity of watching movies, a favorite pastime among the prisoners, had restrictions. Before a movie could be shown to the Germans it had to be approved by the ASF and the PMGO. Once given the green light the camp commander could still veto an approved film and prevent the prisoners in his camp from viewing that picture.

The availability of the film itself created a second obstacle. The War Department heavily censored movies to be viewed by the prisoners. Movies that portrayed Nazism or racism in a positive light obviously did not make the cut. Numerous German produced movies including "The Pride of the Third Company" and "The Making of a King" wound up on the banned list. By late 1945 officials authorized 36 German made pictures and over 100 American movies. Many Germans preferred American Westerns.[11]

Most camp commanders made the POWs procure their own equipment and space. An empty cafeteria or recreation room usually served adequately, but getting equipment presented a problem. The more fortunate POWs rented projectors from the guards if available. Relief agencies seldom donated this equipment because of expense, but occasionally the prisoners received outdated equipment. Some POWs pooled their money and ordered the projector and the film through the canteen or camp commander. Watching a movie in the camp proved to be a lengthy and expensive procedure. In order to recoup the money spent, the prisoners often charged moviegoers a nominal fee.[12]

Fortune seemed to shine on the Germans at Fort Knox who enjoyed two movies per week shown on a 16-millimeter projector that they borrowed temporarily from the Post Signal Office. The camp commander supported the film endeavor and ultimately ordered two projectors, one for the permanent use of the Knox men and one for their brethren temporarily housed at the Jeffersonville Quartermaster Depot in Indiana. When not enjoying films, the Knox prisoners also had fifteen radios and one record player with classical and light music from which to choose.[13] Heino Erichsen, a former POW at Knox, remembered that the POWs and Americans both agreed on two of their favorite songs, "Don't Fence Me In" and "Sentimental Journey."[14]

The men at Campbell's Compound DD and VW shared a projector. Both groups of men preferred watching films on history, documentaries, and light fare. They had approximately one radio to each company of 250 men. Their classroom also housed one large communal radio sorely in need of repair. Military officials reported that these "anti-Nazis" listened to news broadcasts intently.[15] In another contrast, the Nazis housed at Campbell's XO Compound owned their own projector.[16] Former POWs Fritz Nessler remembered that at Campbell they eventually "had American and German movies one every night."[17]

Participatory activities provided a departure from the sedentary watching of movies and listening to the radio. Kentucky's POWs took an active role in the performing arts, including musicals, orchestras, and plays. U.S. officials, at first, cast a doubtful eye on these endeavors, arguing that much of this material, especially the costumes and props, could be used in an escape. Eventually they relented and the POWs began constructing, bartering, and buying the needed materials.[18] The YMCA proved especially helpful in donating some art supplies, scraps for props, and discarded and used musical instruments.

Probably no compound in Kentucky took as much pride in their theatre as Compound XO at Campbell. These men constructed a 250 seat audience section, an orchestra pit to house the fifteen musicians, and a revolving stage complete with dressing rooms below. In November 1944 five more men joined to the orchestra. Gathering materials, construction of stages and props, and hours of rehearsal demonstrated the labor of love put into these projects as the POWs did it for free and after their normal work day. Soon makeshift billboards around the camp announced the upcoming activities. They performed classics and favorites, with "Carnival of Love" being one of the more popular plays.[19] Walter Schoenstedt, conducting a military inspection of the camp, commented that these troubadours often perform "German classics as do not stand in contrast to the Prussian concept of 'Kultur'."[20] He added that this is "mixed with a few Nazi songs, not known to the American personnel" the sound of which "carries across the camp and is heard by the anti-Nazis to their dismay." On the contrary, the other compounds lacked sufficient material, both in musical instruments and scrap lumber to put on performances. Compound DD had five musical instruments, VW had none.[21]

The POWs also partook of fine art, sculpting, painting, and sketching. Some of these art projects are among the few traces of the POWs that remained after their repatriation. As with most other things the prisoners used their own time and money to procure items for art-work, but donations came in more regularly than musical instruments. Some of the POWs lent their fledgling abilities to drawing cartoons and comics for their camp operated newspaper. Others tried their hand at carving and some made other trinkets with scrap metal and materials. Americans who had access to the POWs seemed eager to purchase an Iron Cross made out of soap, a snake-skin belt, or authentic German prisoner made wooden figurines. The prisoners seemed to enjoy the pastime and looked forward to the illicit exchange with the guards that might include under the table cash, useful for escapes, or other favors like purchasing things not readily available within the camp.[22]

Knox housed some graffiti artists and pranksters as well as more skilled craftsmen. Some of the current U.S. officers living at Knox unwittingly inherited pieces of the POW legacy. Sometime during their captivity there between 1944 and 1945 camp officials had the prisoners repair the roofs and chimneys of some of the officer's houses. The Germans eagerly went to work repairing roofs and constructing chimneys. When they finished they left a clearly visible sign that still remains on over a dozen houses. They carved the symbol of the Afrika Korps on the chimneys; a palm tree with a sun. Apparently this remained a private joke for nearly sixty years. Matthew Rector, the Historic Preservationist at Fort Knox, pointed out to the current officials of Fort Knox and the residents in these houses what the symbol meant and who created it. Other graffiti artists carved their names on bridges at the nearby L&N train depot when they worked there doing repairs.[23]

Some men at Knox exhibited a much more developed talent. A group of POWs created miniature stone castle replicas of German castles. They built at least three of these at Knox, placing the larger two near the fire station on post. Colonel Maur, one of the U.S. chaplains on post received the third one as a gift from the prisoners. Maur served in Europe as a translator and apparently "a bunch of prisoners . . . surrendered themselves to him" despite his being "unarmed."[24] After being transferred to Knox, Maur continued to minister to and translate for the prisoners, becoming one of the favored men in U.S. uniform among the POWs. The castle, built from stones gathered on base and from work details, became a tribute to him for his efforts. Unfortunately, Maur did not keep the castle, but gave it to a friend. The final resting place of this castle is the front yard of central Kentuckian, Barbara James, who has preserved the relic and understands "the uniqueness and importance" of this artifact. Although it attracts questions from company, few neighbors realize the origin of the work.[25]

The castle created at Fort Knox stands about three feet tall and is about three to four feet in diameter. It is intricate with towers and windows and what appears to be a moat. German Prisoners of war across the U.S seemed to enjoy creating these models. Others are known to exist in Iowa and the American Foreign Policy Center in Ruston, Louisiana has one of the many constructed at Camp Ruston. The Kentucky castle, unlike the one at Ruston, Louisiana, is outdoors and has obviously weathered the test of time and the elements. It continues to serve a vigilant watch as a yard ornament and one of the few remaining artifacts that mark that Kentucky once housed thousands of POWs.

Other prisoners spent their time at Fort Knox creating line drawings. The POWs at the camp collected many of these into a booklet titled "PW Camp, Fort Knox, Kentucky." The spokesmen of all three compounds wrote a dedication in the front of the book and presented it to U.S. POW camp commander Lieutenant-Colonel Lloyd L. Hamilton. The dedication is as follows:

> The time of being a prisoner of war will leave a continual remembrance in each one of us. To deepen these remembrances is the aim of this booklet. Together with the personal occurrences there will stay with us the remembrance of the extremely fair treatment here in Camp Fort Knox and its branch camps. We are obliged to thank the officers and men of these camps. As a small sign of gratefulness we would like to devote this souvenir album to the Commanding Officer of the Prisoner of War

Camp, Fort Knox, Kentucky, Lt. Col. Lloyd L. Hamilton.[26]

Drawings depict the various activities surrounding camp life including a truck making a delivery passing through the barbed-wire fence, an aerial view of the barracks, soccer games, the barber shop, a scene from a POW play, their gardens, and many others. These drawings are extremely well done and well preserved.[27]

The prisoners at Camp Breckinridge, however, seemed to be the most artistic of the Germans held in Kentucky. André Vulliet, one of the representatives from the War Prisoners' Aid of the YMCA, reported that as early as October 11, 1943, "each company has its own workshop, which means that there are 4 workshops in every compound." He added that power tools had just arrived for handicrafts and "it was quite welcome as the prisoners were looking to the days when they could make their own chess figures, etc."[28] In addition to woodworkers Vulliet noted a large number of painters and sculptors. He reported that "there is plenty of talent in this camp. Exhibitions have already been organized and the prisoners plan to have some more" however, they were sorely in need of additional supplies.[29]

Breckinridge also houses the greatest artistic legacy left in Kentucky, the murals painted by one of its prisoners of war. These murals, currently housed at *The James D. Veatch Camp Breckinridge Museum & Arts Center*, are quite simply breathtaking. Nearly two dozen murals depict the German countryside, castles, and rural life. These originally adorned the officer's club at Breckinridge, which now serves as part of the museum. The staff at Breckinridge carefully preserved these portraits and also reproduced them as equally handsome postcards.[30] This artwork remains an appreciated and talked about part of Western Kentucky and Breckinridge history.

The story behind the creation of these murals left another legacy to Kentucky. For a long time no one knew who was responsible for the paintings. Officials and newspapers debated the so-called "Mural Mystery." The murals were originally credited as the work of Peter Heinz, which some, including his tombstone, erroneously called Heinz Peter.[31] Heinz, a paratrooper, fell into Allied hands on June 7, 1941, during the D-Day invasion. He arrived at Breckinridge on March 21, 1942. Rumors circulated that Heinz had a free and unsupervised hand to paint in the U.S. officers' mess and this led to the other prisoners eventually murdering him.[32] This claim certainly fit into the pattern of Nazi violence against those who fraternized with the American guards, but officials recorded his death as due to natural causes. Ron Wormald, a manager at the Earle C. Clements Job Corps Center that occupied Breckinridge after the closing of the camp, conducted research on Heinz. Unable to contact any family members, Wormald contacted the American Legation in Switzerland through the Department of German Affairs for a copy of Heinz's military record. Wormald examined Heinz's incarceration dates and had "doubts that in just over seven months between his confinement and his death at Breckinridge" he "could have painted many, if any, of the pictures."[33]

Decades later interviews with former Breckinridge POWs and employees confirmed that Daniel Meyer, a 36 year old member of the Afrika Korps captured in Tunisia on April 23, 1943, had painted most, if not all of the murals.[34] Most recalled Meyer working unsupervised, coming and going as he pleased. One reporter made the doubtful claim that Meyer visited Morganfield unescorted to buy materials.[35] His colleagues remembered that he was a troubled man broken by the war and captivity. Former POW Heiner Traeger recalled that Meyer's "heart was broken, he was a simple person, quiet and polite . . . he worried about his family in the Sudetenland." According to Traeger "even our understanding and compassion, which we all gave him, and our reassurances that everything would be all right, could not tear him away from his thoughts. Not his body, but his mind broke and one day he didn't want to do anything else and didn't."[36]

Many wondered if Meyer painted from memory or if he used postcards. But a letter to his wife Hermina and six year old daughter Martha on July 3, 1944 cleared that up when he wrote his wife that "I made myself an oil painting from a photograph that you sent me."[37] In an earlier letter written on October 11, 1943, not long after he arrived at Breckinridge, he told his wife that "my spare time is spent in artwork for which I have a big interest for further use in the future."[38] On July 17, 1944, he wrote, "by the way I am healthy and very busy with pictures, painting."[39] Meyer contracted pneumonia and died at Breckinridge on September 21, 1945.

Nearly fifty-five years later Meyer's daughter, Martha Bolg, visited the Camp Breckinridge site, her father's murals, and his grave. She remembered her father's postcards, but "then the letters stopped" and "because of a problem with the mail, the typewritten letter announcing her father's death didn't reach her mother until August 1946."[40] Meyer's last mural was of Castle Werneck. Considered his "masterpiece," the 20' by 30' painting still adorns the former officers club at Camp Breckinridge. Ruth Espy, a civilian employee at Breckinridge, recalled that "toward the end he was barely able to climb the ladder, and could only lift his brush for a few moments at a time."[41] His daughter stated that "from now on when I think of him, I'll just think of this painting."[42]

The prisoners had nearly unlimited access to sources of news and information and the publication of in-camp newspapers served to illustrate to them the ideal of freedom of the press long prohibited in Nazi Germany. The POWs organized their own libraries and stocked them with books and daily newspapers purchased by the prisoners or donated to them by organizations and individuals. The prisoners gained knowledge of the war, through newsreels on movies, radio broadcasts, and newspaper articles, equal to that of any American civilians. They not only followed the course of the war, but they also used the news of an advance to learn something about the fate of their hometowns and the conditions in Germany. They used these methods to gauge the mood within the U.S. concerning the war, home front problems, and the overall feeling towards housing the prisoners.

In their homeland, broadcasts and dailies suffered from so much censorship, restrictions, and propaganda that only the most diehard or desperate put stock in their reports. The Nazis employed roving detection units and a system of "ratting out" neighbors to see who utilized radios to intercept contraband messages. Some Germans risked arrest and possible incarceration by secretly tuning into the BBC to hear accounts of battles, especially following major German reverses on the Eastern Front.

Camp authorities heavily censored any books and newspapers received by the POWs.[43] As a provision of the Geneva Convention a captor nation could not give its prisoners reading material banned in the home nation. In the case of Nazi Germany this simple provision meant that dozens of titles received immediate bans.[44] Any books the Third Reich burned or otherwise prohibited, including works by Jews, Communists, and Socialists, and those of authors critical of the Nazis, the U.S. also outlawed for the Germans in its care.[45] Yet, U.S. officials could not stomach allowing the prisoners access to many of the books allowed by the Third Reich, including *Mein Kampf* and other rabid fascist demagoguery and racist drivel, and prohibited them as well. In a frantic attempt to determine which books POWs could not have access to, the U.S. had banned a total of 225 books by November 1944. In the next months officials added more books to the chopping block.[46] At the same time, however, the Third Reich and legal scholars considered any literature that had a pro-American or democratic bent as an attempt to denationalize the Germans. The Geneva Convention clearly forbade any attempt by the

U.S. to denationalize prisoners. In the early stages of making reading list approvals the U.S. government carefully weighed their decisions against this provision, not wanting to provoke the Third Reich or break international law over the matter of a book or two. By 1945, however, this clause had been clearly circumvented, not only through access the POWs had to literature, but through a secret and voluntary reeducation program. In the meantime, the U.S. also prohibited any books that could aid in escape or sabotage, especially textbooks on geography and chemistry.[47] The process of creating a list of allowed books seemed exhaustive, but the fact that few of these American titles had a German language counterpart made the completion of the task even more complex. The difficulty in finding books that not only fit the requirements of the Geneva Convention, but also those of the Third Reich, and of the U.S. proved so difficult that the U.S. decided to create its own series of books that they felt would meet all of the above criteria.

The War Department answer lay with the publishing of the *Infantry Journal's New World Bookshelf*. The *Infantry Journal* compiled twenty-four books in a series titled "Buecherreihe Neue Welt" or "New World Bookshelf" specifically for the German prisoners of war. The first distribution of these titles came in limited quantities at the late date of May 1945. The POWs who purchased these at the canteen and read some of them at their library seemed quite pleased with the decision and the selection. The limited quantities quickly sold out and the POWs placed orders for thousands more copies.[48] Officials at Camp Campbell conducted a survey among the POW readership and found the titles to be "in great demand."[49]   Each book had been carefully selected, all of them were German language editions, and officials often chose well-known authors. Thomas Mann, for instance, had four of his titles featured: *Lotte in Weimar, Der Zauberberg I, Der Zauberberg II,* and *Der Hauptmann von Koepenick.*[50] Wendell Willkie's *Unteilbare Welt* and Stephen Vincent Benet's *Amerika* were especially sought after for their view of politics and the United States. One prisoner expressed the desire to continue receiving all the books in the affordable series and hoped to take them all home since "our books at home probably have fallen victim to the ravages of war."[51]

As early as March 23, 1943, the ASF and PMGO's broad interpretation of the Geneva Convention allowed nearly any widely circulating national U.S. newspapers, like the *New York Times*, or approved U.S. published foreign language newspapers as well as a wide variety of popular magazine to be read by the prisoners. The camp commander still maintained veto power even if the material had previously been approved by a higher branch.[52]   All reading material designated for the prisoners at any individual camp went first to the camp commander or his representative. After approval these items initially only went to the POW library, no prisoners could have an individual subscription.[53]

German language newspapers published in the U.S. underwent special scrutiny, but nearly 45 gained approval for prisoner consumption. Kentucky's German POWs had access to the relatively local *Cincinatti Freie Presse* or the national *German-American.*[54] ASF and PMGO officials typically did not approve newspapers and magazines published in Germany or other parts of central Europe for fear of their being too slanted towards the Nazi cause. While some of the POWs in the U.S. did get German publications after these underwent the complete scrutiny of the War Department and its branches, there are no records that Kentucky's POWs had them. POWs also received the local English language papers, but many preferred to read the *New York Times* or the *Christian Science Monitor*.[55] Demand for reading material became so great that by February 6, 1945, the War Department relented and allowed newspapers and some magazines for purchase at the canteens. The list of periodicals, however, remained restricted to *Collier's*, *Life*, *Newsweek*, the *Saturday Evening Post*, *Time*, *Reader's Digest*, *Pageant*, *Natural History*, and *Coronet*.[56]

By the end of the war in Europe, prisoners finally had access to a myriad of books, newspapers, and magazines. Achieving this difficult feat required the cooperation of all the War Department agencies, the understanding of the camp commanders, and the efforts of the YMCA, International Red Cross, and other religious and civilian agencies who continually donated materials. The prisoners consumed this material as quickly as they could obtain it and constantly demanded more. They organized libraries to house the communal reading property and to provide a quiet place to absorb the information. This space often came from an extra room, small building, part of the recreation or day room, or entirely new construction made possible through donated POW time and purchase of materials.

Some of these libraries, such as the one in Compound DD at Camp Campbell, had a rudimentary construction. The Germans organized their small library by partitioning the day room and using scrap lumber to construct shelves to house the second hand books. Their library prominently featured two types of books, German to English dictionaries, comprising thirty of the collection's books, and German language books on the United States.[57] Despite the fact that nearly all of the 600 POWs in this compound regularly visited the library, most of them on a daily basis, scant few newspapers supplemented these books. English language material consisted of only three copies of the *New York Times* and six copies of *Life*, supplemented by 25 copies of the German-language paper *Cincinnati Freie Presse* and 50 of the *Staate Herald*.[58] Fritz Nessler, former Camp Campbell POW, recalled that "the 'Staats-Herald,' a German-American newspaper, was delivered to us every day."[59] As late as November 1944 VW, the third compound at Campbell, did not have a library or any books. Officials at Campbell offered the excuse that the Compound had only recently been completed and the newly arrived POWs would soon have equal access to such perks.

Meanwhile, the concurrent visit of First Lieutenant Walter Schoenstedt, of the Special Programs Section, revealed that the XO Compound at Campbell enjoyed an "excellent and comfortable" library.[60] Within the façade of this innocent looking and deceptively relaxing library, however, he discovered some disturbing selections. While the library housed some texts by anti-Nazi authors, these books only masked the existence of numerous titles by Nazi authors on the less prominent shelves. Featured writers included Upton Sinclair and others who, according to Schoenstedt "are critical to the United States."[61] He recommended that "a tactfully conducted revision of the library by the assistant executive officer should be initiated as soon as possible."[62]

Other factors limited the growth of the POW library at Fort Knox. The fact that the camp had recently switched from housing Italian POWs presented a major limitation for German POW intellectual pursuits. As of March 1944 the library consisted of numerous books, magazines, and newspapers largely in Italian and of no use to the majority of Germans. Through the labor and insistence of the Germans, however, they soon had access to a large library and the benefit of an athletic field, something the Italians did not stay long enough to enjoy.[63] The Germans moved swiftly and by December 1944 their library held 450 books. About one hundred titles remained in circulation at one of the many branch camps operated from Knox.

Major Paul A. Neuland, Chief of the Field Service Branch, inspected the library at Knox in December 1944 and discovered problems. The POWs took advantage of the administrative and censorship lag when the Assistant Executive Officer at Knox had been replaced, to order nearly three hundred books that normally would not be allowed. The War Prisoners Branch of the YMCA sent these books, but fortunately military officials caught the ruse and had these books routed to the Education Branch of the POW program for censorship and review. Neuland also had a problem with the four subscriptions of the *Chicago Tribune* being sent to the POW library. Although he did not state the specific infractions or problems inherent with that publication, he recommended to the Camp Commander that these newspapers be banned from the camp. Neuland also found that *Die Saat* the POW operated paper had been "twisting news." He took immediate action on this issue and banned the POWs from further publishing *Die Saat* or any other newspaper.[64]

Allowing prisoners to write and publish their own newspapers seemed a natural extension of this reading and education program. The branches of the War Department agreed to this arrangement as long as the Axis men vowed to prohibit Nazi or anti-American propaganda, that camp commanders or their designated official monitored these activities, and as long as the papers only had camp-wide distribution.[65] The POWs provided their own physical and intellectual material and produced the paper from each issue's conception to its distribution. These limitations posed little problem for the demonstrated craftiness and work ethic of the prisoners. The POWs at Camp Campbell and at Camp Breckinridge took to publishing their newspapers with zeal. Germans at Camp Campbell produced *Der Neue Weg* (The New Way) and *Der Europäer: Kriegsgefangenenzeitschrift* (The European: War Prisoner Periodical). Breckinridge POWs published *Die Brücke* (The Bridge).

The first issue of *Der Europäer* appeared in September 1944, and with some irregularity, monthly thereafter. War Department officials found the newspaper to be "liberal" with "an unusually high level [of thought]" that "advocates a strong, democratic

Europe, without German domination." According to one U.S. official from the Special Projects Branch *Der Europäer* was ". . . the most important newspaper printed and written by German prisoners of war in the United States."[66] A simple glance at the *inhaltsverzeichnis* (table of contents) demonstrates the degree of intellectual debate among some of the POWs at Campbell. A typical issue had several sections. Some articles argued against Nazism and war, such as "Aufbau un Selbsterkenntnis" and "Die preussische Faust" from the October 1944 issue.[67] Anti-Nazi and democratic rhetoric remained the hallmark features of *The European*, but poetry, literature, and articles on music also received ample print space. *Die Saat* published by the prisoners at Fort Knox, just a few hours away from Campbell, stands in stark contrast to its anti-Nazi counterpart *Der Europäer*. Authorities disbanded the paper after the authors disobeyed the rules and "twisted the news."[68] Despite the political tone of *Die Saat* it shared a trait with its sister papers by publishing a Christmas issue.[69]

Many of these intellectual diversion or recreation activities, whether they involved playing sports or publishing newspapers, preceded actual education courses offered behind barbed wire. The concept of soldiers taking correspondence courses existed for some time and certain universities, colleges, and high schools had already established a good working relationship with U.S. military men pursuing these endeavors. The Geneva Convention did not restrict this practice for prisoners and the U.S. and Germany both cooperated with the IRC, YMCA, and each nation's school systems to accept credits for degrees and transfer of credit earned while in captivity.

The prisoners seeking education used whatever space they could find within the compound for their classrooms. These informal settings included the library, recreation room, barracks, outdoor space, and even the chapel. Anywhere that interested POWs and qualified prisoner instructors mutually agreed upon seemed adequate. Some of the POWs were fortunate to have men among them who served as teachers in civilian life or otherwise had qualifications that enabled them to teach. While the transfer of such credit seems questionable, under the circumstances it was accepted as long as the instructor's credentials matched the level of degree being sought.[70] This rudimentary setting became increasingly propelled by POW efforts until finally entire "school systems" with a director and staff of teachers organized within the camps. Eventually military authorities recognized these distinctions and even provided instructors or teachers the same pay as those men working on Kentucky's farms.[71] In some cases, U.S. civilians or military instructors added to the faculty of the POW education program.

The U.S. Armed Forces Institute provided numerous correspondence courses to enlisted men and POWs alike. These courses became so popular that by May 1945 the ASF had to issue Circular 161 explaining to camp commanders the procedures and costs of enrollment. The Germans applied for admittance and paid for the classes, which varied in price according to course and level, at the beginning of the semester or term of enrollment. Offerings ranged from a myriad of history courses through economics, literature, and philosophy. As part of a compensation package to seriously wounded or injured prisoners unable to work, the U.S. military paid for their tuition through a Central Prisoner of War Fund. The Armed Forces Institute offered high school and college classes like those offered by the prisoners within the camps. One limiting factor kept many interested POWs from taking these classes, however, as they required the men to be able to read and write English.[72]

The YMCA War Prisoners' Aid and the International Red Cross, as well as other religiously affiliated groups, provided many of the textbooks.[73] The Lutheran Commission and the War Relief Services Branch of the National Catholic Welfare Conference donated textbooks as well.[74] Fritz Nessler recalled that "they gave us free books for classes in German, French, English, Russian, car repair, history, mathematics, and other subjects."[75]

Between the in-house education offered at the camps, the Armed Forces Institute, and correspondence courses offered at participating schools, and the meticulous records of courses, exams, and grades kept by the camp, the school, and the IRC, the POWs had access to a wide range of possibilities and many of them took advantage of these opportunities to gain a degree or a skill that could be put to use in post-war Germany.[76]

As of November 1944 the educational facilities at Campbell's DD Compound, quite like their library, appeared barely functional. An extra room off of the spokesperson's office provided the "classroom" albeit without the necessities such as chalk or blackboards. While at least twenty-five percent of the men in the compound understood English well enough, none of them enrolled in any correspondence courses, even those offered by German universities. Instead, they asked that Thomas Mann, the famed German writer and 1929 Nobel Prize laureate, come to the camp and offer a class. This request, of course, went unfilled. The VW compound at Campbell also offered in-house classes every day of the week, except Sundays. Like nearly every camp in the U.S., English was prominently featured, but despite nearly a complete lack of textbooks they also offered French, U.S. History, Philosophy, and interestingly a religious hour and a weekly news review and discussion.[77]

XO Compound once again surpassed the other two prisoner compounds at Campbell. These men had a school building with four classrooms and all the material needed to conduct traditional lectures or vocational training. They had a "full-time" staff of four teachers, a director, and the spokesperson for the compound. Thirty of the men from XO enrolled in correspondence courses with German universities. Other prisoners, some skeptical of the length of the programs offered by German schools, prepared for classes with the University of Chicago and other American schools.[78] The men at Breckinridge also organized classes and held them all during the week and the weekend. In addition to English, the Breckinridge Germans enrolled in math and science courses.[79]

POWs at Knox heartily took to organizing and attending their classes. Classrooms filled up fast with an average enrollment of fifteen men in courses held in the mess hall or in an extra barracks and officials looked for more space while quickly filling orders for supplies.[80] Whereas only 5 percent of the POWs at XO Compound at Campbell attended classes, almost 1000 of the men at Knox could be counted among the student population. English language and grammar remained one of the most popular courses at Knox as at other camps, but at Knox they also had an advanced group in the English Literature class reading Shakespeare on par with upper-level U.S. college students. The third most popular class among the Germans was Civics.[81]

Sundays at the camps had special significance as a day of reverence and prayer and many POWs attended religious services. Few other activities took place on Sunday, certainly no labor assignments, and the POWs relaxed and caught up on personal matters during that time. Many POWs spent time reading or writing. Some sent letters to loved ones or friends back home. Afternoon strolls around camp provided time for reflection, a chance for friends to chat, or to meet people within the camp from one's hometown. The most pressing matter for most of the POWs on Sunday, however, was attending Sunday services. The Geneva Convention permitted religious worship and the War and State Department encouraged it. U.S. officials wanted the Germans to have the freedom of religion denied them in Germany and hoped through fostering this it would help "legally" de-Nazify the POWs.[82] Former POW Heino Erichsen stated that "Hitler had suppressed religion, Jewish and Christian alike. In the camp, the SS and other Nazis viewed religion as an anti-Nazi activity, but that didn't stop me from going to the chapel. My friends started coming with me. Our heartsick souls began to heal when we were given a place to practice our faith together."[83]

Despite the U.S. military giving lip service to freedom of religion, the men often did not have adequate space to worship and many camps did not have a chapel. As with many other aspects of camp life when the POWs had to provide for themselves they set about the task with vigor.[84] The Breckinridge POWs used their own funds and labor and built a chapel and altar adorned with Old English style gold lettering containing the 23rd Psalm and parts of John 10. Catholic and Protestant POWs shared the facility by alternating the times of day for their services. The two faiths together brought in approximately 500 worshippers every Sunday.[85]

Finding preachers or priests became the next problem for the prisoners as few among their number had performed in this position either as a civilian or a military chaplain. Most of the men in the Wehrmacht who served in these roles had dual function as political officers and Nazis. These false prophets could not be trusted by most of the men and after segregation many camps lost access to even the small numbers of these men. The War Department permitted the post chaplains serving the U.S. military to also hold services for the prisoners. This, of course, had limitations as well, since these men had busy schedules tending to their own flocks and their use had to be something both they and the camp commander allowed. Even when permitted the prisoners preferred someone from their own number when possible. One of the difficulties for this transnational service lay in the language barrier, services conducted in English ill-served the prisoners.

The Germans also felt uneasy about confessing to the "enemy." In an attempt to satisfy all parties, camp officials often invited clergymen from nearby German communities. Catholic and Lutheran religious leaders, some of whom immigrated in the past generation or two themselves, often volunteered to serve in this role to witness to the men behind the wire.

Catholics at Camp Campbell had to settle for Chaplain Stephen P. Kenney, from the 20th Armored Division. Kenney worked with a German speaking priest to gather basic German skills and create a translation chart with religious phrases so that he could hear confessions, give mass, and converse with the POWs. Chaplain Aloysius C. Ziellinski, who worked with Kenney served on a limited basis and only arrived to give mass twice a month. Chaplain Paul J. Roetling conducted Protestant services in German to the POWs.[86] As more men arrived in the prison camps the demand for additional Sunday and other services increased to the point that suitable prisoners had to serve in supplemental capacities as early as November 1944. One of the U.S. military additions was Chaplain Captain Roberts, a member of the Armored Replacement Training Center who spoke German and oversaw the Protestant services for both the Americans and the Germans, while a POW priest performed additional Catholic services.[87] George Rupprecht, the camp spokesman for both DD and VW compound, also performed religious services at DD compound. Despite the increase in the size of the POW population over the course of the year, the chapel for DD compound still consisted of only a small adjoining room that also served as the classroom.[88]

A rare way to spend one's down time was to get visits from relatives. Many German prisoners had relatives in the United States. Some who served in the German Armed Forces were actually first or second generation German immigrants living in America who had returned to Germany in the 1930s. A visit from a prisoner's American relatives may not have been common, but they could be arranged through the camp commander. Several POWs cited these visits as being lifesavers. Relatives helped break the monotony of the camp, brought hope for the future, and often came bearing small gifts. Of course, a POW had to be careful of the Nazis monitoring the visit and becoming suspicious of their fellows' activities. A POW could have a visitor twice a month and that person had to be a relative.[89] One unnamed Campbell POW enjoyed a reunion with his two sisters who emigrated from Germany to New York before the war. Both of his sisters became U.S. citizens. One of them wanted to visit him on a return trip to Germany, but he was in basic training and the German military prohibited them from seeing each other. She returned to the U.S. just as the war began in 1939. The sister voiced her desire to see her brother turned prisoner to Lieutenant Colonel Carl E. Byrd, commander of the POW camp, and he arranged the visit. He even allowed the family to use his headquarters and released a picture to the press, although he did not release the man's name.[90]

Sometimes there could be too much down time, especially when prisoners used it to plot escapes or get into other mischief. That was the case when four Germans' preparation for a Christmas celebration was cut short. The men had been brewing six gallons of orange juice wine in their barracks when the guards caught the smell of the mixture of sugar and oranges as they passed by and apprehended the men in the act. Two of the men were sent to another camp and two received punishments at Knox. The wine went to waste despite the fact that "the concoction looked powerful, nobody at Knox had the fortitude to taste it, mainly because of the bugs that were floating around on top-either dead or dead drunk."[91]

Egon Hessenthaler recalled one instance of running afoul of the guards at Fort Knox:

> During the weekends when the weather was bad we hung out at the barracks, mostly laying on the beds, and of course, smoking. After the cigarette has burned off, the still-burning butt was flicked onto the floor, which, of course, left burn marks on the nice light wood floor. Since all of us did that, the floor was soon branded with burn marks. During the monthly check of the barracks, a US-officer gave us an order to remove the burn marks within two hours. When he left the barracks, there was a dead silence. Then the work began. We used our razors and scraped and scraped like possessed by devil. After two hours the officer came back. Naturally, we weren't finished and were afraid to be punished. He looked over our work, thanked us politely and demanded we use ash trays in the future. We then removed the rest of the stains. Afterwards, there were never any burn marks on the floor. By the way, one could buy cigarettes 200-count for 90 cents at the

cafeteria (Chesterfield, Lucky Strike, Camel, Old Gold, Pall Mall).[92]

Did these efforts by the U.S. to entertain and educate these men go in vain? Even though some of the men may have taken advantage of the situation or abused the good-will of the U.S., the Intellectual Diversion program met with resounding success. It could be argued that these programs prevented numerous escape attempts or other problems within the camp by keeping the morale of the men high. By the same token knowledge of these camp activities reached Germany and might have had the desired results of ensuring better treatment of American personnel in German hands and of making more of the enemy's active soldiers inclined to surrender. The program certainly proved a natural extension of U.S. adherence to the Geneva Convention and of exceeding its minimum requirements. The U.S not only built on a history of officially calling for good treatment of its prisoners of war and honoring international commitments, but it provided an example for other nations to follow during World War II and future wars. Immediate results could also be attributed, at least in some small part, to these programs. At Camp Campbell, for instance, the POWs decided it was time to give back to the Red Cross for all that they had done for the prisoners. Each man donated from their canteen funds until a total donation of $3,800 had been sent.[93] In addition to this contribution Kentucky POWs joined the cause by purchasing U.S. War Bonds.[94] Even on a local level, when one of the guards wrecked his truck and became pinned underneath it in Little West Creek with only his head above water, ten German POWs made up part of the rescue crew. They provided first aid to the Stocker and the seven passengers of his truck that were thrown when he blew the tire and wrecked.[95] In addition to these efforts German prisoners of war in camps across the U.S. called upon Germany to surrender before it suffered complete capitulation and countless more men on all sides died. These examples of reciprocal humanitarian action demonstrate that enemy prisoners were actually just men, albeit in German uniform.

Chapter 8
Y'all Come Back Now:
Concluding the program

*V*ictory in Europe Day, May, 8, 1945, presented a
watershed in many ways. The war in Europe ended,
allowing the U.S. to focus its military and industrial
efforts on defeating Japan. German POWs received the
news with mixed emotions. One measure of this came
from Camp Breckinridge where a poll returned the
following results:

> Average German Prisoner: "I had expected this
> for some time. It is hard to lose, but now maybe
> I can go home soon."
> Anti-Nazi Prisoner, A PW Company Leader:
> "Am relieved that the war is over. I knew that
> after Stalingrad the war was lost. The Nazi
> party is finished."
> Pro-Nazi Prisoner: "Germany has not been
> defeated. Hitler is not dead. The 3rd Reich will
> rise again."
> Rabid Nazi Prisoner: "Germany could have
> surrendered a year ago. Then the German Army
> would not have been destroyed. Hitler is not
> dead. The Nazi Party will continue to grow."[1]

Regardless of initial reaction, the prisoners, locals, guards, and officials waited anxiously for a word or sign from the War or State Department indicating when the POWs would go home. The anticipation resembled that of a few years earlier when it had been announced that the POWs would arrive. Rumors of the men going began circulating home as early as the summer of 1945. Eventually, the War Department announced that there were no plans to send these men home yet and that labor contacts would continue uninterrupted through the summer. This was good news for farmers, but cold comfort for many prisoners who once again began contract labor work on Kentucky farms in the summer of 1945. Most realized that no serious moves would be made to transport the men until the war with Japan concluded, as the U.S. needed to devote all of its shipping and transport resources to the Pacific. Additionally, military production had not slowed sufficiently, nor had enough military personnel funneled back into the civilian labor pool to allow agricultural labor to return to normal levels. The summer turned to fall and the prisoners began harvesting Kentucky tobacco. Their employers grew nervous that the contracts and use of the German labor would be cancelled with little notice. The military announced, however, that contracts would continue uninterrupted until November 1945.

In November of 1945, the POW camps closed with the same urgency that began the camp construction and housing program. Slowly work contracts were cancelled or not renewed. Branch camps shut down and the men returned to the main base camps. The Lexington Army Depot closed and shifted its several hundred POWs to Fort Knox in the winter of 1946. The branch camp at Maysville continued to operate through that winter but then moved its men to Fort Knox. Other branch camps, temporary in design to follow seasonal needs, closed earlier in 1945 and some only operated through 1944. The branch camp at Eminence, for instance, only operated during the 1943 harvest season.[2] The men from all of Kentucky's 13 branch camps eventually returned to Camp Breckinridge or Fort Knox as Camp Campbell did not operate branch camps. In most cases, once the prisoners tore down the facilities of the branch camp and the grounds had been cleaned, virtually no physical traces remained. Sixty years later few Kentuckians know that their rural counties once housed German prisoners of war. For instance, a baseball diamond and park now exist where POWs stayed at Maysville. Those housed in the tent city at Danville from August 17 to September 16, 1945, left no remnants to mark the existence of the camp.[3]

Throughout the winter of 1945-46 base camps consolidated and as soon as shipping became available, thousands of men poured into familiar ports at Norfolk, Virginia or New York, their points of arrival years earlier. The journey this time took them back to Europe. Other ports, including New Orleans, handled the massive numbers of released prisoners.

The first prisoners shipped back were those who participated in the formal, secret and voluntary reeducation program. Dr. Henry Ehremann, an instructor of this program, later stated that a total of 24,158 men completed the program.[4] If the total number of German prisoners kept in the U.S. was 371,683 as reported by National Archives documents and Army publications, then only 6.5 percent of the total number of POWs underwent this process.[5] When at maximum capacity Kentucky's three base camps held 9,000. This figure does not include the men housed at the various branch camps. In other words, only about 585 Germans housed in Kentucky, could have gone through the program.[6] While it might be possible to trace the number of Kentucky POWs who volunteered for the program it would be extremely difficult. More important to this study is the fact that those selected came from anti-Nazi groups, therefore making those at compounds DD and VW from Campbell the most likely to be recruited. The reeducation program did not take place in any of the Kentucky camps. Once selected these men were transferred to the camps Fort Getty, Fort Wetherhill, and Camp Kearney, all in Rhode Island, and Fort Eustis, Virginia.[7]

The U.S. Army had high hopes that these special prisoners would aid the American Military Occupation Government in reconstructing and governing postwar Germany.[8] The Germans, sent home beginning in the fall of 1945, were the only prisoners returned directly to Germany. When the former POWs landed in Europe, French officials and the heads of other Western European governments, wanted to intercept and imprison them for use as forced labor to repair their war torn nations. American officers accompanying the men navigated through these nations to ensure that the special prisoners arrived in Germany. Once there, however, not all had to stay in the American zone, and several left Germany within the next few years.

The U.S. repatriated the bulk of the prisoners throughout the spring and summer of 1946. A War Department Press Release declared that all prisoners had to be out of the U.S. by the end of April 1946. By this time, however, the bulk of the prisoners had already been sent to Europe. Given that only small numbers remained and that these men were housed at base camps in areas that still needed the labor planting crops, the War Department extended the deadline. Fort Knox was among the few base camps that continued to operate into the late spring of 1946. Finally, the War Department issued an order that these prisoners needed to be sent home "as practicably as possible" between April and July 1946. On July 22, 1946 the War Department finally declared, with few exceptions, that all of its 435,788 Axis POWs had been repatriated.[9] A small handful of men remained in the U.S. until 1947 or later. Brigadier General Blackshear M. Bryan stated that "the only prisoners-of-war remaining here today [June 22, 1946] are 140 Germans, 15 Italians and one Japanese serving Federal prison sentences for crimes committed while interned; 81 German and three Italian hospital patients who cannot yet be moved; and 28 German and 15 Italian escapees still at large."[10]

The prisoner transfer did not go quite as smoothly as the U.S. hoped. Negotiations with U.S. allies produced two results that affected the prisoners. The first agreement required that the men ultimately return to their home towns within Germany or their nation of origin. As Germany had been divided up into four zones, that meant many of these men would go to the Soviet zone. Additionally, all of the men from the Soviet Union that served within the German military would have to go back to Russia or Eastern Europe. Many former Soviet citizens, realizing that torture or death for treason awaited them, rioted and some actually committed suicide. Many Germans slated to return to Eastern Germany and Soviet rule also expressed their discontent, but others simply tried to lie or escape sometime during transit. Others, once in Germany, used the mass confusion and lackadaisical attitude of guards or officials to slip away from train depots or other areas of transit.[11]

The second agreement proved more traumatic, if one was from Western Germany. It prohibited the men from going directly back to Germany. They had to remain in the Western Allied nations where they stayed prisoners and worked alongside other POWs in rebuilding efforts. This second clause came as a shocking surprise for many POWs. This forced labor service ended for most of the POWs held in Western Europe by the end of 1948, depending on which Allied nation held them and how quickly they could release the hundreds of thousands of POWs they already held. Their final release in 1948 was predicated by an agreement reached in 1947 at the Moscow Foreign Minster Conference.[12]

When the Germans finally made it back to their home country, they found destruction on a far greater scale than anything they had previously experienced, perhaps with the exception of those who witnessed the ruins of cities on the front such as Stalingrad. Howard Tromp, a former POW, who underwent the reeducation program and returned to Germany in early 1946, recalled that he "was surprised when I got back to Germany about the damage done by Allied air raids.

Especially in Cologne, my home town, the damage was indescribable . . ."[13]

Few Kentuckians or prisoners realized the extent of damage, economic disruption, and numbers of refugees and other "displaced persons" within Germany.[14] Little remained of major urban areas like Cologne and Dresden. The economy had been ruined, few jobs existed, and the German Mark was nearly worthless. The Germans, now living under Allied rule, lost their autonomy. According to historian Frank Biess "former soldiers and POWs were not the only group to experience the consequences of defeat. Total defeat brought back to ordinary Germany the violence that Germans had previously meted out all over the European continent."[15] Former POW Egon Hessenthaler returned to the economic ruin of Germany and recalled his POW camp pay. The remainder of the coupons was paid out in a check to all former POWs. This became a running joke between Egon and his father. Egon admitted that "none of [the prisoners] believed that the check should have any value for us," he therefore "kept it as a souvenir." At his father's urging, however, Egon tried to cash the check and received a total of 800.00 DM for the $200.00 check, or the equivalent "to a four-month wage of a foreman."[16]

Over the years the former POWs began thinking about their time in captivity, about the size and prosperity of the U.S., and about the humane and relatively friendly treatment that they received. Many corresponded with their former employers, guards, and family members in the U.S., and sympathetic Americans sent food and other care packages to German families. Some like the Smith Broadbent family from Cadiz, Kentucky, maintained lifelong correspondence and actually traveled to Austria to visit with their prisoners turned friends. [17]

Alfred Liest, a former POW, who worked on the Mason County, Kentucky, farm of Ray and Marie Meyer, continued to correspond with them long after the war. Liest and his family struggled in Eastern Germany and declined several offers by the Meyers to return to the U.S., citing financial difficulties which were coupled with probable health problems of one of his children. He informed the Meyers that "if I can take you up on your kind offer at a later time, I would come for sure. I love farming and would do my best to satisfy you." [18] Liest never returned and the Meyer family eventually lost contact with him. [19]

Prisoners, like Howard Tromp, who went through the reeducation program had such a deep appreciation for the U.S. that he applied for and received a Visa in 1949. This former member of the Luftwaffe joined the U.S. Air Force in 1950 and after his time as part of the U.S. garrison in Paris, France ended, he opened up a restaurant in Miami, and eventually married. When he finally retired he moved up the coast to settle down. [20]

Fritz Nessler, a member of the Afrika Korps held at Camp Campbell returned to the U.S. in the 1960s. Nessler's daughter married an American stationed in Germany and when they returned to Fort Campbell, Nessler and his wife followed them. Like many other former POWs he visited the camp and described the POW program to camp officials and newspaper reporters years later. [21]

Former POW Horst Blumenberg, held in Camp Ruston, Louisiana, and other camps, visited the places of his former captivity and then moved back to the U.S.[22] Rather than live in Louisiana he made the Bluegrass State his retirement home. Two former POWs at Knox also returned to the U.S. The first was Walter Breitkopf who moved to Minnesota.[23] The second was Heino Erichsen, who had worked for the British occupation force as a translator before finally getting approval to move to the U.S. in 1953. He moved to Texas where he currently resides and runs Los Niños, an international adoption agency. Erichsen has visited Fort Knox several times since returning to the U.S.[24] This pattern continued as dozens of other former prisoners immigrated to the U.S.. These men, with few exceptions, returned not to the place of their captivity, but to the nation that offered them so much freedom behind the wire.

During World War II the U.S. successfully held over 425,000 Axis personnel in 155 base camps and more than 500 branch camps within the continental United States. As demonstrated in this work, this was a difficult, time-consuming and costly endeavor. Some critics might argue that it was not worth the effort and that the Germans POWs were "coddled" in the U.S. despite the fact that they were enemies who committed atrocities in Europe. This work, however, shows that the positive benefits of the program helped not just the prisoners, but Kentucky and the U.S. as a whole.

The U.S. agreed to abide by the Geneva Convention and stayed the course despite the problems arising within the camps and those perpetrated by the brethren of the POWs in Europe. Never before or since has the U.S. carried out such a large prisoner of war operation so successfully as in World War II. It set an international example of adhering to international law and humane treatment despite the many difficulties in implementing the program and controlling the POWs.

In addition to adhering to its legal obligations the U.S. hoped that good treatment of Germany's POWs would lead to reciprocal treatment of the thousands of Americans in German hands. Prisoners held in the U.S. communicated with family and loved ones through letters and the Red Cross. These contacts served the purpose of informing the Third Reich and the people of Germany that the U.S abided by and even exceeded the requirements of the Geneva Convention. The U.S. certainly had much to gain from this proper treatment. The government hoped that investigations of its POW camps and correspondence from Germans to Germany would provide sufficient guarantee that Germany would uphold their end of the Geneva Convention by treating U.S. personnel taken prisoner humanely. Kentucky soldier William Fortner, taken prisoner during the Battle of the Bulge, can attest to benefiting from this reciprocity. Fortner was wounded in the leg and narrowly missed a fatal chest wound that lodged in the *Bible* that he still owns. When the Germans came upon him, the officer "asked if I knew where Ft. Campbell was, which I did. He told me he had two brothers who were prisoners of war" there "and ordered the guy with the gun not to shoot me. I guess he thought it would go better for his brothers."[25]

While exceptions do exist, the Third Reich attempted to provide U.S. personnel with the same food quantity, shelter, protection, and clothing as given to its active duty soldiers. As the war progressed the quality of life of American prisoners declined on par with that of their German captors. It became increasingly difficult to supply adequate food and even to locate these men in areas away from the front when it became shorter with every Allied advance and constant air raids.

This same communication going from German POW camps to the Third Reich also led to a greater willingness of Wehrmacht soldiers to surrender to the Americans. Letters and statements from captured German personnel demonstrate an understanding that the U.S. would abide by the Geneva Conventions. Some prisoners wrote home that they had gained weight while a prisoner in America. An accurate statement if one only compared the caloric allowance in the U.S., which at one point soared as high as 3,000 per day, to that of an active duty German soldier, which may have been as low as 1,000 with substandard food. If the U.S. treated its German captives in the same manner that the Soviets did, the results may have been similar to those experienced on the Eastern Front where often no quarter was asked and none was given. These men on both sides often fought to the death because they knew that poor treatment, malnourishment, torture and slave labor operated as the norm. Yet, near the end of the war whole units surrendered to American forces.

While housing German prisoners, U.S. officials looked towards the post-war world and they saw several major benefits coming from within the prisoner compounds. The first of these post war considerations included the imminent American occupation of Germany. Proper treatment hopefully would lead to these soldiers being more cooperative once they returned home. The formal reeducation program certainly pulled some of Kentucky's POWs to these special camps in the northeast and provided post war training for future officials, translators, and police. As stated earlier, however, relatively few Kentucky POWs could have gone through this program. The process of recreation, education, and freedom behind barbed wire, albeit with a heavy dose of censorship, served as a primer to the goodwill of Kentuckians and an introduction to American democratic ideals. These reeducation efforts within the camp were met by a total de-Nazification, reeducation, and restructuring of the American zone in Germany during the post war period.[26]

The U.S was also looking towards the Cold War which was looming before World War II ended. Proper treatment of the prisoners not only created a cadre of future post war German officials who would appreciate U.S. democracy and American values, but those who would cooperate against the Soviet Union. If the U.S. hoped to gain German allies during the Cold War then the Soviet Union's treatment of its POWs certainly helped drive the Germans into the Western camp.

Housing the prisoners of war added another dimension to the Kentucky landscape and psyche. One could argue that it was bringing the war home. While true, most Kentuckians already clearly understood the war and its effects. Beset by labor problems, fear of farms failing and an ever present rationing system, Kentuckians knew the daily operations of living under wartime conditions. Few Kentuckians did not know someone who went off to war and the need for war workers further drained areas of its young men and women. Those living nearby Fort Knox, Camp Campbell, or Camp Breckinridge became accustomed to the sight of men in uniform, of caravans of military trucks carrying men and supplies down the highways, and the normal bustle of military bases. Even citizens living in more rural parts of Kentucky, like Monroe McGhee who still lives in Buffalo, a small community without a post office nestled between the equally small communities of Cerulean and Gracey, could not escape the sights of war. McGhee remembers seeing military cargo loaded on a seemingly endless line of train cars passing nearby his home as he cut tobacco or rested in the evening. All Kentuckians living at the time could recall the indignation and disgust when they heard of the Pearl Harbor attack. For Kentuckians, the war was already home.

The arrival of prisoners of war, however, added another dimension to the reality of war. For the first time locals, those too young, too old, unfit, or unable to serve could see the "superior race" up close. The arrival of these men, according to War Department policy, was supposed to be a secret and their activities subject to media blackout. That theory did not last long. Indeed, newspapers provide one of the best sources available on what the POWs were doing. National, state, and local papers seemed to provide ample coverage of their activities, which served as a stark contrast to what was happening in Europe. At first many Kentuckians were fearful, apprehensive, and often angry about having Germans housed in the country, emotions expressed by Americans across the nation. These prisoners represented not only enemy combatants, but men who likely killed loved ones. One of the greatest fears on the minds of locals was what if they escaped? Yet, despite this, the arrival of POWs became a media event and was often the biggest thing happening in most areas. When the trains arrived they were greeted by dozens of spectators, newspaper reporters, and photographers. Even when the trains were just rolling through stations for a brief stop and the POWs were not allowed off, people lined up to get a glimpse of these men from the Afrika Korps or elsewhere. Fort Knox was one of the few exceptions as the rail line ran right into camp. At branch camps, however, with the men housed in smaller groups and closer to the community, there was little safety from the prying eyes of young boys or teenage girls. The POWs at Maysville became a prime target for spectators who watched them from a slightly wooded hill that overlooked the camp.

Eventually the prisoners visited local towns either under guard while on work details, getting supplies, or getting food, or sometimes as escapees. While the excitement of having these prisoners close by never wore off for most, the fear did. Newspapers covered the work details of the men, listed the camps that they were housed at, and reported on some of the more humorous and unsuccessful escape attempts. Many Americans never overcame their anger and resentment of the POWs good treatment and better food than local citizens. That these former combatants potentially committed some of the heinous atrocities uncovered in Europe only exacerbated these emotions. On the other hand, there is the case of one woman from

Madison County whose family refused to hire forced POW labor.[27]

The POW labor force, however, benefited Kentucky by providing, statistically, a relatively benign, cooperative, and hard-working labor force. Farm records, newspapers, and personal recollections state that the POWs saved hundreds of thousands of dollars of tobacco and corn crops over the three year period between 1943 and 1946 that otherwise would have been destroyed. These men worked largely in Kentucky's agriculture, which mostly consisted of those two crops, but they also helped in other ways as well. Near Henderson prisoners picked peaches, while those in Owensboro shifted back and forth across the Ohio River into Indiana to do factory work. They also worked constructing buildings for their own upkeep and doing general repair work on the military bases. The POWs at Fort Knox worked on the L& N Railroad and repaired the roofs of houses along a street on base. They left their mark at both places. Some names were scrawled near the railroad that today look just like grafitti. They adorned all the chimneys with the Afrika Korps symbol which still exists and is plainly visible if you know where to look, although many spectators today don't know what it stands for and don't know that it is prominent along the entire street.

This labor overall, not only helped the state immensely, but earned the POWs the respect of local farmers, farm hands, and others who realized the benefit that these men provided to the state. This was a time of both small and big farmers and sharecropping was not uncommon. The McGhees of Buffalo had a small operation, not large enough to afford hiring prisoners from Campbell, but the lack of available free hands still impacted their operation. The Mathis family of Christian County, Kentucky, were sharecroppers who worked the POWs in much the same way they worked other labor. According to C.J. Mathis this meant labor sharing between families "neighbors would get together and you know cut tobacco and help each other . . . you didn't have the money to hire a lot of people."[28] The prisoners who worked for the Mathis family performed quite well and were cost-effective.

While nearly everyone seemed to know about the prisoners, and that certain farmers were hiring them, a lot of people knew very little else about them. Paul Gardener of Cerulean, Kentucky said he knew that they worked out of Campbell for the Broadbents but didn't know much else. Margaret Rudd of Lyon and later Trigg County said the same thing, but added "I have heard stories since," but otherwise we "in fact we hardly knew they were here."[29]

Working these men in local communities brought the average Kentuckian closer to a captured German or other Axis prisoner than they ever would be. Kentuckians realized that they were mostly just boys, not hardcore Nazis. These men shared pictures and souveniers with their employers. When the food rations of POWs were cut the farmers lobbied for their cause. Farm work was hard and all men, regardless of national origin, needed sustenance to perform that labor. Many Americans first looked at them as just the enemy, but as one researcher has titled his work, they soon discovered "they were people just like we were."[30]

Walter Mathis had the rare experience of having prisoners work on his farm when he was a boy and then later when he was stationed in Germany with the U.S. Special Forces he encountered some of the former prisoners that worked on his family farm. Mathis had purchased a radio from another American soldier being discharged. Mathis said that selling goods bought overseas was not that uncommon as it cut down on moving expenses when returning to the States. The radio blew one of the tubes and Mathis was unable to replace it on base. He went into town to a local electronics store, but none of the employees could speak English. Eventually they got the owner who surprised Walter with his very clear English. Walter asked where he learned to speak so fluently and the man informed him that he was a former POW held at Camp Campbell, Kentucky. Mathis told him that he was not only stationed at Campbell as part of the 101st, but is from the area as well. After a long conversation both men realized that the German had been one of the men who worked on the Mathis family farm. Speaking of the incident and World War II decades later, he felt that "in hindsight World War II was probably never about differences between Americans and the Germans or the Japanese as it was about the differences in the leadership of those two countries and its leaders, it was not about the people."[31]

After six decades, however, memories fade, the labor benefit is forgotten, just as the experience of housing prisoners of war in the Bluegrass State has become a mere historical footnote or oddity. Many of the former prisoners have died, or are in their eighties or older. U.S. guards and officials were typically much older than then seventeen to twenty four year old Europeans that they guarded and they too have passed.

Still, there are those who hired these men and those prisoners out there who are still around and willing to talk. Children of farmers who were teenagers or even younger vividly recall this experience of encountering the enemy. Youths who only saw these men at train stations have a recollection of that moment. Those in the World War II generation knew that they were part of something big, unfortunately few today truly appreciate it. Many former prisoners maintained contact with guards and employers. Often these are letters dust covered and boxed up in the attic. The distances of time and space have erased many of these memories. Few physical artifacts remain to mark the presence of the Axis invasion of the Bluegrass State. Most branch camps were temporary to begin with and once cleaned or vacated returned to the empty warehouses, fairgrounds, or Civilian Conservation Corps buildings that they once were.

Even base camps like Breckinridge eventually closed. At that camp the lasting legacy is a land dispute between the military and those who claim that their deceased relatives had the land taken from them.[32] The prisoners at Breckinridge, however, painted several large and beautiful murals on the walls of the officers' quarters. These works of art have been preserved and are now part of the Camp Breckinridge Museum. Stone walls that marked the entrance to the Prisoner of War compound at Breckinridge are now an entrance to a local county club. There are no markers or other indications that these pillars were originally constructed by German hands.

At Fort Knox, which is still an active base today, the remnants of the men are fewer. There is a

216

cemetery that holds the remains of the men who died at Knox and Breckinridge. Artifacts like those left on the chimneys and L&N railroad still remain, but are difficult to locate. One of the POW castles, a seemingly common pastime nationally, built at Knox is owned by a central Kentucky family. In the last years interest in the POW experience at Knox has grown. Most of the research done, however, has been by middle school students whose buildings and sports field rests on the former site of the camp. The occasional visiting former POW generates press, but again these visits are becoming fewer and fewer. Even the Patton Museum, housed at Knox does not mention the fact that there was once a prisoner of war camp there. The library houses some scant information, but getting access to it is more difficult than visiting the National Archives which contains much more useful information.

Even less remains at Fort Campbell, called Camp Campbell during the war. The three POW barracks were a mixture of existing facilities and hastily constructed security measures including barbed wire fences and guard towers. Once the war was over, these were torn down or converted to another purpose for the expanding base. Eventually, even the barracks were torn down. Only a few of the World War II type buildings existed into the 1990s and these were not POW buildings but barracks for U.S. soldiers later converted to education buildings. A modern education facility on base which houses programs from several of the surrounding area colleges replaced these outdated facilities. Even a well plotted out cemetery to house deceased prisoners of war gave way to the base expansion. Only five of the POWs at Campbell actually died while interned, theoretically fewer than officials expected and certainly fewer than the facilities allowed. After the war, the cemetery was moved to make way for a Family Resource Center. The deceased were interred on a very remote location nestled off of a gravel road and in a clearing in the woods. They share the new cemetery with another individual buried there in the late 1800s. Few know of this cemetery, but the Clarksville Edelweiss Club maintains it and they hold a memorial service there every November.

With few exceptions the memory of this experience on Kentucky, and on the nation in general, has been forgotten. Despite burgeoning interest in World War II and Kentucky history, this aspect of the war did not deal with sweeping battles and tactics or larger than life generals. Yet, as this study has demonstrated it is still an important and vital part of our history and culture. So, was it worth the time, expense, and struggle to operate the POW program? The answer is an obvious and resounding yes.
In the end the U.S. demonstrated several its commitment to humanitarian treatment and adherence to international law to the global community and Kentucky's role was paramount. Unlike all the other belligerents during World War II the U.S. transported its prisoners' halfway around the world to enter captivity within the continental U.S. in places as far removed from North Africa or Normandy as Henry, Christian, or Fayette Counties in Kentucky. If President Woodrow Wilson led our nation to war in 1917 to "make the world safe for democracy," the POW program operated under President Franklin D.

Roosevelt certainly showed the strength and value of democracy in a time of war. The difficulties encountered during this global war demonstrated that in future wars, nations could implement similar programs and should adhere to a policy of humane treatment and international law. It is with heavy heart that one can look at the difficulties overcome during the Second World War and then to see how far we as a nation have departed from these practices in more modern conflicts.

Photo Appendix

One of the many officer housing chimneys at Fort Knox
adorned with the Afrika Korps placed there by POWs.

Camp Campbell as it appeared in 1943.
Photo Courtesy of John O'Brien,
Don F. Pratt Museum, Fort Campbell

POW sketch of Fort Knox.
Photo Courtesy of Matthew Rector,
Historical Preservation Office, Fort Knox.

Fort Knox POW sketch.
Photo Courtesy of Matthew Rector,
Historical Preservation Office, Fort
Knox.

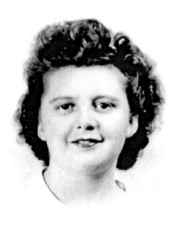

Photograph (left) was used by Camp Campbell POW to create chalk drawing (right). Carmine "Johnny" DeName, camp guard, commissioned a POW to complete this drawing of Frances Thomas, who later became his wife.
Courtesy of Shea Godwin and Thomas Harper and Tony DeName.

One of several miniature castles built by Fort Knox POWs, Located in the yard of a central Kentucky resident.

Cartoon taken from Der Neue Weg published by POWs at Camp Campbell. Artist's distress at not going home is clearly displayed as this appeared in the January 1946 edition. Notice the prisoner is housed in the VW (anti-Nazi) compound.

Fort Knox POW canteen.
Photo Courtesy of Matthew Rector,
Historical Preservation Office, Fort Knox.

Carving done by Fort Knox POW.
Photo Courtesy of Matthew Rector,
Historical Preservation Office, Fort Knox.

Postcard image of mural in former Breckinridge Officer
Club, now James D. Veatch Museum and Art Center.
Postcard courtesy of James D. Veatch Museum and Art
Center.

Location of POW Camp

Courtesy of Matthew Rector,
Fort Knox Cultural Resources Office

Courtesy of Matthew Rector,
Historical Preservation Office, Fort Knox.

Guard tower at Camp Campbell.
Photo courtesy of John O'Brien, Don F. Pratt Museum,
Fort Campbell.

Bibliography

Books

Albertson, Hans-Albert Smolinski. *My Memories of the Prisoner of War Camp in Crossville, Tennessee.* Draft, 8 March, 1993.

Arndt, John, ed. *Microfilm Guide and Index to the Library of Congress Collection of German Prisoner of War Newspapers Published in the United States from 1943-1946.* Mass: Clark University, 1965.

Asada, Teruhiko. *The Night of A Thousand Suicides: The Japanese Outbreak at Cowra.* St. Martin's Press, 1972.

Bailey, Ronald H. *Prisoners of War.* Chicago: Time-Life Books, 1981.

Bangerter, Lowell A. *German Prisoners of War in Wyoming.* Wyoming: Wyoming Council for the Humanities, 1979.

Bartov, Omar. *Hitler's Army: Soldiers, Nazis, and War in the Third Reich.* New York: Oxford University Press, 1991.

Barnouw, Dagmar. *The War in the Empty Air: Victims,Perpetrators, and Postwar Germans.* Bloomington, Indiana University Press, 2005.

Beck, Earl R. *Under the Bombs: The German Home Front, 1942-1945*. Lexington: The University of Kentucky Press, 1986.

Biess, Frank. *Homecomings: Returning POWs, and the Legacies of Defeat in Postwar Germany*. Princeton: Princeton University Press, 2006.

Billinger, Robert D., Jr., *Hitler's Soldiers in the Sunshine State: German POWs in Florida*. Gainesville: University of Florida Press, 2000.

Billinger, Robert D., Jr. *Nazi POWs in the Tar Heel State*. Gainesville: University of Florida Press, 2008.

Bosworth, Allan R. *America's Concentration Camps*. New York: W.W. Norton & Company, Inc., 1967.

Buck, Anita. *Behind Barbed Wire: German Prisoner of War Camps in Minnesota*. MN: North Star Press of St. Cloud, Inc., 1998.

Carlson, Lewis H. *We Were Each Other's Prisoners: An Oral History of World War II American and German Prisoners of War*. New York: Basic Books, 1997.

Carr-Gregg, Charlotte. *Japanese Prisoners of War in Revolt: The Outbreaks at Featherstone and Cowra During World War II*. Palgrave Macmillian, 1978.

Cooper, Herston. *Crossville*. United States: Adams Press, 1965.

Cooper, Matthew. *The German Army 1933-1945*. Chelsea, MI: Scarborough House, 1991.

Cowley, Betty. *Stalag Wisconsin: Inside WWII Prisoner-of-War Camps*. Oregon, Wisconsin: Badger Books, Inc., 2002.

Davis, Calvin DeArmond. *The United States and The Second Hague Peace Conference: American Diplomatical and International Organziation, 1899-1914*. Durham, NC: Duke University Press, 1975.

Davis, George J. *The Hitler Diet: As Inflicted on American P.O.W.'s in World War*. CA: Military Literary Guild, 1990.

Dennett, Carl. *Prisoners of The Great War*. Boston: Houghton Mifflin Company, 1919.

Dobbs, Michael. *Saboteurs: The Nazi Raid on America*. New York: Vintage Books, 2004.

Doyle, Michael W. *Ways of War and Peace: Realism, Liberalism, and Socialism*. New York: W.W. Norton & Company, 1997.

Ellis, John. *Brute Force: Allied Strategy and Tactics in the Second World War*. New York: Viking-Penguin Books, 1990.

Erichsen, Heino R. *The Reluctant Warrior: Former German POW Finds Peace in Texas*. Austin, TX: Eakin Press, 2001.

Fiedler, David. *The Enemy Among Us: POWs in Missouri During World War II*. Saint Louis, MO: Missouri Historical Society Press, 2003.

Flory, William E.S. *Prisoners of War: A Study in the Development of International Law*. Washington, D.C.: American Council on Public Affairs, 1942.

Foy, David A.. *ForYou The War is Over: American Prisoners of War in Nazi Germany*. New York: Stein and Day, 1984.

Gaertner, Georg and Arnold Krammer. *Hitler's Last Soldier in America*. New York: Stein and Day, 1985.

Gansberg, Judith M. *Stalag: U.S.A.: The Remarkable Story of German POWs in America*. New York: Thomas Y. Cromwell Company, 1977.

Geiger, Jeffrey E. *German Prisoners of War at Camp Cooke, California: Personal Accounts of 14 Soldiers, 1944-1946*. North Carolina: McFarland and Company, Inc., 1996.

Goebeler, Hans with John Vanzo. *Steel Boats, Iron Hearts: A U-boat Crewman's Life aboard U-505*. London: Chatham Publishing, 2005.

Gordon, Harry. *Voyage of Shame: The Cowra Breakout and Afterwards*. Specialized Book Services, 1994.

Green, Vincent S. *Extreme Justice*. New York: Pocket Books, 1995.

Hörner, Helmut. *A German Odyssey: The Journal of a German Prisoner of War*. Translated and edited by Allan Kent Powell. Colorado: Fulcrum Publishing, 1991.

Hull, William I. *The Two Hague Conferences and Their Contributions to International Law*. Introduced by Warren F. Kuehl. New York: Garland Publishing, Inc., 1972.

Jackson, Robert. *The Prisoners, 1914-18*. Routledge, Kegan & Paul, 1989.

Jaworski, Leon. *After Fifteen Years*. Gulf Publishing Company, 1961.

Jaworski, Leon. *Confession and Avoidance*: *A Memoir*. Anchor Press, 1979.

Johnson, Clarence. *Prisoners of War*. Los Angeles: The University of Southern California Press, 1941.

Koller, Berneda. *An Ironic Point of Light: The Story of a German from Russia who Survived an American World War II Prisoner of War Camp.* South Dakota: Pine Hill Press, Inc., 1994.

Koop, Allen V. *Stark Decency: German Prisoners of War in a New England Village.* Hanover: University Press of New England, 1988.

Krammer, Arnold. *Nazi Prisoners of War in America.* New York: Scarborough House, 1979.

Luck, Hans von. *Panzer Commander: The Memoirs of Colonel Hans von Luck.* New York: Praeger, 1989.

May, Lowell A. *Camp Concordia: German POWs in the Midwest.* Kansas: Sunflower University Press, 1995.

Moore, Bob and Kent Fedorowich. *The British Empire and Its Italian Prisoners of War, 1940-1947.* New York: Palgrave, 2002.

Moore, Bob and Kent Fedorowich. *Prisoners of War and their Captors in World War II.* Oxford: Berg, 1996.

Moore, John Hammond. *The Faustball Tunnel: German POWs and Their Great Escape.* New York: Random House, 1978.

Pabel, Reinhold. *Enemies are Human.* Philadelphia: The John C. Winston Company, 1955.

Parnell, Wilma and Robert Taber. *The Killing of Corporal Kunze.* New Jersey: Lyle Stuart Inc., 1981.

Pictet, Jean. *Development and Principle of International Humanitarian Law.* Netherlands: Martinus Nijhoff Publishers, Dordrecht, and Henry Dunant Institute, Geneva, 1985.

Powell, Allan Kent. *Splinters of a Nation: German Prisoners of War in Utah.* Salt Lake City: University of Utah Press, 1989.

Ready J. Lee. *The Forgotten Axis: Germany's Partners and Foreign Volunteers in World War II.* Jefferson, NC: McFarland & Company, Inc., 1987.

Reid, Major Pat, and Maurice Michael. *Prisoner of War.* New York: Beaufort Books, 1984.

Riconda, Harry P. *Prisoners of War in American Conflicts.* Lanham, MD: The Scarecrow Press, Inc., 2003.

Robin, Ron. *The Barbed-Wire College: Reeducating German POWs in the United States During World War II.* New Jersey: Princeton University Press, 1995.

Seydewitz, Max. *Civil Life in Wartime Germany: The Story of the Home Front.* New York: The Viking Press, 1945.

Schmid, Walter. *A German POW in New Mexico.* Translated Richard Rundell, Edited by Wolfgang T. Schlauch. Albuquerque, NM: University of New Mexico Press, 2005.

Stimson, Henry. *The Henry Stimson Diaries.* Yale University Library, Manuscripts and Archives, New Haven, 1973, Microfilm.

Tent, James F. *Mission on the Rhine*: "Reeducation" and Denazification in American-Occupied Germany. University of Chicago Press, 1984.

Thompson, Glenn. *Prisoners on the Plains: German POWs in America.* Nebraska: Phelps County Historical Society, 1993.

Treaties and Alliances of the World: An International Survey covering Treaties in Force and Communities of State, ed. Kessing's Publications Ltd. New York: Charles Scribner's Sons, 1968.

Towle, Philip, Margaret Kosuge, and Yoichi Kibata, Editors. *Japanese Prisoners of War.* London: Hambledon and London, 2000.

Unknown Unteroffizier. *And Still We Conquer! The Diary of a Nazi Unteroffizier in the German Africa Corps who was Captured by the United States Army, May 9, 1943 and imprisoned at Camp Shelby, Mississippi.* Stanley Hoole, Editor. University of Alabama: Confederate Publishing, 1968.

Vulliet, Andre. *Preliminary Report of the War Prisoners Aid Young Men's Christian Associations During World War II.* Geneva, Switzerland: International Committee of the Young Men's Christian Association, 1946.

Walker, Richard P. *The Lone Star and the Swastika: Prisoners of War in Texas.* Austin, Texas: Eakin Press, 2001.

Wall, Randy. *Inside the Wire: Aliceville and the Afrika Corps.* South Carolina State Museum, Courtesy of Alabama Heritage, December 7, 1991-January 4, 1993.

Ward, Leslie A. *History of the Concordia Prisoner of War Camp.* Concordia, KS: The Kansan Printing House, Inc., 1969, 1982.

Wheaton, Henry. *History of the Law of Nations in Europe and America from the Earliest Times to the Treaty of Washington, 1842.* Albany: WM & A. Gould & Co., 1845.

Whittingham, Richard. *Martial Justice: The Last Mass Execution in the United States.* Chicago: Henry Regnery Company, 1971.

Wilcox, Walter W. *The Farmer in the Second World War.* Ames, Iowa: The Iowa State College Press, 1947.

Vance, Jonathan F., Editor. *Encyclopedia of Prisoners of War and Internment.* California: ABC-CLIO, Inc., 2000.

Zollo, Burt. *Prisoners.* Chicago: Academy Chicago Publishers, 2003.

Unpublished Material

Pluth, Edward J. "The Administration and Operation of German Prisoner of War Camps in the United States during World War II." Ph.D. Dissertation, Ball State University, 1970, 457 p.

Mallet, Derek R. "They were just people like we were: World War II German and Italian prisoners of war in Missouri." M.A. Thesis, Truman State University, 1997.

Thompson, Antonio "Men in German Uniform: German Prisoners of War Held in the United States during the Second World War." Ph.D. Dissertation, University of Kentucky, 2006.

Thompson, Antonio "German POWs in the United States during World War II with a focus on Kentucky and Tennessee." M.A. Thesis, Western Kentucky University, 2001.

Thompson, Antonio "Colonel George Chescheir and the Operation of Axis POW Camps in the American South." Paper presented at the Ohio Valley History Conference, Johnson City, TN., October 2006.

Thompson, Antonio "Entertaining the Afrika Korps in America: German POW Camp Life in Kentucky." Paper presented at the Ohio Valley History Conference, Murray, KY., October 2005.

Thompson, Antonio "Working for the Enemy? German POW Labor in Kentucky and Tennessee during World War II." Paper presented at the Ohio Valley History Conference, Cookeville, TN., October 2004.

Weldon, Melissa. "Restoring the Light: Ministry to German Prisoners of War in America During the Second World War." M.A. Thesis, University of Richmond, 1993. 122 p.

Government Documents

"Amelioration of the Condition of the Wounded and the Sick of Armies in the Field (Red Cross Convention)," *Convention Between the United States of America and Other POWs, Treaty Series, No. 847*. Washington, D.C.: United States Government Printing Office, 1-47.

"Army Service Forces Organization," *Army Service Forces Manual M301, Headquarters, Army Service Forces*. Washington, D.C.: United States Government Printing Office, 15 August 1944.

Bevans, Charles I., ed. "Amelioration of the Condition of the Wounded and the Sick of Armies in the Field (Red Cross Convention)," *Treaties and Other International Agreements of the United States of America, 1776-1949, Vol. 2. Multilateral, 1918-1930*. Washington, D.C.: Department of State Pubication, (1969), 965-982.

Bevans, Charles I., ed. "Convention Relative to the Treatment of Prisoners of War," *Treaties and Other International Agreements of the United States of America, 1776-1949, Vol. 2. Multilateral, 1918-1930*. Washington, D.C.: Department of State Publication, (1969), 932-964.

Doyle, Robert C. "Making Experience Count," *The Harmon Memorial Lectures In Military History, United States Air Force Academy*, No. 43, 2000, U.S. Government Printing Office, Washington, D.C., 20402. 34 p.

"Escape of Officers and Men from German Ships Interned in the United States" Supplement: Diplomatic Correspondence Between the United and Belligerent Governments Relating to Neutral Rights and Commerce in *The American Journal of International Law* Vol. 10, No. 4

FBI History. "George Dasch and the Nazi Saboteurs," *Federal Bureau of Investigations, Famous Cases*. www.fbi.gov 6 p.

"Handbook for the Director of Civilian Training," *War Department, Army Service Forces, Office of the Quartermaster General*. Washington, D.C.: United States Government Printing Office, (August 1943), 104 p.

"Handbook for Work Supervisors of Prisoner of War Labor," *War Department, Army Service Forces Manual, M-811*. Washington, D.C.: United States Government Printing Office, (July 1945), 1-17.

Lewis, George and John Mewha "History of Prisoner of War Utilization by the United States Army, 1776-1945. Washington, D.C.: Center of Military History, United States Army, Washington, D.C.

Millet, John D. "The Organization and Role of the Army Service Forces," *United States Army in World War II* . Washington, D.C.: Office of the Chief of Military History, Department of the Army, (1954), 494 p.

"Population Lists, June 1942 Thru June 1944, Weekly Report on Prisoners of War," Prisoner of War Operations Division, Office of the Provost Marshal General. Microfilm compilation.

"Safe Work Practices for Prisoners of War (German)," *M805, Army Service Forces Manual, Headquarters, Army Service Forces.* Washington, D.C.: United States Government Printing Office, (22 September 1944), 23 p.

"Technical Manual-Enemy Prisoners of War," *TM 19-500,War Department*. Washington, D.C.: U.S. Government Printing Office, 15 January 1945.

"The Military Police Activities in Connection With the Evacuation and Detention of Prisoners of War, Civilian Internees, and Military Personnel Recovered from the Enemy," *The General Board, United States Forces, European Theater, Provost Marshal Section 11, Study Number 103*

United States. Defense Advisory Committee on
Prisoners of War. "POW, the Fight Continues
After the Battle; the Report on the Secretary of
Defense's Advisory Committee on Prisoners of
War." (August 1955), 82 p.

U.S., Office of the Provost Marshal General, Prisoner
of War Operations Division, "Weekly Reports
on Prisoners of War," *Prisoner of War
Population Lists June 1942 to June 1944.*
Washington, D.C.: GPO.

"Wartime Supervision," *Army Service Forces, Office of
the Quartermaster General.* Washington, D.C.:
U.S. Government Printing Office, (June 14,
1948), 116 p.

Special Collections/Archival Materials

National Archives

Office of the Provost Marshal General, Record Group
389, Entry 457-Subject Correspondence File,
1942-46 (Subject Correspondence File Relating
To The Construction of And Condition in
Prisoner of War Camps, 1942-1946), Boxes
1419-1440

Office of the Provost Marshal General, Record Group
389, Entry 458-Policy File, 1942-45 (Policy and
Procedural Records Relating To The
Supervision of Prisoners of War and Their
Camps, 1942-1945), Boxes 1441-1448

Office of the Provost Marshal General, Record Group 389, Entry 459A-Decimal File, 1943-46 (Special Projects Division, Administrative Branch Decimal File, 1943-1946), Boxes 1593-1655

Office of the Provost Marshal General, Record Group 389, Entry 439A-Historical File, 1941-1958, Boxes 1-5.

Office of the Provost Marshal General *Historical Monograph*, Prisoner of War Operations Division, Office of the Provost Marshal General: with appendices and supplement, 1945-1946. *National Archives II, Modern Military Branch.*

Records of the War Manpower Commission, RG 211, Entry 114-Records of the Reports and Analysis Service, Records of the Foreign Labor Market Section, Manpower Reports 1940-1944, Boxes 1-4

"Descriptive Lists of Monthly Progress Reports of Headquarters Army Service Forces, September 1942-May 1946. National Archives Library.

"Historical Monograph, Prisoner of War Operations Division, Provost Marshal General's Office," National Archives, *RG 389 Historical File 1941-1958, Box 36 Prisoner of War Operations Vol. I, Folder "Prisoner of War Operations Vol I of III.*

"Prisoner of War Circular No. 1 (Wahington, D.C., *War Department*, 24 September 1943): 5-6, National Archives, RG 389, Entry 439A--Historical File, 1941-1958, Box 41-Regulations Governing Prisoners of War.

"April 22, 1942 Manual, Civilian Enemy Aliens and Prisoners of War" National Archives, RG 389 Historical File 1941-1958."

Military History Institute, Carlisle, Pennsylvania

Nationality and Age of German Armed Forces, Prisoners Captured in Northern France, Early August to 10 September 1944.

Western Kentucky University

Record, Kenneth S. *WWI and WWII Axis Burials in the Continental United States and Canada,* 1998, CS403 R42X, Manuscripts, Kentucky Building, Western Kentucky University, Bowling Green, Kentucky.

"Various letters," World War II and Prisoner of War Documents, Manuscripts and Folklife Archives, Kentucky Building, Western Kentucky University, Bowling Green, Kentucky.

Fort Knox, Patton Museum Archives

POW Sketchbook.

"Various Documents," *German POWs at Fort Knox.* Fort Knox Archives, File 3, 91-142-01, (Box 49-2). Fort Knox, Kentucky.

"Various Documents," *POW Daily Time Records.* Fort Knox Archives, File 2, (Box 54-2). Fort Knox, Kentucky.

Photographs.

Fort Knox, Cultural Resources Center

POW Sketchbook.

Egon Hessenthaler, "Memoirs," German copy.

Various Documents.

Photographs.

Kentucky Historical Society, Library and Book Room

"Various Documents," World War II, General Files of Kentucky History, Library, Kentucky Historical Society, Frankfort, Kentucky.

Peyton, Heady. *History of Camp Breckinridge, KY.*
Hites Imperial Printing, 1987, Library,
Kentucky Historical Society, Frankfort,
Kentucky.

Kentucky Historical Society, Special Collections

The George Chescheir Collection.

Oral History Collection.

Fort Campbell

Don F. Pratt Museum, "The History of the 101st
Airborne Division (Air Assault) and Fort
Campbell, Kentucky." Ed. Installation History
Department, Fort Campbell, Kentucky. Fort
Campbell, Ky., GPO.

"Various Documents," *German POWs at Fort
Campbell.*

Fort Campbell Archives, Folder 1. Fort Campbell,
Kentucky.

Photographs.

Personal Collections

E.T. "Hammer" Smith Collection Henry County, KY.

Smith Broadbent Family Collection, Trigg County, KY

Patricia Ellis Collection, Fayette County, KY.

Walter Mathis Collection, Christian and Madison
  Counties, KY.

Articles

Anderson, Chandler P. "Agreement Between the
  United States and Germany Concerning
  Prisoners of War." *The American Journal of
  International Law*, vol. 13, no. 1 (January
  1919): 97-101.

Ansbacher, H.L. "Attitudes of German Prisoners of
  War: A Study of the Dynamics of National-
  Socialistic Followership." *Applied
  Psychological Monographs: General and
  Applied* vol. 62, no. 1 (1948): 1-42.

Balsamo, Larry T. "Germany's Armed Forces in the
  Second World War: Manpower, Armaments,
  and Supply." *The History Teacher* vol. 24, no. 3
  (May 1991): 263-277.

Breycha-Vauthier, A.C. "Reading for Prisoners of War
  as Seen From Geneva." *The Library Quarterly*
  vol XI (1941): 442-447.

Brown, John Mason. "Prisoners from the Master
  Race." *Infantry Journal* no. 53 (December
  1943): 39-42.

Bondy, Curt. "Observation and Reeducation of German Prisoners of War." *The Harvard Educational Review* vol. 14 (January-December 1944): 12-19.

Burdick, Charles. "Prisoners as Soldiers: The German 999th Penal Division." *The Army Quarterly and Defense Journal* vol. 102 (October 1971-July 1972): 65-69.

Casady, Edwin. "The Reorientation Program for POWs at Fort Eustis, Virginia." *The American Oxonian* (July 1947): 146-154.

Cassidy, Henry C. "What to do With German Prisoners: The Russian Solution." *The Atlantic Monthly* vol. 174, no. 5 (November 1944): 43-45.

Coker, Kathy Roe. "World War II Prisoners of War in Georgia: German Memories of Camp Gordon, 1943-1945." *The Georgia Historical Quarterly* vol. 76, no. 4 (Winter 1992): 837-861.

Curt, Bondy. "Problems of Internment Camps." *Journal of Abnormal and Social Psychology* vol. 38 (1943): 453-475.

Davis, Gerald H. "Prisoners of War in Twentieth-Century War Economies." *Journal of Contemporary History* vol. 12, no. 4 (October 1977): 623-634.

Dahms, Steven V. "World War II Prisoners of War and the Missouri Synod." *Concordia Historical Institute Quarterly* vol. 68, no. 3 (Fall 1995): 120-132.

Ehrmann, Henry W. "An Experiment in Political Education." *Social Research* (September 1947): 304-20.

Fahey, John. "John Fahey on Reeducating German Prisoners During World War II." *Oregon Historical Society* vol. 93, (1992): 368-393.

Fay, Sidney B. "German Prisoners of War." *Current History* vol. 8, no. 43 (March 1945): 193-200.

Fecurka, Peter R. "Se Hable Espanol Comrade?: The Spanish Blue Division in Operation Barbarossa." *Command: Military History, Strategy & Analysis* no. 27 (March-April 1994):

Fickle, James E. and Donald W. Ellis. "POWs in the Piney Woods: German Prisoners of War in the Southern Lumber Industry, 1943-1945." *The Journal of Southern History* vol. 56, no. 4 (November 1990): 695-724.

Fisher, Paul. "Repatriation Labor: A Preliminary Analysis." *The Quarterly Journal of Economics* vol. 60, no. 3 (May 1946): 313-339.

Flynn, Eleanor C. "The Geneva Convention on
   Treatment of Prisoners of War." *The George
   Washington Law Review* (June 1943): 505-520.

Haase, Norbert. "Anti-Prisoners of War in American
   Prison Camps: The Example of Fort Devans,
   Massachusetts, *Traces*, www.traces. org.

Holl, Richard E. "Swastikas in the Bluegrass State:
   Axis Prisoners of War in Kentucky, 1942-46."
   The Register of The Kentucky Historical Society
   vol. 100, no. 2 (Spring 2002): 139-165.

Hoover, J. Edgar. "Alien Enemy Control." *Iowa Law
   Review* vol. 29 (March 1944): 396-408.

Jones, Calvin N. "Views of America and Views of
   Germany in German POW Newspapers of
   World War II." *Yearbook of German-American
   Studies* vol. 17 (1982): 63-70.

Kirwan, William E. "German Prisoners of War."
   *Bulletin of the Bureau of Criminal Investigation,
   New York State Police* (August 1944): 1-6.

Krammer, Arnold. "American Treatment of German
   Generals During World War II." *The Journal of
   Military History* vol. 54, no. 1 (January 1990).

Krammer, Arnold. "German Prisoners of War in the
   United States." *Military Affairs* vol. 40 (April
   1976): 68-73.

Krammer, Arnold. "Hitler's Legions in America: POWs on the home front." *American History* vol. 18, no. 4 (June 1983): 54-64.

Krammer, Arnold. "Japanese Prisoners of War in America." *Pacific Historical Review* 52 (February 1983): 67-91.

Kruse, Arthur M. "Custody of Prisoners of War in the United States." *The Military Engineer* vol. 38, no. 244 (February 1946): 70-74

Laurie, Clayton D. "The "Sauerkrauts" German Prisoners of War as OSS Agents, 1944-1945." *Prologue: The Journal of the National Archives* vol. 26, no. 1 (1994): 49-61.

Levie, Howard S. "The Employment of Prisoners of War." *The American Journal of International Law* vol. 57, no. 2 (April 1963): 318-353.

Levie, Howard S. "Penal Sanctions for Maltreatment of Prisoners of War," *The American Journal of International Law* vol. 56, no. 2 (April 1962): 433-468.

Levy, David M. "The German Anti-Nazi: A Case Study." *American Journal of Orthopsychiatry* vol. 16 (1946): 507-515.

Lunden, Walter A. "Captivity Psychosis Among Prisoners of War." *The Journal of Criminal Law and Criminology* vol. 39, no. 6 (March-April 1949): 721-733.

MacKenzie, S.P. "The Treatment of Prisoners of War in World War II." *The Journal of Modern History* vol. 66, no. 3 (September 1944): 487-520.

Marguiles, Newton L. "Proper Treatment of War Prisoners." *Vital Speeches of the Day* no. 15 (May 15, 1945): 477-480.

Mason, John Brown. "German Prisoners of War in the United States." *American Journal of International Law* vol 34 (April 1945): 198-215.

McKnight, Major Maxwell S. "The Employment of Prisoners of War in the United States." *International Labour Review* vol. 50 (July-December 1944): 47-64.

Merill R. Pritchett and William L. Shea. "Axis Prisoner-of-War Camps." *Journal of the West* vol. 18, no 2 (April 1979): 30-34.

Miller, Clarence L. "The Prisoner of War Program." *The New History of Shelby County, Kentucky* Shelbyville, KY: Harmon House Publishers): 515-519.

Moulton, William G. "Our Profession in Reverse: Teaching English to German Prisoners of War." *The Modern Language Journal* vol. 32, no. 6 (October 1948): 421-430.

Peak, Helen. "Some Observations on the Characteristics and Distribution of German Nazis." *Psychological Monographs: General and Applied* vol. 59 (1947): 1-44.

Peak, Helen. "Some Psychological Problems in the Re-Education of Germans." *The Journal of Social Issues* vol. 2, no. 3 (August 1946): 26-39.

Powers, James H. "What to Do With German Prisoners: The American Muddle." *The Atlantic Monthly* vol. 174, no. 5 (November 1944): 46-50.

Radford, R.A. "The Economic Organization of A P.O.W. Camp." *Economica* 11 (November 1945): 189-201.

Reiss, Matthias. "Bronzed Bodies behind Barbed Wire: Masculinity and the Treatment of German Prisoners of War in the United States during World War II." *The Journal of Military History* 69 (April 2005): 475-504.

Richter, Anton, ed. "A German P.O.W. at Camp Grant: The Reminiscences of Heinz Richter." *Journal of the Illinois State Historical Society* vol 76, No. 1 (Spring 1983): 61-70.

Rock, Kenneth W. "Unsere Lute: The Germans from Russia in Colorado." *The Colorado Magazine* vol. 54, no. 2 (1977): 155-183.

Rosen, Stephen Peter. "Military Effectiveness: Why Society Matters." *International Security* vol. 19, no. 4 (Spring 1995): 5-31.

Rundell, Walter, Jr. "Paying the POW in World War II." *Military Affairs* vol. 22, no. 3 (Autumn 1958): 121-134.

Shea, William. "A German Prisoner of War in the South: The Memoir of Edwin Pelz." *Arkansas Historical Quarterly* vol. 1 (Spring 1985): 42-55.

Spidle, Jake W. "Axis Prisoners of War in the United States, 1942-1946: A Bibliographical Essay." *Military Affairs* (April 1975): 61-66.

Stuart, Graham H. "War Prisoners and Internees in the United States." *American Foreign Service Journal* vol. 21 (October 1944): 530-31, 568, 571-573.

Tureen, Louis L. and James O. Palmer. "Some Group Differences in Personal Values between American Soldiers and German Prisoners of War." *The Journal of Social Psychology* vol. 42, (1955): 305-313.

Tuttle, William. "Professors into Propagandists: German POWs and the Failure of Reeducation." *Reviews in American History*, vol. 25, no. 1 (March 1997): 121-126.

Vance, Jonathan F. "Men in Manacles: The Shackling of Prisoners of War, 1942-1943." *The Journal of Military History* vol. 59, no. 3 (July 1995): 483-505.

Walzer, Michael. "Prisoners of War: Does the Fight Continue After the Battle?" *The American Political Science Review* vol. 63, no. 3 (September 1969): 777-786.

Wilson, Robert R. "Escaped Prisoners of War in Neutral Jurisdiction." *The American Journal of International Law* vol. 35, no. 3 (July 1941): 519-523.

Worall, Janet E. "Prisoners on the Home Front: Community Reactions to German and Italian POWS in Northern Colorado, 1943-1946." *Colorado Historical Society* no. 1 (1990): 32-47.

Magazines

"Anger at Nazi Atrocities is Rising, but U.S. Treats Prisoners Fairly." *Newsweek* (May 7, 1945): 58.

Blennemann, Ulrich. "Hitler's Other Foreign Legions." *Command: Military History, Strategy & Analysis* no. 35 (November 1995):

"Boss of 200,000 Enemies." *American Magazine* vol. CXXXVII (January 1944-June 1944): 131.

Byrd, Martha H. "Captured by the Americans." *American History Illustrated* 11 (February 1977): 24-35.

"Conditions of Employment of Prisoners of War." *Monthly Labor Review* 56 (May 1943): 891-895.

Cook, F.G. Alletson. "Democratic ABC's for Nazi PW's." *The New York Times Magazine* (November 11, 1945): 8, 32.

Cook, F.G. Alletson. "Nazi Prisoners are Nazis Still." *New York Times Magazine* (November 21, 1943): 12, 38.

Davis, Jerome. "Millions Behind Barbed Wire." *Survey Graphic* (August 1942): 345-347.

"Death and Treason." *Newsweek* (February 5, 1945): 47-48.

Devore, Robert. "Our Pampered War Prisoners." *Collier's* (October 14, 1944): 14, 144.

"Escape in Arizona." *Time* (January 8, 1945): 16.

Deutsch, Albert. "German PWs Living Better Than our War Workers." *PM* [New York] (15 May 1945): 6

Frost, Meigs O. "Afrika Korps Veteran Flays Nazism, Tells of Torture." *The Times-Picayune Sunday Magazine*, New Orleans, Louisiana (September 23, 1945): 2.

Frost, Meigs O. "New Orleans Test Tube for German Democracy." *The Times-Picayune Sunday Magazine*, New Orleans, Louisiana (September 15, 1945): 1-2.

"German Atrocities Raise Questions: Are Nazi POWs 'Coddled' Here?," *Newsweek* (May 7, 1945): 60-61.

"German Prisoners." *Army and Navy Register* Vol. 66, No. 3412 (April 28, 1945): 20.

"German Propaganda." *Army and Navy Register* Vol. 66, No. 3410 (April 14, 1945): 8.

Hoover, J. Edgar. "Enemies at Large." *The American Magazine* (April 1944): 17, 97-99.

Hoover, J. Edgar. "Recaptured Prisoners." *The American Magazine* (May 1944): 4.

Humphrey, Yvonne E. "On Shipboard With German Prisoners." *Journal of Nursing* vol. 43, no. 9 (September 1943): 821-22.

Kretzmann, P.E. "The Lutheran Commission for Prisoners of War." *The Lutheran Witness* (December 1943): 421-426.

Kunzig, Robert Lowe. "360,000 PW's-The Hope of Germany." *American Magazine* no. 142 (November 1946): 23, 132-137.

"Last of the Supermen." *Newsweek* (April 5, 1946): 20.

Lerch, Major General Archer. "The Army Reports on Prisoners of War." *The American Mercury* (May 1945): 536-547.

Lerch, Archer. "Handling German Prisoners in the United States." *Prisoners of War Bulletin*, Red Cross, vol. 3, no. 5 (May 1945): 4-5.

Lerner, Max. "The Chances Are Dark for a Democratic Germany." *PM*, New York (March 26, 1945): 2-3.

"Life in a German Prison Camp." *American National Red Cross, 1943-1945, Prisoners of War Bulletin* (February 1944): 4-5.

"Manpower Boost." *Business Week* (May 29, 1943): 20-22.

"Masquerader." *Time* (March 23, 1953): 25.

Meyer, Lawrence B. "A Plea for Prison Camp Literature." *The Lutheran Witness* Vol LXII, No 19 (September 14, 1943): 311.

"Midnight Massacre." *Time* (July 23, 1945): 24.

Mooth, Verla. "Memories of Christmas, 1944." *Good Old Days Magazine* vol. 38, no. 2 (February 2001): 58-59.

Munoz, Antonio J. "Losing World War II: Nazi Racial and Recruitment Policies in the East." *Command: Military History, Strategy & Analysis* No. 35 (November 1995).

"Nazis in the U.S." *Time* (May 1, 1944): 64-65.

"No Converts?" *Time* (December 11, 1944): 24.

Pabel, Reinhold. "It's Easy to Bluff Americans." *Collier's* (16 May 1953): 20-21.

Pierson, Ralph. "The Barbed-Wire Universities." *School and Society* vol. 62, no. 1602 (September 8, 1945): 156-158.

"Points System in Prison Camps." *American National Red Cross, 1943-1945, Prisoners of War Bulletin* (August 1943): 9.

"Policies for Employment of Prisoners of War." *Monthly Labor Review* (July 1944): 93.

"Postwar Policies Regarding Foreign Workers and Prisoners of War." *Monthly Labor Review* (November 1945): 910-912.

"POWs Outbound." *Newsweek* (May 28, 1945): 34.

"Priorities in Allocation of Services of Prisoners of War." *Monthly Labor Review* vol. 58 (June 1944): 1189.

"Prisoners' Dues?," *Business Week* (February 19, 1944): 94.

"Prisoners of War: Non-Germans Want to Go Back and Fight." *Military Police Training Bulletin* vol. 3, no. 1 (January 1945): 33.

"Prisoner of War Labor." *The American City* vol. 59 (March 1944): 87.

"P.W. Camp 168." *The New Statesman and Nation* (July 21, 1945): 4.

"Re-Educating the Nazis." *America* vol. 71, no. 21 (August 26, 1944): 515.

"Reorienting the Supermen." *Newsweek* (January 10, 1944): 78.

"Repatriates Arrive Home from Germany." *American National Red Cross, 1943-1945, Prisoners of War Bulletin* (December 19, 1943): 7.

Roberts, Tim. "POWs Spend Duration of War in Missouri" *Bearfacts* (February 1999).

"Set These Slaves Free." *Christian Century* vol. 63, no. 31 (July 31, 1946): 933-34.

"Seven by the Rope." *Newsweek* (July 23, 1945): 27.

Shafer, Jack. ". . . And Here's How We Treat Captives." *PM* (May 1, 1945): 9

Shays, Eugene. "German Prisoners of War in the U.S.: Observations of A Soldier." *Fourth International* no. 12 (December 1945): 366-371.

Smith, Beverly. "The Afrika Korps Comes to America." *American Magazine* (August 1943): 28-29, 83-84.

Smith, Beverly. "Nazi Supermen Hit the Dirt." *American Magazine* (July 1945): 45, 82.

Smith, T.V. "Behind Barbed Wire." *The Saturday Review of Literature* vol. 29 (May 4, 1946): 5-7, 43-44.

Stenbuck, Jack. "German War Prisoner for Democratic Leadership." *Magazine Digest* (December 1945): 66-72.

Stevens, Leland. "Thoroughly American." *The Lutheran Witness* vol. 116, no. 5 (May 1997): 14-16.

Strong, Tracy. "Prisoners Under the Law." *Christian Century* (April 14, 1943): 455-457.

"Studies and Sports in German Prison Camps." American National Red Cross, 1943-1945, *Prisoners of War Bulletin* vol. 1, no. 4 (September 1943): 1, 5.

"Swastika Over Arizona." *Newsweek* (February 26, 1945): 58.

"The Kriegsmarine Escape." *Newsweek* (January 8, 1945): 33-34.

"The Nation: Enough Nazis." *Newsweek* (May 21, 1945): 38.

"Treatment of War Prisoners." *Army and Navy Register* vol. 66, no. 8413 (May 5, 1945): 8.

"The Captive Enemy." *Newsweek* (March 29, 1945): 32, 34.

"Uncle Sam in the Slave Trade." *Christian Century* (June 12, 1946): 24.

"Utilize Prisoners of War." *Army and Navy Journal* No. 1109 (May 13, 1944): 96.

"War Prisoners Opposed." *Business Week* (January 15, 1944): 96.

"War Over Prisoners." *Newsweek* (November 2, 1942): 24.

Yochum, H.L. "I Went to a POW Camp." *The Lutheran Outlook* (March 1946): 72.

"The YMCA War Prisoners' Aid Offers Educational Assistance." *School and Society* (May 6, 1944): 325.

Interviews and Oral Histories

Heino Erichsen, questionnaire from William T. Ripley, Curator of Natural Science at The Children's Museum of Indianapolis, 23 July 2003.

Egon Hessenthaler, "Memoirs," German copy held at Fort Knox cultural resources, trans. by Natalie DoVanne (March 2007).

Paul James, interview by Gary Kempf, November 1, 2001.

John Edwin McClure, interviewed by Sheila Brown Heflin, 12-17-85, Kentucky Historical Center Oral History Collection.

Conducted by Antonio Thompson

Horst Blumenberg, Spring and Summer 2007.

Bill Columbia, 2005.

Patricia Ellis, Summer 2005.

Heino Erichsen, Summer 2005.

Paul Gardner, 1999.

Barbara James, March 2007.

Mary Ellen Lilly, 2006.

Walter Mathis, Summer 2005.

Junior Mathis, Fall 2005.

Monroe McGhee, 2006.

Myron Pool, May 2000.

Edgar Radford, May 11, 2000.

Margaret Rudd, 2005.

Howard Tromp, May 2006 and August 2005.

Newspapers

Cadiz Record, Cadiz, KY

Cincinnati Post, Cincinnati, Ohio

Clarksville Leaf-Chronicle, Clarksville, TN

Courier & Press, Evansville, IN

Danville Advocate-Messenger, Danville, KY

Henry County Local, New Castle, KY

Kentucky New Era, Hopkinsville, KY

Ledger Independent, Maysville, Kentucky

Lexington Herald, Lexington, KY

Lexington Leader, Lexington, KY

Lexington Herald-Leader (Sunday), Lexington, KY

Louisville Courier-Journal, Louisville, KY

Louisville Times, Louisville, KY

Owensboro Messenger, Owensboro, Kentucky

Park City Daily News, Bowling Green, KY

Union County Advocate, Morganfield, *KY*

Camp Newspapers

Die Brücke (The Bridge), Camp Breckinridge, KY.

Der Europäer: Kriegsgefangenenzeitschrift (The European: War prisoner periodical), Camp Campbell, KY.

Der Neue Weg (The New Way), Camp Campbell, KY.

Die Saat, Fort Knox, KY.

Index

202, 206, 208, 211, 214,
215, 217, 247, 267
canning, 48, 60, 147
Castle, 180, 266
Catholic, 118, 127, 133,
190, 193, 194
Central Kentucky, 59,
65
Christian County,
Kentucky, 24, 38, 46,
47, 49, 50, 52, 63, 70,
76, 80, 88, 91, 157, 161,
214
Church, 71
Cincinnati, Ohio, 185,
266
Clarksville, Tennessee,
31, 46, 159, 161, 162,
218, 266
Columbia, Bill, 69, 265
Communist, 118
contract, 16, 41, 44, 45,
46, 48, 49, 50, 52, 59,
64, 66, 68, 71, 74, 76,
78, 91, 95, 101, 200
corn, 3, 38, 44, 45, 48,
49, 52, 54, 67, 71, 74,
80, 100, 152, 213
correspondence, 3, 12,
64, 98, 132, 188, 189,
190, 191, 206, 208
Danville, Kentucky, 3,
10, 51, 67, 101, 201,
266
Daviess County,
Kentucky, 48, 95, 97

DD Compound, 20, 22,
120, 121, 122, 124, 128,
129, 130, 141, 170, 172,
174, 185, 190, 194, 202
democracy, 4, 12, 13,
28, 34, 36, 73, 119, 129,
167, 210, 218
Der Aue, Helmut von,
154
Der Europäer, 187, 267
Der Neue Weg, 187,
267
Die Brücke, 187, 267
Die Saat, 187, 188, 267
dogs, 120, 143, 147,
152, 162, 164
Dunn, D.Y., 76, 77, 78
Eastern Kentucky, 3, 70
Education, 166, 167,
186, 250, 254
Ellis, Patricia, 39, 87,
231, 248, 265
Elwood, Indiana, 60
Eminence, Kentucky, 3,
10, 51, 55, 56, 57, 66,
92, 201
Erichsen, Heino, 18, 54,
108, 110, 114, 115, 162,
169, 172, 192, 207, 232,
264, 265
escape, 10, 16, 19, 21,
30, 40, 73, 93, 104, 106,
140, 142, 143, 145, 146,
147, 149, 150, 151, 152,
154, 155, 157, 158, 159,
160, 161, 162, 163, 164,

Endnotes

Overlay Quote

* J. Earle Bell quoting Major Hugh M. Patton, Public Relations Officer, Union County *Advocate* (3 May 1945): 8.

Chapter 1

[1] *The Geneva Convention Relative to the Treatment of Prisoners of War*, also called the *Prisoner of War Convention*, and the *Amelioration of the Condition of the Wounded and Sick of Armies in the Field*, shortened to *the Red Cross Convention.*

[2] Charles Bevans, ed. "Convention Relative to the Treatment of Prisoners of War," and "Amelioration of the Condition of the Wounded and the Sick of Armies in the Field (Red Cross Convention)," both in *Treaties and Other International Agreements of the United States of America, 1776-1949, Vol. 2. Multilateral, 1918-1930* (Washington, D.C.: Department of State Publication, 1969): 932-982.

[3] *Treaties and Alliances of the World: An International Survey covering Treaties in Force and Communities of State*, ed. Kessing's Publications Ltd. (New York: Charles Scribner's Sons, 1968): 13.

[4] Jean Pictet *Development and Principle of International Humanitarian Law* (Netherlands: Martinus Nijhoff Publishers, Dordrecht, and Henry Dunant Institute, Geneva, 1985): 30.

[5] Ibid., 31-33.

[6] Bevans, 251.

[7] Numerous instances exist in the literature, but Lewis Carlson does a good job of balancing some of these out as they related to specific accounts of German and American soldiers in *We Were Each Other's Prisoners: An Oral History of World War II American and German Prisoners of War* (New York: Basic Books, 1997).

[8] Office of the Provost Marshal General *Historical Monograph*, Prisoner of War Operations Division, Office of the Provost Marshal General: with appendices and supplement, 1945-1946, p. 51-55. *National Archives II, Modern Military Branch* (NAII,

MMB-hereafter); and George Lewis and John Mewha "History of Prisoner of War Utilization by the United States Army, 1776-1945 (Washington, D.C.: Center of Military History, United States Army, Washington, D.C.): 86.

Chapter 2

[1] Tarleton Collier, "Mute Germans Give Prison Camp Air of Unreality," Louisville *Courier-Journal* (9 July 1943): S2, 1.
[2] Ibid.
[3] It must be noted again that Fort Knox first held Italian POWs and did not begin holding Germans until mid-1944.
[4] Specific accounts of the crossing, screening, and initial treatment were gained from personal interviews conducted by Antonio Thompon with former POWs Howard Tromp (2005 and 2006), Paul Mengelberg (2005), Heino Erichsen (2005) and Horst Blumenberg (2007). Other good personal accounts come from Reihhold Pabel's *Enemes Are Human*; Walter A, Schmid, *German POW in New Mexico*, Trans. Richard Rundell, Ed. Wolfgang T. Schlauch. (Albuquerque: University of New Mexico Press, 2005); Hörner, Helmut. *A German Odyssey: The Journal of a German Prisoner of War*. Trans. and ed. by Allan Kent Powell. Colorado: Fulcrum Publishing, 1991.); Heino R. Erichsen *The Reluctant Warrior: Former German POW Finds Peace in Texas*. (Austin, TX: Eakin Press, 2001); and Yvonne E. Humphrey "On Shipboard With German Prisoners," *Journal of Nursing* Vol. 43, No. 9 (September 1943): 821-22.
[5] Erichsen, 67.
[6] "Fate Brings Former POW Back to Post," Article in archives at Don F. Pratt Museum dated Nov. 22, 1968.
[7] Office of the Provost Marshal General *Historical Monograph*, Prisoner of War Operations Division, Office of the Provost Marshal General: with appendices and supplement, 1945-1946. *National Archives II, Modern Military Branch* (NAII, MMB-hereafter). Additional information on the organization of the camp officers can be found in numerous other primary and secondary sources, many cited in this chapter, for a good additional source see John D Millet,. "The Organization and Role of the Army Service Forces," *United States Army in World War II* (Washington, D.C.: Office of the Chief of Military History, Department of the Army, 1954): 494 p.

[8] "Construction of Prisoner of War Camps," Colonel W.A. Wood, Jr., Director Requirement Division and Colonel Albert Pierson, G.S.C., Chief Construction Brigade, Requirements Division (23 September 1942): 1. NAII, MMB, RG 389, Box 1420, Folder Campbell Kentucky: Construction.

[9] "Prisoner of War and Alien Camps," Captain D.M. McLeod, Assistant Director, In. Scty. Div. (22 January 1943): 1. NAII, MMB, RG 389, Entry 457, Box 1420, Folder Breckinridge, Kentucky: Construction.

[10] Office of the Provost Marshal General *Historical Monograph*, Prisoner of War Operations Division, Office of the Provost Marshal General: with appendices and supplement, 1945-1946. NAII, MMB.

[11] "Memo," Colonel B.M. Bryan, Director, Aliens Division (26 November 1942): 1. Ibid.

[12] "Construction of 3,000 Man Internment Camp," Major S.T.B. Johnson, Corps of Engineers, Executive Assistant (12 October 1942): 1. Ibid.

[13] "Memo to Chief of the War Department," Colonel B.M. Bryan, Chief Aliens Division (28 October 1943): 1. Ibid.

[14] "Entry for the Diary," (24 October 1942): 1. Ibid.

[15] Ibid.

[16] Ibid.

[17] "Layout Plan for 3-1000 Man Internment Camps," Lt. Colonel Earl H. Marsden, Corps of Engineers, Assistant; Operations Branch Construction Division (1 December 1942): 1. NAII, MMB, RG 389, Box 1420, Folder: Campbell, Kentucky-Construction.; and "Layout Plan for 3-1000 Man Internment Camps," Colonel R.G. West, Corps of Engineers, Executive Officer (7 December 1942): 1. Ibid; and "Layout Plan for 3-1000 Man Internment Camps," Major M.S. Webb, Corps of Engineers, Area Engineer (17 December 1942): 1. Ibid.

[18] This number has some variance, secondary sources and Lewis and Mewha list it as 150,000 (86-87) as does Krammer (50), but the PMGO records at the National Archives list in several places, including the Historical Monograph, that the number is 175,000. See both Office of the Provost Marshal General *Historical Monograph*, Prisoner of War Operations Division, Office of the Provost Marshal General: with appendices and supplement, 1945-1946. NAII, MMB; and George Lewis and John Mewha "History of Prisoner of War Utilization by the United States Army, 1776-

1945 (Washington, D.C.: Center of Military History, United States
Army, Washington, D.C.).

[18] Lewis and Mewha, 83-84.

[19] Only one camp, Crossville, TN, held Italians and only one,
Camp McCoy, Wisconsin, held Japanese at this time.
"Breckinridge Helps Hold 36,688 War Prisoners," Louisville
Courier-Journal (5 June 1943): S1, 2.

[20] "Campbell Has No Axis Men," Kentucky *New Era* (22 July
1943): 1.

[21] "Diary," (4 December 1942): 1. NAII, MMB, RG 389, Box
1420, Folder: Campbell, Kentucky-Construction.

[22] "500 Nazi Prisoners Now At Local Camp," Kentucky *New Era*
(24 July 1943): 1, 6; and "First Prisoners of War Arrive At Camp
Campbell," Clarksville *Leaf-Chronicle* (24 July 1943): 1.

[23] Hugh Morris, "Germans From Africa Kept At Breckinridge,"
Louisville *Courier-Journal* (13 June 1943): S1, 1.

[24] Tarleton Collier, "Mute Germans Give Prison Camp Air of
Unreality," Louisville *Courier Journal* (9 July 1943): S2, 1.

[25] "Operation of An Eight Compound Enclosure," 19, NAII,
MMB, RG 389, Entry 439A, Box 29, Folder-POW Enclosure-
Operation of An Eight Compound Prisoner of War Enclosure.

[26] "Prisoner of War Circular No. 1 (Wahington, D.C., *War
Department*, 24 September 1943): 5-6, 18-19; NAII, MMB, RG
389, Entry 439A--Historical File, 1941-1958, Box 41-Regulations
Governing Prisoners of War.

[27] Jonathan F. Vance "Men in Manacles: The Shackling of
Prisoners of War, 1942-1943," *The Journal of Military History*,
Vol. 59, No. 3 (July 1995): 483-505.

[28] "Prisoner of War Circular No. 1," 18-19.

[29] Robb Inez, "Kentucky Camp Is Entertaining Nazi Guests,"
Louisville *Courier-Journal* (20 June 1943): Roto Magazine, 9.

[30] Ibid.

[31] Ibid.

[32] "Operation of An Eight Compound Enclosure,": 8-9, NAII,
MMB, RG 389, Entry 439A, Box 29, Folder-POW Enclosure-
Operation of An Eight Compound Prisoner of War Enclosure.

[33] Ibid., 12.

[34]"Prisoner of War Circular No. 1," 22.

[35] Ibid., 26.

[36] "Prisoner of War Circular No. 1," 44-46.

[37] "Nazi Prisoners Scooped Up By Hundreds," Clarksville *Leaf-
Chronicle* (17 August 1944): 7; and "300,382 War Captives Held

in America," Louisville *Courier-Journal* (5 October 1944): S1, 8; and "Army to Keep 600,000 German War Prisoners," Clarksville *Leaf-Chronicle* (9 June 1945): 1.

[38] "31 MP's Return to Camp With Prisoners of War," Clarksville *Leaf-Chronicle* (17 December 1943): 5.

[39] "Persuading Nazi Prisoners," *Cadiz Record* (8 February 1945): 5.

[40] Ibid.

[41] "Wounded Nazi Prisoners Get Expert Cure," Clarksville *Leaf-Chronicle* (31 January 1944): 1.

[42] "Surrendering Nazis Prepare for Easy Life in US Camps," Kentucky *New Era* (9 May 1945): 1.

[43] "Enemy Likes Our Brand," Union County *Advocate* (3 August 1944): 6.

[44] "What's In A Name?" Union County *Advocate* (18 January 1945): 6.

[45] "War-Prisoner Camp Opened At Fort Knox," Louisville *Courier-Journal* (16 February 1944): S2, 1.

[46] Poucher Coleman, "How Nazis Live at Knox," Louisville *Courier-Journal* (13 August 1944): Roto-Magazine, 8.

[47] Ibid.

[48] F.G. Alletson Cook, "Nazi Prisoners Are Nazis Still," *New York Times Magazine* (21 November 1943): 12, 38.

[49] Ibid., 38.

[50] Tracy Strong, "Prisoners Under the Law," *Christian Century* (April 14, 1943): 455.

[51] James H Powers, "What to Do With German Prisoners: The American Muddle," *The Atlantic Monthly* Vol. 174, No. 5 (November 1944): 46-50.

[52] "Use for German Prisoners Suggested," *New York Times* (28 December 1944): C7, 18.

[53] "No German Blood Wanted," *New York Times* (2 January 1945): C7, 18.

[54] "Prisoners of War Present Pressing and Delicate Problems," Clarksville *Leaf-Chronicle* (29 January 1946): 2.

Chapter 3

[1] Hugh Morris, "Germans From Africa Kept At Breckinridge," Louisville *Courier-Journal* (13 June 1943): S3, 1. Morris was among the first reporters allowed to visit a POW camp in the U.S.

and he printed the first picture of POWs from Breckinridge to accompany his article.

[2] Ed Radford, interview by Antonio Thompson, May 11, 2000.

[3] Walter Mathis, interview by Antonio Thompson, Summer 2005.

[4] Walter Mathis, interview by Antonio Thompson, Summer 2005, and Junior Mathis, interview by Antonio Thompson, Fall 2005.

[5] Patricia Ellis, interview by Antonio Thompson, Summer 2005.

[6] Hugh Morris, "Germans From Africa Kept At Breckinridge," Louisville *Courier-Journal* (13 June 1943): S3, 16.

[7] Robb Inez, "Kentucky Camp Is Entertaining Nazi Guests," Louisville *Courier-Journal* (20 June 1943): Roto Magazine, 8.

[8] Ibid.

[9] Tarleton Collier, "Prisoners Make Camp Look Lived-In," Louisville *Courier-Journal* (14 July 1943): S1, 2.

[10] Ibid.

[11] Inez, 9.

[12] Collier, S1, 2.

[13] Inez, 9.

[14] Collier, 2.   Although Inez said the farm was actually 50 acres, Robb Inez, "Kentucky Camp Entertaining Nazi Guests," Louisville *Courier-Journal* (20 June 1943): Roto-Magazine, 8.

[15] "War Prisoners Will Cultivate 240-Acre Crop," Union County *Advocate* (18 May 1944): 3.

[16] Union County *Advocate*, 3 May 1945: 8.

[17] Morris, S3, 1.

[18] "Prisoner of War Camps, By Location and Principle Types of Work As of December 1, 1944," Headquarters Army Service Forces, Office of the Provost Marshal General, Prisoner of War Operations Division, NAII, MMB, RG 389.

[19] Poucher Coleman, "How Nazis Live at Knox," Louisville *Courier-Journal* (13 August 1944): Roto-Magazine, 8.

[20] "War Prisoners to Work Farms," Kentucky *New Era* (July 30, 1943): 1; "Local Farmers May Contract For Prison Labor," (30 July 1943): 1.

[21] "Prisoners Can Be Worked 25 Miles From Camp," Clarksville *Leaf-Chronicle*, (10 August 1943): 3, and "Farmers Given Regulations On Working Prisoners of War Here," Kentucky *New Era* (16 August 1945): 1, 8

[22] "Prisoners Soon To Be Available For Farm Work," Clarksville *Leaf-Chronicle* (12 August 1943): 3.

23 "Farmers Given Regulations On Working Prisoners of War Here," Kentucky *New Era* (16 August 1945): 1, 8.   The nine

farmers were named in the article: J.W. Sholar, Lucian Dade, Kendrick Van Cleave, John Thurmond, J.C. Sandford, M.O. Kimmerling, W.D. Duncan III, Ben Adams, and G.H. Giles. According to a follow up article the first men to actually employ the men were: Charles Garnett, M.O. Kimerling,James Garnett, Ben S. Adams, and A.B. Hull.

[24] "50 German Prisoners of War Sucker and Cut Tobacco Here," Kentucky *New Era* (19 August 1943): 1.

[25] John Edwin McClure, interviewed by Sheila Brown Heflin, 12-17-85, Kentucky Historical Center Oral History Collection.

[26] "Prisoners May Do More Work," Kentucky *New Era* (25 September 1943): 1.

[27] "German Prisoner Work Explained To Kiwanis," Clarksville *Leaf-Chronicle* (20 October 1943): 1.

[28] Ibid.

[29] "Colonel Byrd is Bureau Speaker," Kentucky *New Era* (27 October 1943): 1.

[30] "Farm Bureau Praised For Plan Used In Prisoner of War Work," Kentucky *New Era* (1 November 1943): 1.

[31] My emphasis. "Farm Bureau Praised For Plan Used In Prisoner of War Work," Kentucky *New Era* (1 November 1943): 1.

[32] "Farmers Use Prisoners of War," *Cadiz Record* (8 June 1944): 2.

[33] "New Contract Made For Local PW Labor," Kentucky *New Era* (12 July 1944): 1.

[34] "Prisoner-Labor Rule Announced," Kentucky *New Era* (6 September 1944): 1.

[35] Ibid.

[36] "War Prisoners To Aid Farmers," Union County *Advocate* (27 April 1944): 1.

[37] "Farmers Urged To Ask For Prisoner Of War Help Now," Union County *Advocate* (5 October 1944): 1.

[38] Heino R. Erichsen, *The Reluctant Warrior: Former German POW Finds Peace in Texas* (Eakin Press: Austin, Texas, 2001): 68.

[39] Ibid, 71.

[40] Counties that closed schools included Jessamine and Madison.

[41] "War Prisoners May Help Harvest Kentucky Tobacco," Louisville *Courier-Journal* (16 September 1944): S1, 7.

[42] "Farmers Lack Housing For Prisoners of War," Louisville *Courier-Journal* (17 September 1944): S1, 12.

[43] "State Seeks to Locate Housing Sites For War Prisoners Aiding Farmers," Louisville *Courier-Journal* (18 September 1944): 9.

[44] "Nazi Prisoners Set to Harvest Burley Crop," Louisville *Courier-Journal* (19 September 1944): S2, 1.

[45] "250 German Prisoners Quartered At Eminence To Help In Farm Work," *Henry County Local* (22 September 1944).

[46] Ibid. The first farmers were named: R.R. Mason, Martin Baskett, P.G. Harrell, Clay Roberts, James Perry, John M. Foree, I.C. Smith, and G.L. Cureton.

[47] "Editor Up Early Wednesday To See Farmers Off With Prisoners," *Henry County Local* (22 September 1944).

[48] Ibid.

[49] Ibid.

[50] "Prisoners May Stay," *Henry County Local* (6 October 1944).

[51] These counties included: Fayette, Harrison, Bourbon, Scott, Madison, Clark, Garrard, Boyle, Mercer, and Jessamine, source Joe Reister "560 Nazi Prisoners Helping Harvest Burley In 10 Counties Prove Slow, But Quite Willing," Louisville *Courier-Journal* (24 September 1944): S1, 16.

[52] "Nazi Prisoners Set to Harvest Burley Crop," Louisville *Courier-Journal* (19 September 1944): S2, 1.

[53] Joe Reister "560 Nazi Prisoners Helping Harvest Burley In 10 Counties Prove Slow, But Quite Willing," Louisville *Courier-Journal* (24 September 1944): S1, 16

[54] Ibid.

[55] Ibid.

[56] Ibid.

[57] "Urges Use of War Prisoners," Union County *Advocate* (21 December 1944): 1.

[58] Ibid.

[59] Christine Denham, "Conference Held on May 5, 1944, Relative to Prisoners of War for Food Processing in Region V and VI," (6 May 1944). NAII, MMB, RG 211, Entry 175, Box 1, Folder Region V.

[60] Ibid.

[61] "German and U.S. Soldiers Help Can Indiana Tomatoes," Louisville *Courier-Journal* (26 September 1943): Roto-Magazine: 5.

[62] "German Prisoners May Build Plant," Sunday *Herald-Leader* (7 January 1945): 2; and "Nazi Prisoners May Help Build Powder Plant," Louisville *Courier-Journal* (7 January 1945): S1, 14.

[63] "1,000 Prisoners Assigned To Rocket Powder Jobs," Louisville *Courier-Journal* (23 May 1945): S1, 4.

[64] Richard Renneisen "Nazis Workd at Jeffersonville Depot," Louisville *Courier-Jou*rnal (25 February 1945): S1, 1.

[65] Ibid.

[66] Poucher Coleman "Nazi Prisoners Work and Seem to Like it," Louisville *Courier-Journal* (1 April1945): Roto-Magazine, 8.

[67] Ibid.

[68] "Farmers Hear Rules On Use of Prisoners At Farm Bureau Meet," Kentucky *New Era* (2 April 1945): 1.

[69] "320 Prisoners Allotted Section," Kentucky *New Era* (8 June 1945): 1.

[70] "Kentucky Gets 3,100 Prisoners For Work," Kentucky *New Era* (20 July 1945): 1.

[71] Ibid. It also says that the 5th Service Command, Kentucky, West Virginia, and Ohio had a total of 7,600 allotted for work.

[72] "Prisoners May Help Harvest Leaf," Louisville *Courier-Journal* (29 July 1945): S3, 6.

[73] "Prisoners Available," *Henry County Local* (15 June 1945).

[74] "War Prisoner Camp Likely," *Henry County Local* (20 July 1945).

[75] "Prisoners Of War Aid To Farmers Here," *Henry County Local* (26 October 1945).

[76] "Prisoners To Begin Tobacco Work Today," Lexington *Herald* (13 August 1945): 1; and ""Prisoner Labor Procured," Sunday *Herald-Leader* (19 August 1945): 5.

[77] "P.O.W. Labor Camps Set Up At Lexington and Frankfort," Louisville *Courier-Journal* (12 August 1945): S4, 6; and "German Prisoners Will Harvest Burley," Sunday *Herald-Leader* (12 August 1945): 1.

[78] "More Help Needed In Woodford County," Lexington *Herald* (3 September 1945): 6.

[79] "60 Prisoners Allotted To Harrison County," Lexington *Herald* (3 September 1945): 6.

[80] "War Prisoners Help Scott County Farmers," Lexington *Herald* (24 September 1945): 3.

[81] "Paris Will Have War Captives Camp," Lexington *Herald* (13 August 1945): 5; "Prisoners Arrive Today at Paris," Lexington *Herald* (15 August 1945): 5.

[82] "Paris Will Have War Captives Camp," Lexington *Herald* (13 August 1945): 5.

[83] "War Captive Labor Available in Boyle," Lexington *Herald* (17 August 1945): 19.

[84] "Tented City Erected On Hustonville Road For German POWs," *Danville Advocate-Messenger"* (17 August 1945): 1. "POWs To Leave AS Leaf Harvest Ends," *Danville Advocate-Messenger* (7 September 1945), and Richard Brown *History of Danville and Boyle County* p. 122; "Captives Expected in Boyle Next Week," Lexington *Herald* (9 August 1945): 2.

[85] "25 Prisoners Work in Garrard County," Lexington *Herald* (3 September 1945): 6

[86] "Lexington Depot To Release 175 P.O.W.'s to Farms," Louisville *Courier-Journal* (23 August 1945): 2.; and "Avon Prisoners To Aid Farmers," Lexington *Herald* (23 August 1945): 1.

[87] Bill Columbia, interview by Antonio Thompson, 2005.

[88] Ibid.

[89] "440 Will Lose Jobs At Avon," Lexington *Herald* (18 September 1945): 1.

[90] "More German Prisoners To Assist In Harvest," Lexington *Herald* (29 August 1945): 8.

[91] "Harvesting Of Tobacco Crop Is Moving Swiftly," Lexington *Herald* (5 September 1945): 1.

[92] Myron Pool, interview by Antonio Thompson, May 2000

[93] Margaret Rudd, interview by Antonio Thompson, 2005.

[94] Monroe McGhee, interview by Antonio Thompson, 2006

[95] Smith Broadbent, Jr. as told to Joe Creason, "Sentimental Journey," 1. From Broadbent Family Collection.

[96] Ibid, 2.

[97] Ibid.

Chapter 4

[1] Thomas Jefferson in a Letter to Madison January 1787 on Shay's Rebellion.

[2] "Axis Prisoner Labor the Answer?," Kentucky *New Era* (15 July 1945): 4.

[3] Ibid.

[4] Ibid.

These sentiments can be found in most newspapers as editorials or articles and also appear in both the Records of the Provost Marshal General (RG389) and the Records of the War Manpower

Commission (RG211), both housed at the National Archives II. Modern Military Branch.

[6] Office of the Provost Marshal General *Historical Monograph*, Prisoner of War Operations Division, Office of the Provost Marshal General: with appendices and supplement, 1945-1946, p. 123, NAII, MMB, RG 389.

[7] Ibid.

[8] "Floors Consider Prison Labor," Kentucky *New Era* (4 December 1944): 1, 8.

[9] "200 War Captives May Aid Redryers," Lexington *Herald* (16 January 1945): 1-2, and "Possibility of Using Prison Labor in Redryers Considered," Lexington *Leader* (16 January 1945): 3.

[10] "200 War Captives May Aid Redryers," Lexington *Herald* (16 January 1945): 1-2

[11] "Leaf Sale Holiday Threatens; Prisoner Camp Site Protested," Lexington *Herald* (17 January 1945): 1; and "Residents of Lafayette Area Protest Camp," Lexington *Leader* (17 January 1945): 1. J. Lee Alloway was the man commenting.

[12] Ibid.

[13] Ibid.

[14] Ibid.

[15] "Leaf Sale Holiday Threatens; Prisoner Camp Site Protested," Lexington *Herald* (17 January 1945): 1.

[16] Ibid.

[17] "Situation Hopeless, Leaf Men Say, Unless War Captives Aid," Lexington *Herald* (18 January 1945): 1 and "Leaf Sale Holiday Threatens Prisoner Camp Site Protested," Lexington *Herald* (17 January 1945): 1.

[18] "Prisoner Labor May Be Okayed To Process Leaf," (18 June 1945): 1.

[19] "Situation Hopeless, Leaf Men Say, Unless War Captives Aid," Lexington *Herald* (18 January 1945): 1

[20] Ibid.

[21] "Plan to Use War Prisoners At Leaf Redryers Is Dropped," Louisville *Courier-Journal* (20 January 1945): S1, 5; and "Captive Labor Plan Abandoned," Lexington *Herald* (20 January 1945): 1.

[22] "Prisoner Use Protested," Louisville *Courier-Journal* (12 November 1944): S3, 10.

[23] "Not To Use PWs When Other Labor Is Available," The Union County *Advocate* (9 August 1945): 6; "Prisoner Use Protested," Louisville *Courier-Journal* (12 November 1944): S3, 10; and

"Farmers Urged To Apply Now For Any P.W. Labor In Fall,"
Union County *Advocate* (16 August 1945): 1.
[24] Myron Pool, interview by Antonio Thompson, May 2000.
[25] Ibid.
[26] "German War Prisoners' Strike At Campbell June 5-6
Revealed," Clarksville *Leaf-Chronicle* (1 December 1944): 1.
[27] Major General J.A. Ulio, The Adjutant General,
"Administrative and Disciplinary Measures," AG 383.6 (13 Oct
43) OB-S-A-M War Department, Washington, D.C., 27 October
1943. Historical Monograph," ., National Archives II, Modern
Military Branch; see also Major General J.A. Ulio, The Adjutant
General, "Prisoner of War Labor" AG 383.6 (23 Sep 43) War
Department, Washington, D.C. (16 November 1943): 1. Office of
the Provost Marshal General *Historical Monograph*, Prisoner of
War Operations Division, Office of the Provost Marshal General:
with appendices and supplement, 1945-1946, National Archives II,
Modern Military Branch; and Article 55 of the Geneva
Convention. Lewis and Mehwa suggest that this condition of
restricted diet could be continued without stop, at the discretion of
the Camp commander, until the POWs agreed to work as long as
medical inspections approved of the condition, see p. 151, "thus,
the PW could be given a full meal or a day's ration or more and
then placed again on the restricted diet, provided the conditions
which warranted its imposition continued to exist."
[28] "Congressional Report Reveals Camp Prisoner Of War Strike,"
Kentucky *New Era* (1 December 1944): 1; and "German War
Prisoners' Strike At Campbell June 5-6 Revealed," Clarksville
Leaf-Chronicle (1 December 1944): 1.
[29] "Congressional Report Reveals Camp Prisoner Of War Strike,"
Kentucky *New Era* (1 December 1944): 1;
[30] "Feeding Prisoners of War," *Cadiz Record* (1 July 1943): 1.
[31] Ibid.
[32] J. Earle Bell, "Changes At PW Camp," Union County *Advocate*
(3 May 1945): 1.
[33] Drew Pearson "Pearson Studies Prisoners' Food Question,"
Sunday *Herald-Leader* (4 February 1945): 10; and Drew Pearson
"The Washington Merry-Go-Round: U.S. Treatment of German
Prisoners," The *Cadiz Record* (22 February 1945): 2.
[34] Ibid.
[35] "The Feeding of Prisoners," Lexington *Herald* (16 February
1945): 2.
[36] Ibid.

[37] See, George J. Davis *The Hitler Diet: As Inflicted on American P.O.W.'s in World War II* (CA: Military Literary Guild, 1990) and Lewis H. Carlson, *We Were Each Other's Prisoners: An Oral History of World War II American and German Prisoners of War.* New York: Basic Books, 1997.

[38] Howard Tromp, interview by Antonio Thompson, May 2006 and August 2005.

[39] "War Prisoners' Diet Explained," Clarksville *Leaf-Chronicle* (23 June 1945): 1. "War Prisoners' Menu Changed," Clarksville *Leaf-Chronicle* (28 March 1945): 3.

[40] Special Collections Patton Museum Archives, Box 42, File 3, 91-142-01, German POWs at Fort Knox.

[41] Numerous sources indicate these reasons, file X in the PMGO records of the NA, editorials in the *New York Times* and other state and local papers, and POW personal accounts.

[42] Patricia Ellis, interview by Antonio Thompson, Summer 2005.

[43] Edgar Radford , interview by Antonio Thompson, May 2000.

[44] Special Collections Patton Museum Archives, Box 42, File 3, 91-142-01, German POWs at Fort Knox., "War Prisoner Rations Called Unsatisfactory," Clarksville *Leaf-Chronicle* (16 June 1945): 1; "Complains Prisoners Need More Food To Do Hard Work On Farm," Kentucky *New Era* (16 June 1945): 1; "Rations Unsatisfactory," Louisville *Courier-Journal* (16 June 1945)

[45] Ibid.

[46] "Complains Prisoners Need More Food To Do Hard Work On Farm," Kentucky *New Era* (16 June 1945): 1

[47] Ibid.

[48] "War Prisoners' Diet Explained," Clarksville *Leaf-Chronicle* (23 June 1945): 1.

[49] "Not Kentucky Breakfast," Louisville *Times* (21 June 1945).

[50] "Nazi Prisoner Menus Unchanged By Protest," *Courier-Journal* (21 June 1945): 1, 8

[51] "Germans Are Animals," Louisville *Times* (18 June 1945)

[52] "Menu for War Prisoners In Kentucky Stepped Up," Louisville *Courier-Journal* (29 June 1945): S1, 1.

[53] "Menu for War Prisoners In Kentucky Stepped Up," Louisville *Courier-Journal* (29 June 1945): S1, 1.

[54] "Warning Given As To Safety At Campbell," Kentucky *New Era* (2 November 1944): 8.

[55] "Camp Traffic Warning Given," Kentucky *New Era* (27 November 1944): 1.

[56] "Farmers Get Camp Warning," Kentucky *New Era* (30 July 1945): 1.

[57] Ibid.

[58] "Safe Work Practices For Prisoners of War (German)," *Army Service Forces Manual M805* (22 September 1944): 1-23.

[59] "Handbook for Work Supervisors of Prisoner of War Labor," *Army Service Forces Manual M811* (July 1945): 13.

[60] "Prisoners May Stay," *Henry County Local* (10 June 1944).

[61] "Man Killed, Germans Hurt By Lightening," Sunday *Herald-Leader* (2 September 1945): 1.

[62] Office of the Provost Marshal General *Historical Monograph*, Prisoner of War Operations Division, Office of the Provost Marshal General: with appendices and supplement, 1945-1946, p. 125-126, NAII, MMB, RG 389. Some POWs tried to sue the U.S. Government for larger benefits or life-long benefits to be effected even after repatriation, but War Department lawyers stated that the U.S. commitment to these men expired once they were repatriated and no longer in POW status.

[63] Ibid., 125, see also Article 27 of the Geneva Convention

[64] Kenneth S. Record *WWI and WWII Axis Burials in the Continental United States and Canada,* 1998, 1-8, CS403 R42X, Manuscripts, Kentucky Building, Western Kentucky University, Bowling Green, Kentucky.

[65] Ibid.

[66] Office of the Provost Marshal General *Historical Monograph*, Prisoner of War Operations Division, Office of the Provost Marshal General: with appendices and supplement, 1945-1946, p. 109, NAII, MMB, RG 389.

[67] "Prisoner of War Circular No. 1," NAII, MMB, see also Walter Rundell, Jr., "Paying the POW in World War II," *Military Affairs* Vol. 22, No. 3 (Autumn 1958): 122-124; and Antonio Thompson, "Men in German Uniform: German Prisoners of War Held in the United States During World War II,". Dissertation completed at the University of Kentucky, Spring 2006, 169.

[68] The Labor Committee to Major D.M. McLeod "Use of Prisoners-of-War in Agricultural Labor in Daviess and Adjoining Counties," (20 December 1943): 1. NAII, MMB, RG 211, Entry 175, Box 1, Folder Region V.

[69] The Labor Committee to Major D.M. McLeod "Use of Prisoners-of-War in Agricultural Labor in Daviess and Adjoining Counties," (20 December 1943): 1. Ibid.

[70] R. Murray Hagan to Major Paul e. Moore (5 January 1944): 1-2; Ibid.

[71] Ibid, 2.

[72] B.J. Killian, Manager, U.S. Employment Service "Need for War Prisoners and Prison Encampment" (21 January 1944): 1. Ibid.

[73] Ibid.

[74] Ibid, and "To Major D.M. McLeod (7 February 1944): 1. Ibid.

[75] R.L. Shaw, Acting Chief, Division of Placement, War Manpower Commission Region V "Need for War Prisoners and Prison Encampment at Owensboro, Kentucky." Ibid.

[76] R.L. Shaw to Robert Goodwin, "Need for War Prisoners and Prison Encampment at Owensboro, Kentucky," (19 February 1944): 1. Ibid.

[77] Robert C. Goodwin to Major McLeod (19 February 1944): 1. Ibid.

[78] "War Prisoner camp May Be Moved Shortly," Clarksville *Leaf-Chronicle* (5 June 1944): 1.

[79] Robert C. Goodwin, Regional Director "Allocation of Prisoners-of-War for Kentucky," (3 June 1944) NAII, MMB, RG 211, Entry 175, Folder-Region V; and Robert Goodwin, War Manpower Commission "Memo to Major D.M. McLeod," (3 June 1944). Ibid.

[80] Robert C. Goodwin, Regional Director "Allocation of Prisoners-of-War for Kentucky," (12 June 1944). Ibid.

[81] Robert C. Goodwin, Regional Director "Allocation of Prisoners-of-War for Kentucky," Ibid.

[82] "Plan to Move War Prisoner Labor North Is Hit," Louisville *Courier-Journal* (11 June 1944): S3, 8.

[83] "Rumor Spiked on POW Labor," Kentucky *New Era* (5 May 1945): 1.

[84] "No More German Prisoners to Come to U.S." (10 May 1945): 3

[85] "No Orders To Send PWs Home," Union County *Advocate* (9 August 1945): 1.

[86] "Boyle County Leaf Harvest Near End," Lexington *Herald* (10 September 1945): 3.

[87] "Fayette's Prisoner Labor To Be Reduced," Lexington *Herald* (7 September 1945): 1; and "227 War Prisoners To Leave Here Today," Sunday *Herald-Leader* (16 September 1945): 1.

[88] "Labor Situation In Bourbon Improved," Lexington *Herald* (10 September 1945): 3.

[89] "PW Camp Disbanded Near Owensboro," Union County *Advocate* (4 October 1945): 1.

[90] "War Prisoner Labor Halted in Montgomery," Clarksville *Leaf-Chronicle* (4 January 1946): 1.

Chapter 5

[1] Louis L. Snyder *Encyclopedia of the Third Reich* (New York: Marlowe & Company, 1976): 378,

[2] See "Brigadier-General Blackshear M. Bryan, Assistant PMGO, "Attention: Lieutenant Colonel William P. Gray," (17 May 1944): 1-2. NAII, MMB, RG 389, Entry 439A, Box 35, Folder Prisoners of War Letters and Directives; see also John Hammond Moore *The Faustball Tunnel: German POWs and Their Great Escape* (New York: Random House, 1978), "Escape in Arizona," *Time* (January 8, 1945): 16; and "Swastika Over Arizona," *Newsweek* (February 26, 1945): 58.

[3] Ibid.

[4] See all of the following for information on Kunze: Richard Whittingham, *Martial Justice: The Last Mass Execution in the United States* (Chicago: Henry Regnery Company, 1971).; Wilma Parnell and Robert Taber, *The Killing of Corporal Kunze* (New Jersey: Lyle Stuart Inc., 1981).; Leon Jaworski, *After Fifteen Years* and *Confession and Avoidance*. Vincent Green, *Extreme Justice* (New York: Pocket Books, 1995).
The five men accused and put to death included Walter Beyer, Berthold Seidel, Hans Demme, Willi Scholz, and Hans Schomer, see also "Death and Treason," *Time* (February 5, 1945): 47-48; and "Seven by the Rope," *Newsweek* (July 23, 1945): 27; and Antonio Thompson "Men In German Uniform: German POWs from World War II held in the United States," Dissertation, University of Kentucky, May 2006.

[5] See Michael R. Waters, *Lone Star Stalag: German Prisoners of War at Camp Hearne* (Texas: Texas A&M University Press, 2004).

[6] Heino R. Erichsen *The Reluctant Warrior: Former German POW Finds Peace in Texas* (Austin, TX: Eakin Press, 2001): 64.

[7] Historian David Fiedler put the number of murders at 300, see David Fiedler, *The Enemy Among Us: POWs in Missouri During World War II* (Saint Louis: Missouri Historical Society Press, 2003): 43.

[8] Brigadier General B.M. Bryan, Asst Prov Marshal General "Segregation of German Prisoners of War, Memo for G-2:" 2. NAII, MMB, RG389, Entry , Box 1428, Folder-Camp Campbell, Kentucky-Misc.

[9] Howard Tromp, interview by Antonio Thompson, May 2006 and August 2005.

[10] Erichsen, 69.

[11] Major John L. Warrick, "Transfer of German Prisoners of War," (20 November 1944): 1. NAII, MMB, RG 389, Box 2481, Folder-Knox, Fort, Kentucky.

[12] Ibid.

[13] Colonel C.D. Parmelee, Director of Security and Intelligence, "to the Provost Marshal," (23 November 1944): 1. Ibid.

[14] Captain Clair Scott, "Prisoner of War Mail," (19 January 1944): 1. NAII, MMB, RG 389, Box 2476, Folder.-Breckinridge, Camp, Kentucky.

[15] Frank Reisinger, et. al., "P.O.W. Co. # 1," (17 January 1943): 4. Ibid.

[16] Captain Clair Scott, Adjutant to Lt. Col. Chester, "Political Groups," (18 June 1943): 1-2. Ibid.

[17] The Anti-Nazis at Breckinridge, "The History of POW Camp, Breckinridge." NAII, MMB, RG389, Entry 459A, Box 1608, Folder-253.9/General.

[18] The Anti-Nazis at Breckinridge, "The History of POW Camp Breckinridge." NAII, MMB, RG389, Entry 459A, Box 1608, Folder-253.9/General.

[19] The Anti-Nazis at Breckinridge, "The History of POW Camp Breckinridge." Ibid.

[20] Ibid., 56.

[21] Ibid.

[22] J.A. Ulio, Major General, the Adjutant General, "Segregation of Prisoners of War," (February 18, 1943): 1. NAII, MMB, RG389, Box 1428, Folder-Camp Campbell, Kentucky-Misc; and Brigadier General B.M. Bryan, Asst Prov Marshal General. Ibid.

[23] Ibid.

[24] Captain Elbert E. Foster, Director, S+I Division, "Political Activities of Prisoners of War, Including Future Plans re Underground Organization upon Return to Germany, PW Camp, Camp Forrest, Tennessee.": 1. RG 389, Entry 459A, Box 1614-Camp Cambridge to Camp Clinton, Folder-255 (Camp Forrest) Gen., National Archives II, Modern Military Branch; and Edward F. Witsell, Brigadier General, Acting the Adjutant General,

"Screening of German Prisoners of War of Polish, French, Czechoslovakian, Belgian, and Luxembourg Origin," 383. 6, 28 November 1944; RG 389, Entry 439A, Box 35, Folder-Prisoners of War, Letters and Directives, National Archives II, Modern Military Branch.
[25] Colonel R.C. Jacobs, Jr., Executive Officer, G-2 "To Commanding General, Army Service Forces, War Department,"(2 March 1944): 1-2. NAII, MMB, RG389, Entry , Box 1428, Folder-Camp Campbell, Kentucky-Misc
[26] Friedrich W. Schiltz, VW Compound, "Letter to Major Mims, Executive Officer, P.W. Camp, Camp Campbell, Kentucky." (10-29-44): 2. NAII, MMB, RG389, Entry 459A , Box 1611, Folder-255 Camp Campbell-General.
[27] Ibid.
[28] Ibid.
[29] For some general accounts see Lewis H. Carlson *We Were Each Other's Prisoners: An Oral History of World War II American and German Prisoners of War* (New York: Basic Books, 1997).
[30] Camp McCain, Mississippi was also an anti-Nazi camp for some time but ceased functioning in that capacity after authorities and inmates realized the German government may have known its purpose, similar sources point to Camp Ruston having a like history. See also Haase, Norbert "Anti-Prisoners of War in American Prison Camps: The Example of Fort Devans, Massachusetts, *Traces*, www.traces. org. accessed on June 12, 2007.
[31] Various documents cite this or refer to this in this group: NAII, MMB, RG389, Entry 459A , Box 1611, Folder-255 Camp Campbell-General.NA Folder 255 Campbell.
[32] Lt. Colonel Earl Edwards, Assistant Director, Prisoner of War Division "Anti-Nazi German Prisoners of War," (22 April 1944): NAII, MMB, RG 389, Entry 439A, Box 35, Folder Prisoners of War Letters and Directives
[33] Lt. Colonel Carl B. Byrd "Segregation of Anti-Nazis Prisoners of War," (20 March 1944): 1, NAII, MMB, RG389, Entry , Box 1428, Folder-Camp Campbell, Kentucky-Misc.
[34] Major D.M. McLeod, "The Segregation of Anti-Nazi Prisoners of War, for the Provost Marshal General," (20 March 1944): 1. Ibid.

[35] Captain Clair Scott, "Transfer of Anti-Nazi Prisoners of War," (1 May 1944): 1. NAII, MMB, RG 389, Box 2476, Folder.-Breckinridge, Camp, Kentucky.

[36] Rudolf Tirk "Letter to the Free Austrian Movement: New York," (12 October 1943): 1. NAII, MMB, RG389, Entry 459A , Box 1621, Folder-255 Cp Ruston, General.

[37] Ibid.

[38] First Lt. Walter Schoenstedt, Special Program Section, Special Projects Branch, "Memorandum for Chief, Special Projects Branch," (14 November 1944): 1. NAII, MMB, RG389, Entry 459A , Box 1611, Folder-255 Camp Campbell-General.

[39] Friedrich W. Schiltz, VW Compound, "Letter to Major Mims, Executive Officer, P.W. Camp, Camp Campbell, Kentucky." (10-29-44): 2. Ibid.

[40] Carl B. Byrd, "Transfer of Prisoners of War," (31 March 1944): 1. Ibid.

[41] Rudolf Schwanse, "Application for Enlistment in the Czech Legion," (5 May 1944): 1. RG 389, B 2477, Camps-Campbell to Crook, Folder-Campbell, Camp.

[42] Josef Obermayer, letter to Czechoslovakian Embassy, Washington (3 June 1944): 1. Ibid.

[43] Viktor Schroeffer, letter to the War Department, (15 September 1944): 1. Ibid.

[44] Robert Durant, Ewald Luthin, Augustin Remy, Antoine Schneider, and Jean Seiler, letter to the Free French Committee, (% June 1944): 1. Ibid.

[45] Paul Hollerbach, Fritz Stroiwas, and Karl Hease, letter to the Free French Committee, Washington, D.C., (5 November 1944): 1, ibid.

[46] Undersigned, "To the Representative of the Free French Committee," 1. Ibid.

[47] Wolfgang Mursa, Sgt. "Statement," (17 May 1944): 1. Ibid.

[48] Private Eduard Pannek, "Application," Camp Campbell (25 April 1944): 1. NAII, MMB, RG389, Entry 459A, Box 1608, Folder-253.9/General.

[49] PMGO "Petition of German POW Georg Rupprecht, Sgt.," (10 October 1944): 1. Ibid.

[50] First Lt. Walter Schoenstedt, Special Program Section, Special Projects Branch, "Memorandum for Chief, Special Projects Branch," (14 November 1944): 1. NAII, MMB, RG389, Entry 459A , Box 1611, Folder-255 Camp Campbell-General.

[51] Ibid.

[52] Ibid.

[53] Ibid., 1-2.

[54] Ibid., 2.

[55] Ibid.

[56] The German "Anti-Nazis" "To the German American" (September 1944): 1. "Memorandum for Chief, Special Projects Branch," (14 November 1944): 2. NAII, MMB, RG389, Entry 459A , Box 1611, Folder-255 Camp Campbell-General.

[57] Ibid.

[58] Ibid.

[59] Friedrich W. Schiltz, VW Compound, "Letter to Major Mims, Executive Officer, P.W. Camp, Camp Campbell, Kentucky." (10-29-44): 2. Ibid.

[60] These camps were Fort Philip Kearney, Forty Getty, and Fort Wetherhill, Rhode Island, and Fort Eustis, Virginia.

[61] First Lt. Walter Schoenstedt, Special Program Section, Special Projects Branch, "Memorandum for Chief, Special Projects Branch," (14 November 1944): 2. NAII, MMB, RG389, Entry 459A , Box 1611, Folder-255 Camp Campbell-General

[62] Ibid.

[63] Major D.M. McLeod and Lt. Col. Carl B. Byrd, "Transfer of Prisoners of War Within Camps," (3 June 1944): 1-2. NAII, MMB, RG 389, Box 2477-Camps-Campbell to Crook, Folder-Campbell, Camp.

[64] "Transfer of Pro-Nazi Prisoners of War," (8 June 1944): 1. NAII, MMB, RG 389, Box 2477-Camps-Campbell to Crook, Folder-Campbell, Camp.

[65] "Evaluation of PW Alois Antes, Sgt.," (28 April 1944): 1. NAII, MMB, RG389, Entry 459A, Box 1608, Folder-253.9/General.

[66] Ibid.

[67] Carl B. Byrd, "Transfer of Prisoner of War,"(8 May 1944): 1. NAII, MMB, RG 389, Box 2477-Camps-Campbell to Crook, Folder-Campbell, Camp.

[68] "Disposition of Pro-Nazi German Prisoners of War," (10 June 1944): 1. Ibid.

[69] Statement of POW Hans Stephan, Pfc. (9 May 1944): 1. Ibid.

[70] "Report on POW Stephan, Hans, Pfc., 6WG-1895, POW Co. No. 10," (6 May 1944): 1-2. Ibid.

[71] Lt. Colonel Carl B. Byrd, "Request for Disposition of Prisoner f War," (18 October 1944): 1-2. Ibid.

[72] "Report on POW Schmitz, Wilhelm, Cpl., 6WG-1091, POW Co. No. 10," (8 May 1944): 1. Ibid.

[73] Wilhelm Schmitz, "Request," (9 May 1944): 1. Ibid.

[74] "Report on POW Schmitz, Wilhelm, Cpl., 6WG-1091, POW Co. No. 10," (8 May 1944): 1. Ibid.

[75] "Report on POW Schmitz, Wilhelm, Cpl., 6WG-1091, POW Co. No. 10," (8 May 1944): 1. Ibid.

[76] Wilhelm Schmitz, "to the American Headquarters of the P.W. Camp Alva, Oklahoma," (19 July 1944): 1. Ibid.

[77] Carl B. Byrd, "Pro-Nazi Prisoners of War," (6 April 1944): 1. Ibid.

[78] Ibid.

[79] Ibid.

[80] Earl L. Edwards, Lt. Colonel, C.M.P, "Memorandum for the Assistant Chief of Staff, G-2 and For The Provost Marshal General," (11 May 1944): 1. Ibid.

[81] Erwin Ebeling, letter to the War Department (1944): 1. Ibid.

[82] See Chapter 6 for their escape.

[83] Major D.M. McLeod, Memo to the Provost Marshal General, (6 October 1944): 1. Ibid.

[84] "Petition of 29 German Prisoners of War of POW-Camp Campbell (DD) to be transferred to a regular POW-Camp," (18 November 1944): 1. Ibid.

[85] First Lt. Walter Schoenstedt, Special Program Section, Special Projects Branch, "Memorandum for Chief, Special Projects Branch," (14 November 1944): 8. NAII, MMB, RG389, Entry 459A , Box 1611, Folder-255 Camp Campbell-General.

[86] Ibid., 7-8.

Chapter 6

[1] Reinhold Pabel, "It's Easy to Bluff Americans," *Collier's* (16 May 1953): 20-21.

[2] Robb Inez, "Kentucky Camp Is Entertaining Nazi Guests," Louisville *Courier-Journal* (20 June 1943): Roto 8.

[3] "Prisoner of War Circular No. 1 (Wahington, D.C., *War Department*, 24 September 1943): 9, 18-19; NAII, MMB, RG 389, Entry 439A--Historical File, 1941-1958, Box 41-Regulations Governing Prisoners of War.

[4] Office of the Provost Marshal General *Historical Monograph*, Prisoner of War Operations Division, Office of the Provost

Marshal General: with appendices and supplement, 1945-1946, p. 42-46. *National Archives II, Modern Military Branch.*

[5] "Operation of An Eight Compound Enclosure," 50-53; NAII, MMB, RG 389, Entry 439A, Box 29, Folder-POW Enclosure-Operation of An Eight Compound Prisoner of War Enclosure.

[6] For specific and general examples of the methods of prisoner escape see any of these references, more examples are found in specific folders from the National Archives and newspaper articles individually referenced in the remainder of this chapter. See, John Hammond Moore. *The Faustball Tunnel: German POWs and Their Great Escape* (New York: Random House, 1978); Ulrich Steinhilper and Peter Osborne. *Ten Minutes to Buffalo: The Story of Germany'sGreat Escaper* (Great Britain: Independent Books, 1991); Martin F. Auger "The HARIKARI Club: German Prisoners of War and the Mass Escape Scare of 1944-45 at Internment Camp Grande Ligne, Quebec," *Canadian Military History* Vol. 13, No. 3 (Summer 2004): 49-67; William E. Kirwan "Escape Tactics of German War Prisoners," *Journal of Criminal Law and Criminology* Vol. 35, no. 5 (Jan.-Feb. 1946): 357-366; Robert R. Wilson "Escaped Prisoners of War in Neutral Jurisdiction," *The American Journal of International Law*, Vol. 35, No. 3 (July 1941): 519-523; 'Escape in Arizona," *Time* (January 8, 1945): 16; and "The Kriegsmarine Escape," *Newsweek* (January 8, 1945): 33-34.

[7] See Charlotte Carr-Gregg *Japanese Prisoners of War in Revolt: The Outbreaks at Featherstone and Cowra* During World War II (Palgrave Macmillian, 1978); Harry Gordon *Voyage of Shame: The Cowra Breakout and Afterwards* (Speciallized Book Services, 1994); and Teruhiko Asada *The Night of A Thousand Suicides: The Japanese Outbreak at Cowra* (St. Martin's Press, 1972). Surprisingly the leaders of the breakout commanded their escapees not to attack Australian civilians, and none were killed or injured.

[8] Ibid.

[9] The women were Tsuruko "Toots" Wallace, Florence "Flo" Shivze Otani, and Billie Shitara Tanigoshi.

[10] "Jap Girls Face Treason Charge," Kentucky *New Era* (8 August 1944): 8; and "Three Japanese Sisters Convicted For Conspiracy," Clarksville *Leaf-Chronicle* (11 August 1944): 1.

[11] "Recaptured Nazi Prisoners And Girls Who Aided Them," Kentucky *New Era* (24 July 1944): 1.

[12] "8 Soldiers, 5 WACS, Involved In Escape," *New York Times* (10 May 1944): C3, 10.

[13] See Office of the Provost Marshal General *Historical Monograph*, Prisoner of War Operations Division, Office of the Provost Marshal General: with appendices and supplement, 1945-1946,. *National Archives II, Modern Military Branch*; and "Operation of An Eight Compound Enclosure," NAII, MMB, RG 389, Entry 439A, Box 29, Folder-POW Enclosure-Operation of An Eight Compound Prisoner of War. Some sources say two, others three. Some say the guard had to fire a warning shot, others say this was more of a courtesy.

[14] "Prisoner of War Circular No. 1 (Wahington, D.C., *War Department*, 24 September 1943): 44-45, National Archives, RG 389, Entry 439A- Historical File, 1941-1958, Box 41-Regulations Governing Prisoners of War.

[15] These men arrived in two groups of four, the first on June 13 and the second on June 17, 1942.

[16] FBI History. "George Dasch and the Nazi Saboteurs," *Federal Bureau of Investigations, Famous Cases*. www.fbi.gov. 1-6 p; and Robert E. Cushman "The Case of the Nazi Saboteurs," *The American Political Science Review* Vol. 36, No. 6 (Dec. 1942): 1082-1091, see also Dobbs *Saboteurs*.

[17] J. Edgar Hoover, "Alien Enemy Control," *Iowa Law Review* Vol. 29 (March 1944): 396.

[18] Ibid.

[19] J. Edgar Hoover, "Enemies at Large," *The American Magazine* (April 1944): 97.

[20] "Fort Knox Soldier Who Killed 2 Nazis Acquitted of Murder," *Louisville Courier-Journal* (19 November 1944): 21, and "Kills 2 War Prisoners," *New York Times* (6 November 1944): 21.

[21] The men were POWs Hand Ricahard Jonat (27) and Karl Luft (19) and internee Paul Theodore Hitzegard (38); in reality, however all three were alien interness,

[22] "Nazi Prisoners Make Escape," Park City *Daily News* (5 November 1942): 1.

[23] "Aliens Escaped Train Here On Wednesday," Park City *Daily News* (6 November 1942): 1.

[24] Ibid.

[25] Ibid., 1-2.

[26] "Aliens Escaped Train Here On Wednesday," Park City *Daily News* (6 November 1942): 1-2.

[27] "German Aliens Taken Back to Camp," Park City *Daily News* (8 November 1942): 1, 5.

[28] "German Prisoners Dig Escape Tunnel," Kentucky *New Era* (8 November 1943): 1.

[29] "German War Prisoner Flees Camp Campbell," Clarksville *Leaf-Chronicle* (2 February 1945): 1; "German Prisoner Makes Escape Today," Kentucky *New Era* (2 February 1945): 1; "German Prisoner Surrenders At Pembroke," (3 February 1945): 1; "German Prisoner of War Gives Himself Up," Kentucky *New Era* (3 February 1945): 1; and "Escaped Nazi Prisoner is Captured" Park City *Daily News* (4 February 1945): 11

[30] "Two Prisoners Flee Stockade," Kentucky *New Era* (26 February 1945): 1; and "Two Camp Campbell Soldiers Capture Nazi Prisoner of War," Kentucky *New Era* (8 February 1944): 1; and "Soldiers on Leave Capture Escaped Nazi at Sturgis," *Cadiz Record* (10 February 1944): 1.

[31] "Prisoners Found Hidden Under Hay," Kentucky *New Era* (28 February 1945): 1; and "German Prisoners Retaken In Barn," Louisville *Courier-Journal* (1 March 1945): S1, 12.

[32] "Nazi Prisoner Captured Here," Kentucky *New Era* (13 July 1944): 1.

[33] "Escaped Nazi Prisoner Returns to Campbell," Louisville *Courier-Journal* (7 July 1945): S1, 9.

[34] "English-Speaking Nazi Captive Escapes Camp Breckinridge," Louisville *Courier-Journal* (19 January 1944): S1, 5; and "Bus Driver Captures Escaped German," Louisville *Courier-Journal* (20 January 1944): S1, 11.

[35] "German Prisoner At Breckinridge Escapes," *Cadiz Record* (13 April 1944): 3.

[36] "Nazi Prisoner's Romance Wrecked," Union County *Advocate* (10 January 1946): 1.

[37] "Public Warned To Watch Out For Escaped Nazi War Prisoners," Kentucky *New Era* (20 August 1945): 1.

[38] "'Fanatical Nazi' Flees Stockade At Campbell," Louisville *Courier-Journal* (19 September 1944): S1, 3.

[39] "German Prisoner Is caught Near Camp," Kentucky *New Era* (19 September 1944): 1.

[40] Newspaper articles and editorial letters throughout the nation made these types of claims.

[41] "Peeper's Imagination Took Flight But Prisoners of War Didn't," Louisville *Courier-Journal* (22 June 1944): S2, 1.

[42] "'PW' Signs No Joke," *New York Times* (26 April 1945): C2, 25.

[43] "2 Nazis Flee Breckinridge Prisoner Camp," Louisville *Courier-Journal* (13 June 1944): S1, 12; and "Two German Prisoners Repeat Escape Act," Louisville *Courier-Journal* (3 August 1944): S2, 1.

[44] "2 More German Prisoners Flee," Kentucky *New Era* (3 July 1944): 1.

[45] "10-Year Old Girl Helps Father Capture German War Prisoner," Kentucky *New Era* (8 July 1944): 1.

[46] "German Prisoner Captured Here Friday, July 7," *Cadiz Record* (13 July 1944): 1.

[47] "German Prisoner Captured Here Friday, July 7," *Cadiz Record* (13 July 1944): 1; see also "Two War Prisoners Seized In State," Louisville *Courier-Journal* (8 July 1944): S2, 9; and "German Prisoner Is Recaptured," Kentucky *New Era* (8 July 1944): 1.

[48] "Fourth German Is Sought Here," Kentucky *New Era* (17 July 1944): 1; "2 Campbell Prisoners Use Jeep to Escape," Louisville *Courier-Journal* (25 November 1944): S1, 3.; "Campbell Fugitives Taken in Nashville," Kentucky *New Era* (27 November 1944): 8; and "Nazi PW Captured Here Last Summer Escapes Again, Captured In Nashville," *Cadiz Record* (30 November 1944): 1.

[49] "Escaped German Prisoner Caught," Kentucky *New Era* (26 December 1944): 1; and "2 Nazi Prisoners Escape From Campbell," Louisville *Courier-Journal* (31 March 1945): S1, 4.

[50] "Two Nazi Prisoners Escape From Campbell," Owensboro *Messenger* (6 October 1944): 8; "Two Prisoners Escape Campbell," Kentucky *New Era* (4 October 1944): 1; "Two Prisoners Camp Campbell," *Cadiz Record* (12 October 1944): 1; and "2 German War Prisoners Flee Camp Campbell," Clarksville *Leaf-Chronicle* (4 October 1944): 1.

[51] "Two Escaped War Prisoners Caught Here," Clarksville Leaf Chronicle (5 October 1944): 1.; "Two Escaped Germans Taken," Kentucky *New Era* (5 October 1944): 1; and "Two Nazi Prisoners Recaptured," Louisville *Courier-Journal* (6 October 1944): S2, 1.

[52] "Four German War Prisoners Captured Here," Clarksville Leaf-Chronicle (23 December 1944): 1; and "Corporal Herds In Prisoners," Park City *Daily News* (3 January 1945): 6.

[53] "Four Germans Flee Stockade At Fort Knox," Louisville *Courier-Journal* (16 February 1945): S2, 1.; and "4 Nazi Prisoners At Knox Get 5-Year Terms," Louisville *Courier-Journal* (6 May 1945): S4, 12.

[54] "Nazi Escapee Found on Farm After 4 Months," Louisville *Courier-Journal* (19 February 1944): S2, 1.

[55] "2 German Prisoners Flee Camp Campbell," Louisville *Courier-Journal* (9 August 1945): S2, 1; and "2 German Prisoners Flee Camp Campbell," Louisville *Courier-Journal* (9 August 1945): S2, 4

[56] "Public Warned To Watch Out For Escaped Nazi War Prisoners," Kentucky *New Era* (20 August 1945): 1.; and "Escaped German Eludes Police At Hopkinsville," Louisville *Courier-Journal* (21 August 1945): S1, 7.

[57] "Escaped German Is Recaptured," Kentucky *New Era* (23 August 1945): 1.

[58] "German War Prisoner Taken At Holt Home," Clarksville *Leaf-Chronicle* (27 August 1945): 1.; and "2 Escaped Germans At Campbell Recaptured," Louisville *Courier-Journal* (28 August 1945): S1, 8.

[59] "Nazi Prisoner of War Shot in Kentucky," *New York Times* (29 January 1945): C2, 21; "Campbell Guard Kills Prisoner," Kentucky *New Era* (23 January 1945): 1; "War Prisoner Fleeing Guard Killed At Depot," Clarksville *Leaf-Chronicle* (22 January 1945): 1; "German Prisoner of War Shot Fatally," Park City *Daily News* (24 January 1945): 2; "War Prisoner Fleeing Guard, Killed At Depot," Clarksville Leaf Chronicle (22 January 1945): 1; "Slain German Prisoner Was Being Removed," Clarksville *Leaf-Chronicle* (23 January 1945): 1.

[60] "Kills 2 War Prisoners," *New York Times* (6 November 1944): 21.

[61] Heino R. Erichsen, *The Reluctant Warrior: Former German POW Finds Peace in Texas* (Austin, TX: Eakin Press, 2001): 72-74.

[62] "German Aliens Taken Back to Camp," Park City *Daily News* (8 November 1942): 1, 5.

Chapter 7

[1] Andre Vulliet *Preliminary Report of the War Prisoners Aid Young Men's Christian Associations During World War II* (Geneva, Switzerland: International Committee of the Young Men's Christian Association, 1946): 110.

[2] These camps were Fort Kearney, Fort Wetherhill, and Fort Getty, Rhode Island; and Fort Eustis, Virginia

[3] Office of the Provost Marshal General *Historical Monograph*, Prisoner of War Operations Division, Office of the Provost Marshal General: with appendices and supplement, 1945-1946; 143. NAII, MMB.

[4] Memorandum for the Fiscal Director, Army Service Forces (Attention: Major J.K. Cranmer, Fiscal Control Branch) NAII, MMB, RG 389, Entry 461-POW Information Bureau, Reporting Branch, Subject File, 1942-46, Box 2468-Activities to Athletic and Recreational Equip., Folder-Athletic and Recreational Equipment.

[5] Ibid.

[6] Heino R. Erichsen *The Reluctant Warrior: Former German POW Finds Peace in Texas* (Austin, TX: Eakin Press, 2001): 68.

[7] Egon Hessenthaler, "Memoirs," German language copy held at Fort Knox cultural resources, trans. by Natalie DoVanne (March 2007).

[8] Ibid.

[9] "Visit by Mr. Paul Schnyder," Prisoner of War Camp, Fort Knox, Kentucky (26 April 1946): 2. NAII, MMB, RG 389, Entry 459A, Box 1616, Folder 255 (Fort Knox, KY) Gen.

[10] "Field Trip to Camp Campbell," Memorandum for Chief, Special Projects Branch (14 November 1944): 7. NAII, MMB, RG 389, Entry 459A, Box 1611, Folder 255 Cp. Campbell, General.

[11] See "German Synopsis," NAII, MMB, RG 389, Entry 439A, Box 40, Folder Movies Shown to German Prisoners of War, Index. "German Motion Pictures for Prisoners of War," Prisoner of War Circular No. 4 (23 January 1945): 1-2. NAII, MMB, RG 389, Entry , Box 38, Folder PW Circulars, PW Policies Not Covered In Regulation Book.

[12] Office of the Provost Marshal General *Historical Monograph*, Prisoner of War Operations Division, Office of the Provost Marshal General: with appendices and supplement, 1945-1946; 144. NAII, MMB.

[13] "Field Service Report on Visit to Prisoner of War Camp, Fort Knox, Kentucky, 20-21 December 1944," Memorandum for Director, Prisoner of War Special Projects Division (20-21 December 1944): 2. NAII, MMB, RG 389, Entry 459A, Box 1616, Folder 255 (Fort Knox, KY) Gen.

[14] Erichsen, 68

[15] "Field Trip to Camp Campbell," Memorandum for Chief, Special Projects Branch (14 November 1944): 4. NAII, MMB,

RG 389, Entry 459A, Box 1611, Folder 255 Cp. Campbell, General.

[16] Ibid 7.

[17] "Fate Brings Former POW Back to Post," *German POWs at Fort Campbell*, Fort Campbell Archives, Folder 1. Fort Campbell, Kentucky.

[18] Office of the Provost Marshal General *Historical Monograph*, Prisoner of War Operations Division, Office of the Provost Marshal General: with appendices and supplement, 1945-1946; 144. *National Archives II, Modern Military Branch.*

[19] "German Prisoners Have Own Theater, Musical Productions," Clarksville Leaf Chronicle (25 February 1944): 1.

[20] "Field Trip to Camp Campbell," Memorandum for Chief, Special Projects Branch (14 November 1944): 3-5. NAII, MMB, RG 389, Entry 459A, Box 1611, Folder 255 Cp. Campbell, General.

[21] Ibid.

[22] Numerous sources for this include the many primary sources housed at the National Archives, especially camp inspection reports. Other sources include Vulliet *Preliminary Report of the War Prisoners Aid Young Men's Christian Associations During World War II*; Erichsen *The Reluctant Warrior: Former German POW Finds Peace in Texas*; and nearly every monograph and memoir about German POWs in the U.S.

[23] Matthew Rector and I both walked through the area and observed the Afrika Korps symbol, included in this work are pictures of that. I visited the remains of the rail road where the Germans scrawled graffiti.

[24] Paul James, interview by Gary Kempf, November 1, 2001.

[25] Barbara James, interview by Antonio Thompson March 2007. She asked that the address not be revealed due to fear of vandalism as it is in her front yard. I have taken pictures and included them in the appropriate section.

[26] Dedication page, "PW Camp, Fort Knox, Kentucky," sketchbook, copy housed at Cultural Preservation Office, Fort Knox, and Patton Museum Library, Fort Knox.

[27] See photographs in the appropriate section.

[28] André Vulliet, "Report on Visit to camp Breckinridge War Prison Camp (U.S.A.) on October 11th and 12th, 1943," War Prisoners' Aid of the Y.M.C.A. Geneva-1st June, 1944, p. 5. Copy held in the Camp Breckinridge Library and Museum.

[29] Ibid, 6.

[30] See Photo Appendix.
[31] "German POWs left their art at old Army post's officers' club," Louisville *Courier-Journal* (11 May 1998): B3.
[32] Ibid, and Bill Powell, "The Mural Mystery," The *Courier-Journal* (6 July 1980) and reprint on http://www.rootsweb.com/~kyunion/prisoner.htm.
[33] Bill Powell, "The Mural Mystery," The *Courier-Journal* (6 July 1980) and reprint on http://www.rootsweb.com/~kyunion/prisoner.htm
[34] Roger McBain, "Artistic Legacy: German POW Left Behind His Paintings," *Courier & Press*, http://www.breckinridge-arts.org/legacy.html.
[35] Bill Powell, "Letters from Readers", Louisville *Courier-Journal*, (10 August 1980): 17
[36] Powell, "The Mural Mystery," The Courier-Journal (6 July 1980) and reprint on http://www.rootsweb.com/~kyunion/prisoner.htm.
[37] Daniel Meyer to Frau Hermine Meyer, Postcard, July 3, 1944, copy held at the Breckinridge Museum.
[38] Daniel Meyer to Frau Hermine Meyer, Postcard, October 11, 1943, copy held at the Breckinridge Museum
[39] Daniel Meyer to Frau Hermine Meyer, Postcard, July 17, 1944, copy held at the Breckinridge Museum
[40] Roger McBain, "Artistic Legacy: German POW Left Behind His Paintings," *Courier & Press*, http://www.breckinridge-arts.org/legacy.html.
[41] Ibid.
[42] Ibid.
[43] "Prisoner of War Circular No. 1 (Wahington, D.C., *War Department*, 24 September 1943): 59, National Archives, RG 389, Entry 439A--Historical File, 1941-1958, Box 41-Regulations Governing Prisoners of War.
[44] Although it should be noted that the Consultative Committee on Reading Facilities for Prisoners of War and Internees, formed from numerous library representatives from the belligerent countries, assisted the IRC in obtaining and distributing books, as well as determining which ones would be allowed by the Geneva Convention and individual nations, see A.C. Breycha-Vauthier "Reading for Prisoners of War as Seen from Geneva," *The Library Quarterly* Vol. XI, 1941: 442-447.
[45] This restriction was also reciprocal as well, meaning that such titles could not be read by American POWs in Germany, see also

"Chicago Library Compiles Book List for Prisoners of War," *Publisher's Weekly* (22 July 1944): 241.

[46] "German Authors Not Approved For Prisoner of War Camps," Edward F. Witsell, Brigadier General, Acting the Adjutant General, (26 November 1944): 1-5. NAII, MMB, RG 389, Entry 439A, Box 35, Folder-History of the Prisoner of War Division.

[47] Some felt that any restriction on the reading and education or reeducation materials of German POWs ran counter to teaching them democracy. See Dorothy Thompson, "Education or Book Burning," *Forum* (September 1945): 42-43.

[48] 116,000 additional copies were ordered nationwide after the first ones had been distributed to camp canteens.

[49] "Reactions to Buecherreihe Neue Welt," NA, MMB, RG 389, Entry 439 A , Box 40, Folder PW Education Program: 1-6.

[50] Ibid.

[51] Ibid.

[52] "Newspapers and Magazines for Prisoners of War," B.M. Bryan, Brigadier General, Director, Aliens Division (23 march 1943): 1. NA, MMB, RG 389, Entry , Box 38, Historical File, POW Regulations not in Regulations Book.

[53] Ibid.

[54] Ibid., 1-5.

[55] Howard Tromp, interview by Antonio Thompson, May 2006 and August 2005.

[56] "Prisoner of War Circular, No. 7," G.C. Marshall, Chief of Staff and J.A. Ulio, Major General, the Adjutant General, War Department (6 February 1945): 1.

[57] "Field Trip to Camp Campbell," Memorandum for Chief, Special Projects Branch (14 November 1944): 4. NAII, MMB, RG 389, Entry 459A, Box 1611, Folder 255 Cp. Campbell, General.

[58] Ibid, 5.

[59] "Fate Brings Former POW Back to Post," *German POWs at Fort Campbell*, Fort Campbell Archives, Folder 1. Fort Campbell, Kentucky.

[60] "Field Trip to Camp Campbell," Memorandum for Chief, Special Projects Branch (14 November 1944): 4. NAII, MMB, RG 389, Entry 459A, Box 1611, Folder 255 Cp. Campbell, General, 6.

[61] Ibid., 7.

[62] Ibid.

[63] "Visit by Mr. M Perret," From Department of State to Provost Marshal General (25 March 1944): 1-3. NAII, MMB, RG 389, Entry 459A, Box 1616, Folder 255 (Fort Knox, KY) Gen.

[64] "Field Service Report on Visit to Prisoner of War Camp, Fort Knox, Kentucky, 20-21 December 1944," Memorandum for Director, Prisoner of War Special Projects Division (20-21 December 1944): 4-5. NAII, MMB, RG 389, Entry 459A, Box 1616, Folder 255 (Fort Knox, KY) Gen.

[65] Office of the Provost Marshal General *Historical Monograph*, Prisoner of War Operations Division, Office of the Provost Marshal General: with appendices and supplement, 1945-1946; p. 144. NAII, MMB

[66] "Field Trip to Camp Campbell," Memorandum for Chief, Special Projects Branch (14 November 1944): 5. NAII, MMB, RG 389, Entry 459A, Box 1611, Folder 255 Cp. Campbell, General.

[67] *Der Europäer: Kriegsgefangenenzeitschrift* Camp Campbell Oktober 1944 Heft 2.

[68] "Field Service Report on Visit to Prisoner of War Camp, Fort Knox, Kentucky, 20-21 December 1944," Memorandum for Director, Prisoner of War Special Projects Division (20-21 December 1944): 4-5. NAII, MMB, RG 389, Entry 459A, Box 1616, Folder 255 (Fort Knox, KY) Gen.

[69] Fort Knox cultural resources office.

[70] Office of the Provost Marshal General *Historical Monograph*, Prisoner of War Operations Division, Office of the Provost Marshal General: with appendices and supplement, 1945-1946; 140-141. NA II, MMB.

[71] Ibid, 142-143.

[72] ASF Circular, No. 161, (5 May 1945): 1-6. NAII, MMB, RG 389, Entry 439A, Box 35, Folder History of the Prisoner of War Division.

[73] See Vulliet and "The YMCA War Prisoners Aid Offers Educational Assistance," *School and Society* (6 May 1944): 325.

[74] See P.E. Kretzmann "The Lutheran Commission for Prisoners of War," *The Lutheran Witness* (December 1943): 421-426; and Lawrence B. Meyer, "A Plea for Prison Camp Literature," *The Lutheran Witness* (14 September 1943): 311.

[75] "Fate Brings Former POW Back to Post," *German POWs at Fort Campbell*, Fort Campbell Archives, Folder 1. Fort Campbell, Kentucky.

[76] "Studies and Sports in German Prison Camps," American National Red Cross, 1943-1945, *Prisoners of War Bulletin,* vol. 1, no 4 (September 1943): 1.

[77] "Field Trip to Camp Campbell," Memorandum for Chief, Special Projects Branch (14 November 1944): 4. NAII, MMB, RG 389, Entry 459A, Box 1611, Folder 255 Cp. Campbell, General.

[78] Ibid.

[79] "Nazis Kept at Breckinridge," Louisville *Courier-Journal* (13 June 1943): S1, 16.

[80] "Field Service Report on Visit to Prisoner of War Camp, Fort Knox, Kentucky, 20-21 December 1944," Memorandum for Director, Prisoner of War Special Projects Division (20-21 December 1944): 4-5. NAII, MMB, RG 389, Entry 459A, Box 1616, Folder 255 (Fort Knox, KY) Gen.

[81] "Visit by Mr. Paul Schnyder," Prisoner of War Camp, Fort Knox, Kentucky (26 April 1946): 1-3. NAII, MMB, RG 389, Entry 459A, Box 1616, Folder 255 (Fort Knox, KY) Gen.

[82] Office of the Provost Marshal General *Historical Monograph,* Prisoner of War Operations Division, Office of the Provost Marshal General: with appendices and supplement, 1945-1946; p.89. NAII, MMB.

[83] Erichsen, 71.

[84] Office of the Provost Marshal General *Historical Monograph,* Prisoner of War Operations Division, Office of the Provost Marshal General: with appendices and supplement, 1945-1946; p.89. *National Archives II, Modern Military Branch.*

[85] J. Earle Bell "Changes at POW Camp," Union County *Advocate* (3 May 1945): 1.

[86] "German Prisoners Attend Worship At Campbell," Clarksville *Leaf-Chronicle* (20 September 1943): 2.

[87] "Field Service Report on Visit to Prisoner of War Camp, Fort Knox, Kentucky, 20-21 December 1944," Memorandum for Director, Prisoner of War Special Projects Division (20-21 December 1944): 4-5. NAII, MMB, RG 389, Entry 459A, Box 1616, Folder 255 (Fort Knox, KY) Gen.

[88] "Field Trip to Camp Campbell," Memorandum for Chief, Special Projects Branch (14 November 1944): 3. NAII, MMB, RG 389, Entry 459A, Box 1611, Folder 255 Cp. Campbell, General.

[89] Office of the Provost Marshal General *Historical Monograph,* Prisoner of War Operations Division, Office of the Provost

Marshal General: with appendices and supplement, 1945-1946; p. 145. *National Archives II, Modern Military Branch.* This restriction was changed to carry the "must be a relative" in 1944 after Italian POWs had too many friends and friends of the family visiting them on a regular basis

[90] "Nazi Prisoner Sees Sister At Campbell," Clarksville *Leaf-Chronicle* (17 November 1943): 3.

[91] "Nazi Prisoners Caught Making Orange Wine At Fort Knox," Louisville *Courier-Journal* (20 September 1944): S2, 6.

[92] Egon Hessenthaler, "Memoirs," German copy held at Fort Knox cultural resources, trans. by Natalie DoVanne (March 2007).

[93] "War Prisoners At Campbell Give to Red Cross," Clarksville *Leaf-Chronicle* (26 February 1945): 6.

[94] "Prisoners Buy Bonds," Union County Advocate (6 January 1944): 7. Ironically this article ran the same day as the beginning of the D-Day invasion.

[95] "Prisoners Help In Rescue of Driver," Kentucky *New Era* (12 September 1944): 1.

Chapter 8

[1] Heady Peyton, *History of Camp Breckinridge, KY* (Hites Imperial Printing, 1987): 30.

[2] Clarence L. Miller, "The Prisoner of War Program," *The New History of Shelby County, Kentucky* (Shelbyville, KY: Harmon House Publishers): 515-519.

[3] "Tented City Erected On Hustonville Road For German POWs," *Danville Advocate-Messenger"* (17 August 1945): 1. "POWs To Leave AS Leaf Harvest Ends," *Danville Advocate-Messenger* (7 September 1945), and Richard Brown *History of Danville and Boyle County* p. 122.

[4] Henry W. Ehrmann, "An Experiment in Political Education" *Social Research* (September 1947): 304-20, Figures are from page 1 of the article.

[5] George Lewis and John Mewha "History of Prisoner of War Utilization by the United States Army, 1776-1945 (Center of Military History, United States Army, Washington, D.C.

[6] These numbers are only rough estimates based on the figures cited above.

[7] The impact of the actual reeducation program is briefly mentioned in the introduction to this work. I describe it in more

detail in my dissertation "Men in German Uniform: German Prisoners of War Held in the United States During World War II." A wonderful study of this topic has been done by Ron Robin, see *The Barbed Wire College: Reeducating German POWs in the United States During World War II* (New Jersey: Princeton University Press, 1995).

[8] Interestingly the German military's special prisoners, *Sonderkommando*, had a very different meaning.

[9] In this sense "repatriated" refers to being sent back to Europe, not necessarily back to Germany.

[10] "Army Repatriates Final Group of Able-Bodied Prisoners-of-War," War Department Public Relations Division (July 22, 1946): 1. Fort Knox Archives.

[11] The regulations can be found in the Historical Monograph and accompanying documents, and cited in the numerous monographs and memoirs.

[12] Ibid.

[13] Howard Tromp, interview by Antonio Thompson, May 2006 and August 2005.

[14] For a discussion of this see Frank Beiss *Homecomings: Returning POWs, and the Legacies of Defeat in Postwar Germany* (Princeton: Princeton University Press), Dagmar Barnouw *The War in the Empty Air: Victims, Perpetrators, and Postwar Germans* (Bloomington, Indiana University Press), and Earl R. Beck *Under the Bombs: The German Home Front, 1942-1945* (Lexington: The University of Kentucky Press, 1986.

[15] Biess, 5.

[16] Egon Hessenthaler, "Memoirs," German copy held at Fort Knox cultural resources, trans. by Natalie DoVanne (March 2007).

[17] Letters to and from the Broadbent family after World War II prove this as well as the conversations between Antonio Thompson and the Broadbent family.

[18] Wendy Mitchell, "Letters translate German POW's life post WWII," *The Ledger Independent* (29 May 2005).

[19] Ibid.

[20] Howard Tromp, interview by Antonio Thompson, August 2005 and June 2006.

[21] Information on Nessler is held at Don F. Pratt Museum at Fort Campbell and in numerous area newspaper articles including the Clarksville *Leaf-Chronicle*.

[22] Horst Blumenberg, interview by Antonio Thompson , Spring and Summer 2007, also see "German ex-POW donates WWII

memorabilia to Tech," *News @ Tech*, Louisiana Tech University, Ruston, Louisiana.

[23] Heino Erichsen, interview by Antonio Thompson, Summer 2005; and see also *The Reluctant Warrior* 80-81, 154-155.

[24] Ibid.

[25] David Wecker, "One soldier, Almighty had special relationship," *Cincinnati Post*, Online Edition, accessed June 2005.

[26] For another treatment, see James F. Tent *Mission on the Rhine.*

[27] This is a confidential source.

[28] Junior Mathis, interview by Antonio Thompson, Fall 2005.

[29] Paul Gardner, interview by Antonio Thompson, 2001; and Margaret Rudd, interview by Antonio Thompson, 2005.

[30] Derek R. Mallet "They were just people like we were: World War II German and Italian prisoners of war in Missouri," M.A. Thesis, Truman State University, 1997.

[31] Walter Mathis, interview by Antonio Thompson, Summer 2005

[32] Information on this can be found at the Camp Breckinridge Museum.

Printed in the United States
127616LV00004B/1/P

9 781935 290001